Puritanism in north-west England

The diocese of Chester, showing places mentioned in the text

R C Richardson

Puritanism in north-west England

*A regional study of the diocese
of Chester to 1642*

Manchester University Press
Rowman & Littlefield Publishers

Published by the University of Manchester at
THE UNIVERSITY PRESS
316–324 Oxford Road, Manchester M13 9NR

UK ISBN 0 7190 0477 2

USA
Rowman & Littlefield Publishers
81 Adams Drive, Totowa, N. J. 07512
US ISBN 0 87471 093 6

The publication of this book has been assisted by an award from the
Twenty-Seven Foundation

Contents

Preface

Professor Collinson ended the preface to his valuable exploration of *The Elizabethan Puritan Movement* with the hope that his 'necessarily general survey may help to stimulate further local studies of what was, for many of England's provinces, the real rather than the merely formal and constitutional Reformation'. In this, as in most other fields of history, local and regional studies clearly have an important part to play, for it is through them that new approaches can be tried, accepted generalisations tested, and through them that the unique as well as the common characteristics of the social, political, economic and religious organisation of the different regions must ultimately become known. This study of puritanism in the diocese of Chester is intended as a micro-analysis of one particular area.

The book is based on a wide variety of civil and ecclesiastical source material. Central to the whole study were the administrative and judicial records of the diocese and of the archbishopric of York, of which it formed a sizeable part. Particularly important were the enormously informative series of court papers and visitation records. Contemporary correspondence and parochial records were used where available and Quarter Sessions documents occasionally offered insights into specific aspects of puritanism in this region. A study of several hundred original probate records yielded information not only about such tangible matters as books and bequests but also about puritan opinion expressed in their preambles. State papers in the Public Record Office were consulted, and in addition published sermons and puritan devotional literature were widely used.

Most of the research was undertaken in northern archives and libraries—in the Cheshire and Lancashire Record Offices, at the Borthwick Institute in York, in the Archives Department of the Leeds Central Library, and in the Central Reference Library, the University, John Rylands and Chetham's Libraries in Manchester. To the staffs of all these institutions I express my thanks.

This study is based on my doctoral thesis submitted at the University of Manchester in 1968, and for the help and advice given to me as a postgraduate student I am most grateful to my supervisor Dr B. S. Manning. Professor T. S. Willan and Professor P. Collinson also gave me useful advice during the early stages of my researches on puritanism. For help and constructive criticism in preparing my Ph.D. thesis for publication I am indebted to Mr D. H. Pennington and Dr C. Hill of Balliol College, Oxford, to the Secretary of Manchester University Press, and to Dr W. H. Chaloner. I am grateful also to Mr C. W. Chitty for his help in checking the typescript and proofs. But above all I must thank Dr Joan Thirsk of the University of Oxford for reading through the whole of the book in typescript, and for all the assistance and encouragement she has generously given to me on this as on previous occasions.

R. C. Richardson
May 1971

Abbreviations

Chester	County and Diocesan Record Office, the Castle, Chester
Chet. Soc.	Chetham Society
D.N.B.	*Dictionary of National Biography*
E.H.R.	*English Historical Review*
Ec.H.R.	*Economic History Review*
H.M.C.	Historical Manuscripts Commission
Preston	Lancashire Record Office, Preston
P.R.O.	Public Record Office
Rec. Soc. Lancs. and Ches.	Record Society of Lancashire and Cheshire
Trans. Hist. Soc. Lancs. and Ches.	*Transactions of the Historic Society of Lancashire and Cheshire*
Trans. Lancs. and Ches. Antiq. Soc.	*Transactions of the Lancashire and Cheshire Antiquarian Society*
T.R.H.S.	*Transactions of the Royal Historical Society*
V.C.H.	*Victoria County History*
vis.	Visitation records
York	Borthwick Institute of Historical Research, St Anthony's Hall, York.

A classified list of the archive material used in the preparation of this book, and of its location, is given in the opening section of the bibliography.

Note

The spelling, punctuation and capitalisation in all quotations—but not in book titles—have been modernised. Dates are given in the new style.

To my parents

Chapter one

The context and distribution of puritanism

The people, generally devout, are, as I am informed, northward and by the west Popishly affected, which in the other parts are zealous Protestants. . . .

Thomas Fuller, *History of the Worthies of England,* 1662, 105

1 *Basic geographical and religious features of the diocese*

The diocese of Chester was, from its erection in 1541, a poorly endowed, monstrously large and administratively unmanageable ecclesiastical unit.[1] Its territory was principally that of the two counties of Lancashire and Cheshire, but this by no means represented its total extent. In the south the diocese included some Flintshire parishes, and in the north it took in parts of Westmorland and extended into Cumberland as far as Workington. In the east it embraced large areas of Yorkshire. Not until the nineteenth century was the diocese belatedly trimmed to a more realistic size.[2]

For administrative purposes the bishopric was divided at the Ribble into the two archdeaconries of Richmond and Chester, and these in turn were further subdivided into a total of twenty deaneries. The northern archdeaconry of Richmond—as large as

1 Bishop Downham, who held the see of Chester from 1561 until his death in 1577, complained in 1568 that he received 'the least revenue that any man in my calling have in this realm'. (P.R.O., State Papers Domestic. SP 12/48/36.)
  Bishops of Chester during the period which will be surveyed in this book were William Chaderton, 1579–95, Hugh Bellot, 1595–96, Richard Vaughan, 1597–1604, George Lloyd, 1605–15, Thomas Morton, 1616–19, and John Bridgeman from 1619.
  The diocese of Chester formed part of the northern province, which in this period was ruled successively by Edmund Grindal, 1571–76, Edwin Sandys, 1577–88, John Piers, 1589–94, Matthew Hutton, 1595–1606, Tobias Matthew, 1606–28, Samuel Harsnett, 1628–31, and by Richard Neile, 1632–1640.
2 In 1836 its Yorkshire territory was taken to form part of the new diocese of Ripon. In 1847 its Cumberland and Westmorland sections were re-allocated to the see of Carlisle, as also was Lancashire north of the Sands. At the same time the new diocese of Manchester was erected. In 1849 the Welsh parts of the diocese were transferred to St Asaph, and in 1880 the bishopric of Liverpool was founded. (Ollard and Crosse, *Dictionary of English Church History,* 1912, 108.)

many dioceses elsewhere in the country—contained eight deaneries, namely those of Amounderness, Copeland, Furness, Kendal, Lonsdale, Richmond, Catterick and Boroughbridge. The twelve deaneries which comprised the archdeaconry of Chester were those of Middlewich, Frodsham, Chester, Nantwich, Macclesfield, Malpas, Bangor, Wirral, Manchester, Warrington, Blackburn and Leyland.

The parochial structure of the diocese, as we shall see, was equally unmanageable, and the situation was aggravated still further by the fact that a large number of church livings were impropriate.

> There are but a few parishes in my diocese [wrote Bishop Chaderton to Walsingham in 1586], to wit about 248, and of those about 133 have their rectories appropriated and those of the best . . . and no other incumbents than very beggarly vicars and curates . . . And many of the best sort are not resident . . .
>
> I wish with all my heart [Bishop Chaderton continued] the state of the clergy in my diocese were fully known to their Lordships of the Council.[3]

At a later date the puritan divine George Walker showed that he too was well aware of the extent of, and problems caused by, impropriations. He observed that the Lancashire hundred of Furness where he was born:

> which for spacious compass of ground is not much less than Bedfordshire or Rutlandshire . . . has only eight parish churches, and seven of those eight are impropriate and the livings in the hands of laymen, and in some of those parishes which be forty miles in compass [he went on] there is no more ordinary and set maintenance allowed for the ministry of the word and sacraments but ten pounds or twenty nobles yearly.[4]

And William Hinde, the puritan author of the *Life of John Bruen*

3 P.R.O. State Papers Domestic. SP 12/189/12. For the northern province as a whole, it has been estimated that no less than 62.6 per cent of livings were impropriate at this time. For the province of Canterbury the figure was 40 per cent. (W. J. Kaye, 'An ecclesiastical survey of the province and diocese of York, 1603', *Yorks. Arch. Jnl.*, xxxi, 1934, 421–2. Mentioned in C. Hill, 'Puritans and the "dark corners of the land" ', *T.R.H.S.*, fifth series, xiii, 1962, 89.)

As an example of the possible results of impropriation, it can be noted that although in 1636 the Lancashire rectory of Leigh was worth £632 to its lay impropriator, the vicar there received only a paltry net income of £12 11s. 4d. (C. Hill, *Economic Problems of the Church*, Oxford, 1956, 140–1.)

4 Walker, *An Exhortation for contributions to maintain preachers in Lancashire*, in *Miscellany, vol. 1*, Chet. Soc., new series 47, Manchester, 1902, 16.

—a fascinating work which will be much used in the course of this book—denounced such patrons, who:

> being entrusted with the land and living of the Church for the main-
> tenance of the ministry and spiritual provision of God's people, do
> notwithstanding turn their patronage into pillage and their devotion
> into sacrilege cutting short the minister of his means and the people of
> their provision, taking the wheat unto themselves and leaving the straw
> and chaff unto them for their portion only.[5]

Because of impropriations, clerical incomes in the diocese of Chester tended in many cases to be very low. Even as late as 1650, the incumbents of seventeen Lancashire parishes had an income of £40 or less. In the chapelries the position was often even worse; fifty-one Lancashire curates had an annual stipend of £15 or under.[6]

The unsatisfactory state of a great many of the clergy of the diocese was, in part at least, the result of this situation. 'The curates throughout the whole diocese of Chester,' so it was contended in an official report in 1580, 'for the most part are utterly unlearned.'[7] Later, in a puritan survey of the Lancashire clergy made in 1604, only two-fifths of the ministers were described as being preachers. There were many, then, of the other kind. Cartmel in north Lancashire was 'meanly served only with a reading minister'. A Fylde parish, Lytham, had only 'a bare reader, and careless', and the incumbent at Deane, near Bolton, was 'neither preacher himself nor will suffer any other to preach'.[8]

For the authorities, however, there were other disturbing features of the religious condition of the diocese of Chester. One of them was the prevalence—in some areas at least—of irreligion and the obstinate survival of deep-rooted pagan superstitions.

In many isolated communities in the diocese, witchcraft was well woven into the fabric of life.[9] For example, at Great Harwood, near

---

5 Hinde, *A Faithfull Remonstrance of the Holy Life and Happy Death of John Bruen* . . ., 1641, 86.
6 D. Lambert, 'The lower clergy of the Anglican Church in Lancashire, 1558–1642', M.A. thesis, University of Liverpool, 1964, 2, 12–13.
7 P.R.O. State Papers Domestic. SP 15/27/94. An anonymous report.
8 'Certaine briefe observations truly gathered, partly by experience and partly from others, comprehending the whole estate of Lancashire clergy . . .' in *Kenyon Mss.*, H.M.C., fourteenth report, app. IV, 1894, 7, 9, 12. Similar surveys of other counties were made in this year.
9 The existence of witchcraft in this region is explored, for example, in W. Notestein, *A History of Witchcraft in England, 1558–1718*, Washington, 1911, and in M. Tonge, 'The Lancashire witches, 1612 and 1634', *Trans.*

Whalley, in 1590 it was noted that 'Janet Cockshot is supposed to be a witch or a charmer to whom divers resort for counsel'.[10] In 1595 at Stalmine, in the Fylde, one Alice Steven was presented on the charge that she 'has used charms on the eyes [?] of men and does repair to wise men for counsel in witchcraft and such like things'.[11] Similarly, at Halsall, in the western coastal region of Warrington deanery, James and Anne Blundell in 1598 were both 'vehemently suspected for witches and using unlawful prayers'.[12] From roughly the same area came a charge in 1605 against the wife of William Webster of Maghull, who 'said she had cursed Leonard Martin and that there was none that she had cursed that had escaped [sickness] or death'.[13]

As late as 1644 the Yorkshire divine John Shaw, temporarily ministering in north Lancashire, found the inhabitants of that region 'exceedingly ignorant and blind as to religion'. He instanced the case of:

> an old man about sixty, sensible enough in other things, and living in the parish of Cartmel . . . [who when told] that the way to salvation was by Jesus Christ, God–man, who as he was man shed his blood on the cross [answered], 'Oh sir, . . . I think I heard of that man you spake of once in a play at Kendal called Corpus Christi play, where there was a man on a tree and blood ran down!' And after that [Shaw continued] he professed that though he was a good churchman, that is, he constantly went to common prayer at their chapel, yet he could not remember that ever he heard of salvation by Jesus Christ but in that play . . .[14]

Other evidence from these remote parts of the diocese, however, reveals more hostile attitudes. At Pendle, for example—famous for its associations with the Lancashire witches—one Richard Moore was charged in 1626 'for saying that God where he did one good turn did two bad, and that if God were there he would cut off his

---

Hist. Soc. Lancs. and Ches., 83, 1931. More recently the local history of the subject has received some mention in H. R. Trevor-Roper, 'The European witch craze in the sixteenth and seventeenth centuries', in *Religion, the Reformation and Social Change*, 1967, and in A. Macfarlane, *Witchcraft in Tudor and Stuart England*, 1970.

10 York. 1590 vis. RVIA 12, f. 52v.
11 York. 1595 vis. RVIA 15, f. 114v.
12 Chester. 1598 vis. EDV 1/12, f. 136v.
13 Chester. 1605 vis. EDV 1/14, f. 98.
14 *Life of Master John Shaw in Yorkshire Diaries and Autobiographies in the seventeenth and eighteenth centuries*, Surtees Soc., 65, 1875, 137.

head'.[15] While at Barton Cuthbert, in Richmondshire, John Bell was presented in 1630 'for cursing the church and praying the Devil to pull it down'.[16]

But what most alarmed the authorities—civil as well as ecclesiastical in this instance—about the state of religion in the diocese was that Catholicism remained so widely acceptable there and so deeply entrenched.

It was in Lancashire that the old religion had its most extensive ramifications, and recusancy prevailed there on a scale unequalled elsewhere in the country. In a letter from the Privy Council to the Earl of Derby in 1574 Lancashire was described as 'the very sink of Popery where more unlawful acts have been committed and more unlawful persons held secret than in any other part of the realm'.[17] In the late 1580's—when the threat of a Spanish invasion hung over the country—the central government was even more anxious about the county, and although by the end of the century these immediate fears had subsided, the Privy Council's opinion of Lancashire was still basically unchanged. Everywhere, it was convinced, 'seditious spirits' abounded 'whereof there are more harboured in that shire than in any other part, drawing the people from their due obedience to her Majesty and her laws'.[18]

It was in the western part of Lancashire, as we shall see, that Catholicism retained its strongest hold; the Fylde was probably the most staunchly Catholic region in the whole of England. Western Lancashire—a predominantly arable area—was relatively isolated from the main trading network of the county. Its outside contacts were infrequent and largely selective. It was this isolation and this economy which enabled the prominent families of the region, such as the Norrises of Speake, the Blundells of Ince and Crosby, the Irelands of Lydiate and the Molyneux of Sefton, to exercise such extensive authority and influence. Their supremacy as landowners permitted them to dominate the social, economic and religious life of the area in which they lived. 'Great men have their followers of

15 Chester. 1619 vis. EDV 1/22, f. 207v. Cases.
16 York. 1630 vis. RVIA 22, f. 16.
17 *Acts of the Privy Council*, 27 July 1574. The recusancy problem in this region is examined in J. S. Leatherbarrow, *The Lancashire Elizabethan Recusants*, Chet. Soc., new series, 110, Manchester, 1947, in J. Cosgrove, 'The position of the recusant gentry in the socal setting of Lancashire, 1570–1642', M.A. thesis, Manchester University, 1964, and in K. R. Wark, *Elizabethan Recusancy in Cheshire*, Chet. Soc., third series, 19, Manchester, 1971.
18 *Acts of the Privy Council*, 15 March 1599.

their vices as of their persons,' the Lancashire divine Richard Heyricke shrewdly observed in 1641, 'and when they please to be idolatrous, their children, servants, tenants, their poor kindred and idolising neighbours will to the mass with them.'[19]

The government realised that the only way of effectively enforcing conformity in the county was to convert or master the social leaders,[20] for in Lancashire, as elsewhere, Catholicism, deprived of national organisation, sustained itself locally in a seigneurial form. Household religion, taken up in other ways by puritans, remained the surest means of preserving the old religion in these dangerous years. Catholic priests, stripped of their livings, were frequently maintained by co-religionists amongst the gentry and integrated into their households, ministering to the family's spiritual needs and in addition sometimes acting as private tutors.[21]

Encouragement began to come from the seminarist priests in the 1570's and 1580's. Allen's seminary at Douai, founded in 1568, was followed by the establishment of similar institutions at Rome and Seville, and despite the repeated attempts to check the emigration, a steady stream of the sons of the Lancashire gentry went abroad for training there. Although, as Dr Bossy has shown, conflict of emphasis was to develop between the lay and clerical elements of survivalist Catholicism, the seminarists in Elizabeth's reign undoubtedly invigorated the Catholic cause and stiffened the resistance of the recusants.[22] The strength of Catholicism, in fact, remained as great as ever in the first half of the seventeenth century. Richard Heyricke, for example, could write in 1641 that:

Popery has multiplied abundantly. In Lancashire it has superabounded

---

19 Heyricke, *Three Sermans preached at the Collegiate Church in Manchester . . .*, 1641, epistle dedicatory.

20 In 1577, for example, the Privy Council decided that the recusant John Townley of Burnley should be confined to London, 'finding it unmeet that he should return home by reason of his great power in his country'. (*Acts of the Privy Council*, 10 March 1577.)

21 Detailed information about priestly tutors maintained by Lancashire recusants was received by the government in 1592. (P.R.O. State Papers Domestic. SP 12/243/52.)

   The informant declared, for example, that Mr Houghton of Park Hall 'has kept a recusant schoolmaster I think these twenty years; he has had one after another'.

22 Dr Bossy's important study of 'The character of Elizabethan Catholicism' was originally published in *Past and Present*, 21, 1962, but is reprinted in T. Aston (ed.), *Crisis in Europe, 1560–1660*, 1965, 223–46.

above an hyperbole; the mass has outfaced our Christian meetings, Jesuits have jeered our ministers, confronted and abused authority.[23]

And the Lancashire puritan divine John Gee could declare that:

there is not a Popish gentleman in all the country but there is a priest to his steward, and disposer of household and revenues; neither does the owner let or sell any land without the approbation and consent of these pretended spiritual guides.[24]

Such—in the briefest outlines—were some of the most conspicuous features of the religious condition of the diocese of Chester in the later sixteenth and early seventeenth centuries. It was against this background—formidable and unpromising in some ways, but surprisingly conducive in others—that the growth of puritanism took place.

2 The distribution of puritanism

The distribution of puritanism in the diocese of Chester was varied and uneven, reflecting the different conditions which prevailed throughout this large and unwieldy see. Of the twenty deaneries which together made up the diocese, the four most remote—those of Bangor in the south, Copeland in the north-west, and Catterick and Boroughbridge in the north-east—can be at once eliminated from the present survey, since they have been found to contain virtually no evidence of puritanism.[25] Puritanism, in fact, was weak in most of the northern parts of the diocese; in the archdeaconry of Richmond it never developed sufficiently to become a problem. Puritanism was also weak along the western side of the diocese— in the deanery of Malpas, on the Flintshire side of Chester deanery, in the Wirral, in the coastal area of Warrington deanery, in the Fylde and in Furness. Puritan Liverpool was exceptional in this area from a religious as well as from an economic point of view.

23 Heyricke, *Three Sermons . . .*, 1641, epistle dedicatory.
24 Gee, *The Foot out of the Snare . . .*, 1624, 74. Gee was not only a puritan divine but also a renegade Catholic—so he spoke with authority on this point.
25 Only two exceptions to this generalisation have been discovered. The first concerns James Thompson, curate at Moncaster in Copeland deanery, who was charged in the 1633 visitation with various irregularities including his failure to wear the surplice. (York. 1633 vis. RVIA 23, f. 98v.) The second is an isolated charge made in 1623 against five laymen of Downholme in Catterick deanery for failing to kneel at the communion. (Chester. 1623 vis. EDV 1/25, f. 83v.)

B

Its commercial position provided an atmosphere conducive to the development of puritanism, and certainly the town's religious leanings represented a further expression of its general striving for independence.[26]

Puritanism was strongest in Lancashire south of the Ribble and in Cheshire—the main block of territory in the archdeaconry of Chester. And within this area the real stronghold of puritanism was to some extent in the centre but above all in the east. If a line were drawn connecting Ribchester in the north and Wrenbury in the south, and another east from Ribchester to the Yorkshire border, it would be found that this part of the diocese contained the highest proportion of those places for which there is evidence of puritanism. In this area—which occupied little more than a quarter of the diocese—the existence of puritanism amongst either clergy or laity has been discovered in fifty-six parishes and chapelries.[27] In the whole of the remaining three-quarters of the diocese, similar expressions of puritanism have been found in only forty-nine others.[28] The high total for the eastern half of Lancashire and Cheshire is partly explained by the presence within it of the deanery of Manchester, which was, without a doubt, the most strongly puritan of

26 The situation in Liverpool is analysed in chapter four.
27 Arranged under deaneries these are as follows: *Blackburn deanery*—Padiham, Burnley, Samlesbury, Blackburn, Haslingden, Newchurch, Darwen and Whalley; *Amounderness deanery*—Ribchester; *Manchester deanery*—see note 29; *Warrington deanery*—Leigh, Winwick and Warrington; *Frodsham deanery*—Bowdon, Grappenhall, Rostherne, Great Budworth, Knutsford, Over Peover and Witton; *Macclesfield deanery*—Stockport, Alderley, Chelford, Siddington, Macclesfield and Gawsworth; *Middlewich deanery*—Goostrey, Middlewich, Swettenham, Congleton, Astbury, Warmingham and Lawton; *Nantwich deanery*—Coppenhall, Acton, Nantwich and Bartomley.
28 Using the same method of classification by deanery these are as follows: *Richmond deanery*—Brigmel, Melsonby, Marske-in-Swaledale and Richmond; *Catterick deanery*—Downholme; *Lonsdale deanery*—Sedbergh, Tunstall, Areholme, Melling; *Kendal deanery*—Beetham, Burton, Over Kellet and Halton; *Furness deanery*—Coulton, Ulverston and Aldingham; *Copeland deanery*—Moncaster; *Amounderness deanery*—Garstang, Poulton, Kirkham and Preston; *Leyland deanery*—Leyland and Eccleston; *Warrington deanery*—Ormskirk, Wigan, Liverpool, Toxteth, Newton and Prescot; *Frodsham deanery*—Runcorn and Weaverham; *Wirral deanery*—West Kirby, Thurstaston, Bromborough, Stoke and Shotwick; *Chester deanery*—Thornton, Guilden Sutton, Tarvin Tarporley, Chester, Christleton, Farndon and Holt; *Malpas deanery*—Malpas, Cholmondley and Marbury; *Nantwich deanery*—Bunbury.

the entire diocese. In this deanery alone puritan sympathies have been noted in no fewer than nineteen parishes and chapelries.[29] This being the case, then, it will not be amiss to look more closely at puritanism in Manchester.

In a fast sermon preached before the House of Commons in 1646, Richard Heyricke, Warden of the town's Collegiate Church, described Manchester as 'a town famous for religion ever since the Reformation: believe it', he went on, 'it has been a Goshen, a place of light when most places of the land have been places of darkness'.[30] Similarly, another writer later in the seventeenth century spoke of Manchester as 'that ancient famed seat of religion and profession'.[31]

These—and other—writers were correct in stressing the long ancestry of puritanism in Manchester. For example, John Bradford and George Marsh, the only Protestant martyrs from Lancashire to be executed in the reign of Mary, had established strong connections with Manchester in Edward VI's reign and had kept up a correspondence with their lay supporters there.[32] But it would be unwise, of course, to attribute merely to the efforts of these two preachers responsibility for the puritanism that later prospered in Manchester. It was, however, largely through the combined influence of regular preaching and trade that the town moved towards that position in religion which writers such as Heyricke described. It was to Manchester in the 1580's that John Bruen, Esq., of Stapleford in Cheshire—thirty miles away—often resorted to hear sermons, 'all to this end', we are told by his biographer, 'that he might gather manna where he knew it would be rained down'.[33] And it was in this same decade that the Earl of Huntingdon—Lord President of the Council in the North and the most active of aristocratic

29 Puritanism was expressed not only in Manchester itself but in the chapelries of Blackley, Newton, Denton, Birch, Gorton and Didsbury. Outside the parish of Manchester, puritanism was also strong in Bolton (the 'Geneva of Lancashire', as it was termed in the Civil War), Rochdale, Ringley and Oldham. Its existence in this deanery has also been observed at Ashton-under-Lyne, Middleton, Prestwich, Radcliffe, Eccles, Deane, Rivington and Bury.
30 Heyricke, *Queen Esthers Resolves*, 1646, 24.
31 John Howe, in the preface to Chorlton's *Funeral Sermon for Henry Newcome*, 1695.
32 A. Townsend (ed.), *Collected Works of John Bradford*, Parker Soc., 31, 51, 1848–53; A. Hewlett, *Troubles and Martyrdom of the Rev. George Marsh*, Bolton, 1844.
33 Hinde, *Life of John Bruen*, 101.

puritan patrons—described Manchester as 'the best place in those parts' for religion.[34]

The puritan sympathies of the clergy of the Collegiate Church in Manchester were noted in virtually every episcopal and archiepiscopal visitation from 1578, demonstrating beyond doubt that they were giving the town a sustained lead in religion. But the clergy, after all, were not the only channel along which new ideas about religion could flow. Booksellers—who were present in this period in Manchester, Warrington and Chester—were another.[35] But books, and certainly tracts and pamphlets, were sold not only by professional booksellers but also by mercers, who often carried a small stock of popular titles along with their other wares. Pedlars also played an important part in the distribution of low-priced literature in the countryside.

Although he was not the first or only stationer in Manchester, Thomas Smith was particularly active as a promoter of puritanism in the 1630's, and a whole catalogue of charges was directed against him in 1638 in a case dealt with by the Consistory Court.[36] He was charged with refusing to kneel at the communion and with attending conventicles. He was, in short, regarded as 'a hot zealot or a strict nonconformist'. It was due to him, so the charges claimed, that Manchester was supplied with its puritan literature. He was charged with having:

> sold and vented divers Scottish and other schismatical books, containing in them, amongst other things, divers bitter invectives and railings against the government and discipline of the Church of England.[37]

But the study of puritanism cannot be divorced from that of the

34 Francis Peck, *Desiderata Curiosa*, 1779, 110.

35 R. S. Brown, 'The stationers, booksellers and printers of Chester to *c.* 1800', *Trans. Lancs. and Ches. Hist. Soc.*, 83, 1931, and W. H. Rylands, 'Booksellers and stationers in Warrington, 1639–57', *ibid.*, 37, 1885.

36 Chester. Consistory Court papers. EDC 5, 1638. Miscellaneous. Peter Ince, one of the Chester booksellers, was as determinedly puritan as Thomas Smith. See p. 182.

37 The title pages of two works by the Manchester puritan divine Richard Hollingworth and one by Richard Heyricke record that they were 'printed for Thomas Smith and are to be sold at his shop at Manchester'. The works by Hollingworth were *An Examination of Sundry Scriptures* . . ., 1644, and *Certain Queries . . . propounded to such as affect the Congregational Way* . . ., 1646. The book in question by Heyricke was *Queen Esthers Resolves*, the fast sermon which he had preached earlier that year–1646– before the House of Commons.

society against which it grew. And in Manchester it was against a commercial background that puritanism developed. A writer of the mid-seventeenth century declared that the trade of Manchester:

> is not inferior to that of many cities in the kingdom, consisting in woollen friezes, fustians, sackcloths, mingled stuffs, caps inkles, tapes, points, etc, whereby not only the better sort of men are employed, but also the very children by their own labour can maintain themselves. There are besides all kinds of foreign merchandise brought and returned by the merchants of the town, amounting to the sum of many thousands of pounds weekly . . . The people in and about the town [the writer declared] are said to be in general the most industrious in their callings of any in the northern parts of the kingdom.[38]

Manchester was clearly the largest, most prosperous, most economically developed and most puritan town in Lancashire. John Leland had commented on the size of its population and trade, as did Celia Fiennes in the following century. 'Things are very plenty here,' she wrote. 'This is a thriving place.'[39] Manchester was the main distributing centre for the growing textile trade of the east Lancashire countryside, and its merchants, who formed the core of the industry's essential middlemen, were in close contact with London.[40] Some of the larger Manchester firms, such as the Chethams and the Mosleys, maintained permanent factors in the capital. One Manchester businessman—Sir Nicholas Mosley—even became Lord Mayor of London in 1599.[41] Manchester merchants, too, attended the great fairs throughout the country. They were present, for example, at Stourbridge fair on that occasion in Elizabeth's reign when the famous puritan divine William Perkins urged his merchant hearers in his sermon to 'carry home this lesson to your great towns and cities where you dwell'.[42]

Of all towns in this part of the North, Manchester had the closest and most regular ties with London. And the influence of the capital, as Professor Jordan and Dr Hill have observed, was almost as great

38 Quoted in J. Aikin, *A Description of the Country from Thirty to Forty Miles around Manchester*, 1795, 154.
39 C. Morris (ed.), *Journeys of Celia Fiennes*, 1947, 224.
40 A. P. Wadsworth and J. de L. Mann, *The Cotton Trade and Industrial Lancashire*, Manchester, 1931, 8–9.
41 J. S. Booker, *History of Didsbury Chapel*, Chet. Soc., old series, 42, Manchester, 1856, 130–40.
42 Quoted in P. Collinson, 'The puritan classical movement in the reign of Elizabeth', Ph.D. thesis, University of London, 1957, 772.

in religion as it was in commerce.[43] An anonymous writer of the mid-seventeenth century declared that puritanism spread:

> by means of the city of London, the nest and seminary of the seditious faction, and by reason of its universal trade throughout the kingdom with its commodities conveying and deriving this civil contagion to all our cities and corporations and thereby poisoning whole counties.[44]

Dr Howell, for example, has suggested in his book on *Newcastle-upon-Tyne and the Puritan Revolution* that the growth of puritanism in that town can to some extent be viewed as a by-product of its coastal coal trade with London. Manchester and its region were no less profoundly influenced by their commercial relationship with the capital. Merchants are known, for instance, to have used their visits to London as opportunities for hearing sermons and buying religious books. The biographer of the Bolton merchant Richard Heywood, for example, tells that:

> when he was abroad his design and practice was to hear the best preachers; he travelled to London once or twice every year and he constantly heard old Mr Edmund Calamy at Aldermanbury, Mr Thomas Case and such like. His practice at London was to furnish himself with the best books, the most plain, practical, experimental treatises in divinity, such as Calvin, Luther in English, Mr Perkins, Dr Preston, Dr Sibbs, wherein he took much pleasure in reading.[45]

Undoubtedly one of the main themes of seventeenth-century English history was that England was being transformed by the influence of London.[46] But the total impact of London varied according to the strength of economic ties, so within the diocese of Chester it was in the eastern parts of Lancashire, with their close trading links with the capital, that this transformation was most noticeable. The role of Manchester in this respect was of very great importance. The town was significantly described early in the 1640's as 'the very London of those parts, the liver that sends blood into all the coun-

43 W. K. Jordan, *The Charities of Rural England, 1480–1660*, 1961, and *The Social Institutions of Lancashire*, Chet. Soc., third series, II, Manchester, 1962; Hill, 'Puritans and the "Dark corners of the land" '.

44 Quoted in R. H. Tawney, *Religion and the Rise of Capitalism*, Pelican Books edition, 1964, 203.

45 J. Horsfall Turner, *Diaries, etc, of the Rev. Oliver Heywood*, Brighouse, 1882, I, 84.

46 E. A. Wrigley, 'London's importance, 1650–1750', *Past and Present*, 37, 1967.

tries thereabouts'.[47] And so it did, in more ways than one. The Manchester region, interlaced by a complex pattern of commercial and industrial relationships, was dominated by its economic and religious centre to an extent not seen elsewhere in the diocese.

There seems in fact, at least in Lancashire and Cheshire, to be a remarkable correlation between a map of the distribution of puritanism and that of the network of market towns. Professor Everitt has noted that for the country as a whole:

> it is not fanciful to trace a connection between the rapid spread of private trading in the early seventeenth century and the rapid rise of Independency. For Independency was not a rural and static religion like Anglicanism, nor rigid and urban like Presbyterianism, but mobile, virile and impatient of human institutions like the wayfaring community itself.[48]

Market towns—the normal setting of private trading—were not purely business centres. Professor Everitt reminds us that the market town:

> was the focus of the rural life around it. Its squares and taverns provided the meeting place for the yeomen and husbandmen, not only to buy and sell, but to hear the news, criticise the government or organise insurrection.[49]

Market towns were numerous in Lancashire, particularly in the south-east of the county, there being thirty-one in all in this period.[50] In twenty-one of these, signs of puritanism have been discovered.[51] Cheshire had thirteen market towns, and again in religion they overwhelmingly inclined to puritanism, evidence of the latter being found in eight of these centres of trade.[52]

47 Arthur Trevor to the Marquis of Ormonde, 21 December 1642. Quoted in T. Baines, *History of Liverpool*, 1852, 302.
48 A. M. Everitt, 'The marketing of agricultural produce' in Joan Thirsk (ed.), *Agrarian History of England and Wales*, IV, *1500–1640*, Cambridge, 1967, 562.   49 *Ibid.*, 488.
50 Ashton-under-Lyne, Blackburn, Bolton, Burnley, Bury, Cartmel, Chorley, Clitheroe, Colne, Dalton-in-Furness, Garstang, Haslingden, Hawkshead, Hornby, Kirkham, Lancaster, Leigh, Liverpool, Manchester, Ormskirk, Padiham, Poulton, Prescot, Preston, Rochdale, Salford, Ulverston, Walton-le-Dale, Warrington, Whalley, Wigan.
51 Puritanism was expressed by either clergy or laity in Ashton-under-Lyne, Blackburn, Bolton, Burnley, Bury, Haslingden, Kirkham, Leigh, Liverpool, Manchester, Ormskirk, Padiham, Poulton, Prescot, Preston, Rochdale, Salford, Ulverston, Warrington, Whalley and Wigan.
52 Lay puritanism was expressed in the Cheshire market towns of Chester, Congleton, Knutsford, Macclesfield, Middlewich, Nantwich, Stockport and Tarvin.

It is significant that the two most strongly Catholic areas of the diocese—the Fylde and the Wirral—were not intimately involved in the trading network of Lancashire and Cheshire. In the Fylde there were only two market towns—Kirkham and Poulton—and although neither was of prime importance these in fact were the only two towns in the area to have puritan clergy during this period. In the Wirral there were no markets at all. Chester was the nearest important trading centre, just as Preston was for the Fylde. In both the Fylde and the Wirral communications were exceptionally poor, and the economic relationships of these regions in consequence were restricted and largely one-sided. The inhabitants of the Wirral and those of the Fylde must have been obliged to leave their own areas in order to trade, for there were scarcely any inducements or facilities for strangers to come in. In these areas, then, the business of buying and selling—with which the rise of puritanism was so often associated—was mainly carried on outside.

Now it is true that in the northern deaneries of the archdeaconry of Richmond although there were market towns few of them were centres of puritanism. Only three of them, in fact—those of Burton-in-Kendal, Sedbergh and Richmond—seem in any way to have inclined in this direction. But most of these northern markets were of purely local importance, the archdeaconry as a whole being economically undeveloped in the extreme. Professor Jones has written of this situation in the Lake counties and discussed the retarding factors at work in the economy of the region.

> One was distance from markets of any size, which meant that goods taken, for example, to Newcastle or the Midlands had to bear a high cost of carriage by land. There were no navigable rivers to reduce the expense, and, though Cumberland has a long coastline, its harbours were poor until the expansion of the coal trade brought about improvement, especially at Whitehaven.[53]

Commercial links between Cumberland and London were few, the region's involvement in the national trading network was not sufficiently strong to bring in puritanism, and puritan clergy—the most direct channel by which religious ideas could be introduced—were not sufficiently numerous to be influential.

Puritanism, then, took firmest root in the most economically developed areas of the diocese, in the clothing towns, in marketing

53 C. M. L. Bouch and G. P. Jones, *A Short Economic and Social History of the Lake Counties, 1500–1830*, Manchester, 1961, 117.

centres and in the 'industrialising' pastoral regions in the east of the diocese.[54] It was in these areas that the puritan preachers were generally to be found, for although there are exceptions, it was generally true that the ministers were not missionaries.

> They bend not themselves to preach abroad in the country[side], [a critic roundly declared as early as 1585], and where there is greatest need, but in the most populous places, as in market towns, shire towns and cities, where they know that strange devices and novelties finding always most friends and best entertainment they might with less labour sow their contentions.[55]

A further factor which tended to promote the development of puritanism in this region was the ecclesiastical geography of the diocese. For just as noticeable as the enormous size of the see of Chester itself was the vastness of many of its parishes, particularly in Lancashire. 'This shire,' wrote Thomas Fuller, 'though sufficiently thick of people is exceedingly thin of parishes.'[56] The Lancashire-born preacher George Walker had earlier made the same observation, stressing that his native county contained:

> some parishes forty miles in compass to my knowledge, whereas some other shires not much larger than one division or hundred of Lancashire are known and recorded to have two or three hundred parish churches.[57]

In the county as a whole there were no more than sixty-four parishes. Largest of them all was that of Whalley, the extent of which, almost incredibly, was about 106,000 acres. The parish of Rochdale covered about 42,000 acres, while that of Manchester had 35,000, Bolton 33,000 and Ormskirk 31,000.

But the phenomenon was not peculiar only to the Lancashire part of the diocese. Adam Martindale, then ministering at Rostherne, Cheshire, complained that 'the minister of Great Budworth and I had such vast parishes to go through that multitudes of the people would be dead in all probability before we could go once over them'.[58]

54 Dr Thirsk's suggestion in the *Agrarian History of England*, IV, *1500–1640*, 112, that the economic background of pasture and woodland areas was most conducive to the development of puritanism, seems to a considerable extent to be confirmed by this local evidence. The eastern strip of Lancashire and Cheshire—a pastoral area—was the most puritan.

55 A. Peel (ed.), *Tracts ascribed to Richard Bancroft*, Cambridge, 1953, 57.

56 Fuller, *History of the Worthies of England*, 1662, 105.

57 Walker, *An Exhortation . . .*, 16.

58 F. Parkinson (ed.), *Life of Adam Martindale*, Chet. Soc., old series, 4, Manchester, 1845, 122.

The result of this situation for the development of puritanism was that the parish as such was often not a realistic or meaningful unit, either to the authorities, who found that they were in consequence faced with a breakdown of Church organisation and discipline, or to the inhabitants, to whom the parish church might seem impossibly remote. Even before the industrial revolution, then, the parochial organisation of Lancashire seems to have been unable to come to terms with the increasing population of the eastern half of the county and to contain its religious development. So, for the historian of puritanism—just as for the Evangelical Revival of the eighteenth and nineteenth centuries—it is often the smaller and more recently created unit of the chapelry rather than of the parish itself which occupies the centre of interest. In the chapelries, for example, it was common for the clergy to be financially dependent upon their congregations. This being the case, it was in the chapelries that puritan laymen often had greatest scope to exert and express themselves in religion. Certainly by the time of the Civil War it was perfectly clear that the religious tendency of the chapelries was towards Independency rather than towards Presbyterianism.

The importance of the smaller unit of the chapelry in the development and distribution of puritanism will become clearer through a few illustrations. First it can be noted that although there is no evidence of lay puritanism at Whalley itself, there are signs that in some of the fourteen chapelries into which this excessively large parish was subdivided different developments were taking place. For example, in the market town of Haslingden, one of these chapelries, a small puritan element arose within the congregation. Similarly, it is not the parish of Blackburn as such which is of much interest to the historian of puritanism but its chapelry of Darwen, where conventicles are known to have been a regular feature of the organised religious life of the lay puritan element in the congregation. Lay puritanism is known to have been strongest, too, in the outlying and semi-autonomous chapelries of the parish of Prestwich, that is, in Ringley and in Oldham.[59] Again, in the parish of Walton, in western Lancashire, it was not in the vicinity of the parish church that puritanism took hold but in the chapelries of Liverpool and Toxteth.

The case of Toxteth is particularly interesting. The chapelry had been founded some time around 1600, when Toxteth—previously

59 The expression and organisation of puritanism in all these chapelries will be discussed in greater detail in later chapters.

part of the Derby estate—was disparked and settlers were introduced, it seems, from puritan Bolton. Toxteth soon became a centre
of religious enthusiasm, a fact which was eloquently expressed in its
earliest place names. The whole area became known as 'the holy
land', while a stream running through it was called 'Jordan' and
a farm was called 'Jericho'. Prominent landmarks in the district
acquired Biblical names such as 'David's Throne' and 'Adam's
Buttery'.[60]

As an illustration from Cheshire, the case of Goostrey chapel can
be cited. It was here rather than at its parish church of Sandbach
that puritanism was expressed. The nonconformist divine Henry
Newcome was to become curate here in 1648, and he wrote that
'I had the unanimous consent of the whole chapelry testified under
their hands . . . The Lord gave me favour in the eyes of the whole
people.'[61]

3 *The attituude of the authorities*[62]

Puritanism in the diocese of Chester—certainly in Elizabeth's reign
—was also favoured by the ecclesiastical authorities, a state of affairs
which undoubtedly proved conducive to its growth and development. For the existence of puritanism in this region was in no sense
regarded by the authorities as a threat to the safety of the Church.
On the contrary, the prevailing attitude was that puritanism was far
too useful and necessary to be persecuted. The diocese, after all,
ranked as one of the 'dark corners of the land', and, faced with the
constant and alarming threat of Catholicism on the one hand and
of irreligion on the other, Church and government needed to enlist
the able and energetic support of the puritan preachers.

The religious condition of the diocese—and of Lancashire particularly—made preaching not only desirable but essential. Bishop
Aylmer of London, for example, in 1577 saw the possibility of

60 V. Davis, *Toxteth Chapel*, Liverpool, 1884, 1.
61 R. Parkinson (ed.), *Autobiography of the Rev. Henry Newcome*, Chet. Soc.,
    old series, 26–7, Manchester, 1852, 1, 11. For a general essay on the economic
    and social factors influencing the distribution of dissent, see A. M. Everitt,
    'Nonconformity in country parishes' in Joan Thirsk (ed.), *Land, Church and
    People: Essays presented to Professor H. P. R. Finberg*, 1970, 178–99.
62 A much fuller discussion of this subject will be found in my essay on
    'Puritanism and the ecclesiastical authorities: the case of the diocese of
    Chester' in B. S. Manning (ed.), *Politics, Religion and the English Civil War*,
    1972.

ridding the capital of its numerous puritan clergy by using—and exhausting—them in active service elsewhere. He believed that 'they might be profitably employed in Lancashire, Staffordshire, Shropshire, and other such like barbarous counties to draw the people from Papism and gross ignorance'.[63] Similarly, in 1582 the Earl of Huntingdon urged the Bishop of Chester to keep a special watch on the western part of Lancashire. 'The want of diligent and faithful preaching [there],' he wrote, 'does wonderfully hinder the building of our Church and in these north parts it is most apparent.'[64] The Bishop, William Chaderton, received another reminder along these lines from the Privy Council in the following year:

> It is a principal part of your pastoral charge [they told him] to appoint some learned and godly ministers to repair unto such places where it shall be needful, to instruct the people the better to know their duty towards God and Her Majesty's laws and to reduce them to such conformity as we desire.[65]

And so it came about that while in the south of England at this time puritan divines were being harried to conform by Archbishop Whitgift, in the diocese of Chester—as in that of York—there came to exist a working co-operation between the authorities and the puritan clergy.[66] While Whitgift was demanding conformity in his own province, puritanism in the diocese of Chester was being actively encouraged from above.

For example, in 1584 a system of preaching Exercises—regular monthly meetings at fourteen centres—was set up to cover the whole diocese.[67] The purpose of the scheme was to win over the people from Popery and at the same time to improve the educational standards of the lower clergy. But what must be particularly emphasised here is the fact that the scheme took effect with full official approval and direction.

63 J. Strype, *Life and Acts of Bishop Aylmer*, Oxford, 1821, 38.
64 Peck, *Desiderata Curiosa*, 130.
65 *Ibid.*, 113.
66 The development of puritanism in Yorkshire is discussed in R. A. Marchant, *The Puritans and the Church Courts in the Diocese of York, 1560–1642*, 1960, and in J. A. Newton, 'Puritanism in the diocese of York, 1603–40', Ph.D. thesis, University of London, 1956. For a general analysis of the contrast between the theory and local practice of the Elizabethan Acts of Supremacy and Uniformity, see the valuable study by C. Cross, *The Royal Supremacy in the Elizabethan Church*, 1969.
67 Full details of these preaching Exercises are to be found in Gonville and Caius, Cambridge, MS 197, ff. 175–85.

The Exercises of 1584 arose out of an earlier arrangement made in 1582 which provided for thrice-yearly synods to be attended by the Lancashire clergy. The Privy Council wrote to Bishop Chaderton in April 1584 praising the original scheme and recommending its extension. They fully approved of the fact that the clergy:

> have heretofore used an ecclesiastical Exercise in some few places of those countries and that only thrice in the whole year. Forasmuch as the good proceeding or slackness in religion is a cure of no small consequence [they went on] especially in those remote parts of the realm standing dangerously for the enemy and where the Gospel as yet has not been thoroughly planted, we have thought good for increase of knowledge and zeal in the common people, as likewise for the establishing of a learned ministry in the country to commend unto your Lordship's good consideration some further enlargement . . . to have the said Exercises of religion hereafter more frequently and in more places of the diocese . . .[68]

Moreover, their Lordships appended a list of clergymen within the diocese with whom they wished the Bishop to confer. These were not, as might be imagined, those renowned for their orthodoxy, but some of the most prominent nonconformist clergymen in the diocese. Listed here, for example, were Christopher Goodman of Chester, John Caldwell of Winwick, Richard Midgley of Rochdale, William Langley of Prestwich and Edward Fleetwood of Wigan.

Arrangements for the enlarged version of the preaching Exercises were accordingly made. Significantly the document listing them was signed not only by the Bishop of Chester but by the puritans Edward Fleetwood, Leonard Shaw of Bury, William Langley and Richard Midgley.

The Bishop now wrote to the various deans of his diocese informing them of the Privy Council's instructions concerning the enlarging of the scheme of preaching Exercises and of his own discussions with the leading preachers in his charge. He accordingly commanded them to publicise the new arrangements and to make certain that all clergymen and schoolmasters within their respective deaneries were acquainted with them.

The preaching Exercises, then, which were dominated by the puritan divines from the start and which furthered their unity, were officially sponsored. But this was by no means the only decisive intervention from above in favour of the puritan divines of the diocese.

68 *Ibid.*, f. 179.

It was in 1599 that the four Queen's Preachers for Lancashire—each appointment being worth £50 a year—were first established as part of the official effort to win over the county to the reformed religion.[69]

> I have seated the Queen's Preachers in Lancashire [wrote Chaderton's successor Bishop Vaughan to Cecil in 1600 after the first appointments had been made] with as much care as I could, and following the records of presentments made to me and the Judges of Assize of late years, I have put one in every part of the county where there are most recusants . . .[70]

Although it was with Cecil that the scheme originated, the Bishop of Chester had an important share in making the first appointments and thereafter, in fact, was left in complete control of the nominations. Bishop Vaughan particularly wanted Richard Midgley, formerly vicar of Rochdale, to take up one of the preacherships in view of 'his well deserving of the churches in these parts'. Now Midgley was a strict nonconformist, and the Bishop's choice of him may possibly have raised some official eyebrows in the southern province. But Bishop Vaughan stood firm.

> As to Mr Midgley [he declared in the following year], whatever exception may be taken to him, considering the good he has done in the last forty years and the respect in which he is held, I am resolved for his continuance unless by superior authority I am pressed to the contrary.[71]

Bishop Vaughan's choice of Richard Midgley provides a good indication of the peculiarities of the situation in the diocese of Chester. The endowment of the four Queen's Preachers was a royal attempt to further orthodoxy in Lancashire, and in it puritans played the leading part. Of the four preachers first appointed, three—Midgley, William Harrison and William Forster—were inclined to puritanism.[72]

Only in 1590 had an apparently short-lived effort been made to

69 The history of the preacherships—which survived until 1845—is outlined in E. Axon, 'The King's Preachers in Lancashire', *Trans. Lancs. and Ches. Antiq. Soc.*, vol. 56, Manchester, 1944, 67–104.
70 *Salisbury Mss*, H.M.C., x, 41. 20 February 1600. Leigh, Huyton, Ormskirk and Garstang were the places chosen for the preacherships. Appropriately enough, the preachers' stipends, it was agreed, were to come from recusancy fines levied in the county. Catholics were to pay to be converted!
71 *Salisbury Mss*, H.M.C., x, 41.
72 Of the remaining Queen's Preacher—Barnard Adams—virtually nothing is known save that he was well liked by the Bishop. (*Salisbury Mss*, x, 84.) It should be noted that the original character and purpose of the Queen's

bring the Lancashire puritan divines to conformity. This involved not the Bishop of Chester but Archbishop Piers of York, who— possibly acting on instructions from Whitgift—used his metropolitan visitation of the diocese of Chester in that year as a weapon against the puritans.[73] But the issuing and enforcement of orders in six- teenth-century England were two entirely different things. Despite the Archbishop's determination there is no evidence to show that conformity was in fact enforced in the diocese of Chester; the official regulations continued to be neglected by puritan divines. And when at the Hampton Court conference in 1604 a plea was made for a continuation of the traditional policy of studied lenience towards the Lancashire puritan clergy, the initial response was by no means unfavourable.[74]

The official outlook on puritanism in the diocese of Chester began to change in the early seventeenth century, a development which was intimately bound up with the less unyielding attitude which was coming to be shown towards the Catholics. Bishop Morton of Chester (1616–19) tried to reason with the puritan clergy of his diocese and reduce them to conformity.[75] And about the same time James I issued, in 1617, the Declaration of Sports, a document which similarly attacked the puritan position but from a different angle and whose author again was Bishop Morton. Although the Declara- tion—which was issued with Lancashire in mind—was not intended as an edict of toleration for the Catholics, its aim quite clearly was to undermine the authority of the preachers, who by this date were beginning to be considered a greater nuisance than the Catholic recusants they opposed.[76]

Preachers was not maintained throughout the period reviewed in this book. Even in the seventeenth century the positions were tending to become sinecures.

73 Professor Collinson argues that 'the whole episode should probably be under- stood as an effort by Whitgift to bring the administration of the northern province into line with his own'. (*Elizabethan Puritan Movement*, 406.)

74 The plea was made by the Lancashire-born Laurence Chaderton, brother of the Bishop of Chester and Master of Emmanuel College, Cambridge. (W. Barlow, 'The summe and substance of the conference at Hampton Court . . .' in E. Cardwell, *A History of Conferences*, Oxford, 1840, 210–11.)

75 In 1618 the Bishop published an account of his dealings with the puritans, entitling it *A Defence of the Innocencie of the Three Ceremonies of the Church* . . .

76 The text of the 1617 Declaration is printed in E. Axon (ed.), *Manchester Quarter Sessions*, Rec. Soc. Lancs. and Ches., 42, 1901, xxv, and is discussed in J. Tait, 'The Declaration of Sports for Lancashire', *E.H.R.*, 32, 1917.

But despite these clear indications of a fundamental change in the official attitude to both puritans and Catholics, puritanism continued to develop in the diocese of Chester, and a general conformity was not enforced. John Bridgeman, who succeeded Morton as Bishop of Chester in 1619, was as moderate as his sixteenth-century predecessors. It was not until 1633, when outside intervention came in the form of Archbishop Neile's metropolitan visitation, that puritanism in the diocese really came under attack. But mainly because the attack was so late, the results of this attempt to bring the situation in the North into line with that prevailing in the Laudian South were far less impressive than had been intended. Puritanism in the diocese of Chester had been allowed to grow for far too long, and the dividing line between conformity and nonconformity had been left so deliberately vague that no relatively sudden reversal of policy could successfully uproot it.

It is, then, to the largely unmolested growth of puritanism in this region, the forms in which it was expressed and the various forces at work within it, that the main part of this study will be devoted.

Chapter two

The role of the clergy

The Church in these parts has been successively blessed with famous ministers . . .

Oliver Heywood, *Life of John Angier*, Chet. Soc., new series, 97, Manchester, 1937, 45

1. *The forms of clerical nonconformity in worship*

During the period from about 1580 to 1642 at least 160 clergymen in the diocese of Chester can be labelled puritans. In the main this total is made up of those ministers whose nonconformity was noted by the ecclesiastical authorities. Those who, although not presented as such, were regarded as puritans by their colleagues and contemporaries have been included, as also, of course, have those ministers who expressed distinctively puritan attitudes in their published writings. But clearly this total under-estimates the numerical strength of clerical puritanism. The unostentatious, conforming puritan minister who did not publish is an elusive figure who can escape the notice of the historian as he did that of the Church governors in his own day. It was the nonconformist who attracted notice.

Easily the most common expression of clerical puritanism was the failure to wear the surplice as prescribed by the Church canons. The vestment was opposed by puritan ministers as a relic of Popery which the half-hearted Elizabethan Church settlement had failed to remove. This was made clear, for example, in a case heard by the Consistory Court in 1604 concerning Ralph Kirk, a curate in the parish of Manchester. The articles against the nonconformist minister alleged that he:

> denies the wearing of the surplice and he preaches that the surplice is a rag of the Pope and a mighty heresy in the Church and that he who maintains it cannot be saved.[1]

Puritan divines in the diocese of Chester were given an opportunity to justify their position *vis à vis* the surplice—and other

1 Chester. Consistory Court papers. EDC 5, 1604. Miscellaneous.

c

ceremonies—early in the seventeenth century by Bishop Morton. The Bishop required ministers to submit to him a defence of their non-conformity, which he then attempted to refute. The debate—though of course with more space given to the Bishop's views than to those of his adversaries—was later published in 1618.[2] From this book we find that William Hinde, minister at Bunbury in Cheshire at the time, voiced the common view that 'white linen for ministerial apparel was not anciently used in the primitive Church . . .' Since it had no scriptural foundation, the use of the surplice was both unnecessary and unlawful. No respect, it was argued, could be shown for purely man-made ceremonies and regulations.

> These ceremonies imposed [wrote Hinde] are not only not commanded as lawful but prohibited as sinful. For the scriptures, Fathers and ortho-dox writers do condemn as sinful all wit-worship or will-worship proceeding out of the forge of man's fancies . . .[3]

That the failure to wear the surplice was a consistent and deliber-ate policy on the part of the puritan divines is also indicated in the frequency with which the charge was made against the same indi-viduals. The most conspicuous example, perhaps, is that of William Bourne, Fellow of the Manchester College, who was presented for not wearing the surplice on no fewer than six occasions between 1608 and 1633.[4] Not surprisingly, when Bourne was presented for the sixth time on this charge in the metropolitan visitation of 1633

2 The book has already been noted in chapter one. Its full title was *A Defence of the Innocencie of the Three Ceremonies of the Church of England, viz. the Surplice, Crosse after Baptism and Kneeling at the Receiving of the Blessed Sacrament.*

3 *Ibid.*, 204, 28. William Hinde, born in Kendal *c.* 1569 and educated at Queen's College, Oxford, was appointed to the living of Bunbury in Cheshire in 1603. He wrote and edited several works but is principally remembered for his posthumously published biography of John Bruen of Stapleford. In his day Hinde was without doubt the leading puritan divine in Cheshire.

4 Chester. 1608 vis. EDV 1/15, f. 133; Chester. 1611 vis. EDV 1/17, f. 101; Chester. 1614 vis. EDV 1/19, f. 67; Chester. 1622 vis. EDV 1/24, f. 125v; Chester. 1625 vis. EDV 1/26, f. 98v; York. 1633 vis. RVIA 23, f. 602v. Bourne—who has been described as 'the John Knox of Manchester'—became Fellow of the Manchester College in 1600 on the recommendation of the scholars Chaderton and Whitaker at Cambridge. Bourne narrowly missed being appointed Warden in 1609. (F. R. Raines, *Lives of the Fellows of the College of Manchester*, Chet. Soc., new series, 21 and 23, Manchester, 1891, I, 85–95.)

he was suspended. Bourne refused to conform in this matter. It was noted in the visitation report that he was only:

> contented to read prayers without a surplice, saying he refused not as opposing order, but that he was ashamed now to put on the surplice which in thirty years before of his being Fellow there he had not done . . .[5]

It had in fact been normal practice at the Collegiate Church in Manchester, where in 1633 affairs were discovered to be 'altogether out of order', for the use of the surplice to be disregarded. Archbishop Neile wrote in his visitation report that, after being subjected to pressures to conform, the Collegiate clergy—with the notable exception of Bourne—'reformed themselves, came to the prayers in their habits and read the service which they say had not before been seen'. As early as 1578 it was noted in the visitation that at the Manchester College 'the curates do not wear surplices'.[6] John Buckley, one of the Collegiate clergy, was charged in 1590 with not wearing the surplice and, not having conformed, was again presented on this count in 1592.[7] On the same occasion Oliver Carter, the preacher at the College, was also noted as one who did not wear the surplice; twelve years later he was still a nonconformist in this respect.[8]

Surplice cases, then, can provide undoubted evidence of ministerial puritanism, but they must be used critically. Economic as well as religious factors were sometimes involved in the question of the wearing of the surplice. Responsibility for the provision of the surplice rested with the parish, but on account of the expense entailed it was a responsibility that was sometimes shirked. This was made plain, for example, at Kirkham in Lancashire in 1590 when James Smith, the vicar, was presented for not wearing the surplice and explained that 'it is in controversy between him and the parishioners who should provide one'.[9] A surplice was an expensive item and when bought was often made to last an unreasonably long time before it was replaced. Not surprisingly, then, even moderate clergymen might not feel inclined to wear the old, tattered remnants of a surplice which were sometimes offered to them. At the parish church of Eccles, for example, in 1578 it was noted that 'they have

5 P.R.O. State Papers Domestic. SP 16/259/78. Neile to Charles I.
6 York. 1578 vis. RVIA 7, f. 37.
7 York. 1590 vis. RVIA 11, f. 79; Chester. 1592 vis. EDV 1/10, f. 168.
8 Chester. 1604 vis. EDV 1/13, f. 64.   9 York. 1590 vis. RVIA 11, f. 71v.

no surplice good and convenient to be worn'.[10] In 1619 the 'want of a convenient surplice, [the one they had] being torn and ragged', was noted at Wistaston, Cheshire.[11] While at Eccleston, Cheshire, three years later it was observed that the 'surplice [is] old and decayed and the minister will not wear it'.[12]

Cases such as these on the whole can probably be taken at their face value. But where they involve known puritan ministers they ought perhaps to be treated with caution; the failure to provide a decent surplice might be a very convenient excuse for the nonconformity of a puritan minister. In this connection it is worth noting the case of John Broxopp, vicar of Ormskirk, proceedings against whom were opened in the Consistory Court in 1637. Charged with failing to wear the surplice, Broxopp explained:

some few times within the years [mentioned in the articles against him] when he did officiate and minister the holy communion he did not wear the surplice because sometimes it was at washing, sometimes at making and sometimes at mending so as he could not always have the same to put on him.[13]

Broxopp's explanation seems almost too innocent to be true, and it hardly fits in with the other available information concerning him. As will be shown later in the present chapter, Broxopp's extreme nonconformity was undoubted.

Like the surplice, the use of the sign of the cross in baptism was opposed by puritan ministers and their parishioners as a hated relic of Popery for which there was no scriptural foundation.[14] The use of the sign of the cross, in fact, according to puritan reasoning was directly opposed to Biblical teaching.

10 York. 1578 vis. RVIA 7, f. 38v. Details of the actual cost of surplices are occasionally given in churchwardens' accounts. At St Oswald's, Chester, for example, we learn that in 1595 the wardens laid out the sum of 11s 3d for cloth with which to make a new surplice. A replacement was not bought until 1610, when a payment of 18s is recorded 'for twelve yards of Scottish cloth to make a surplice for the vicar'. (Chester. Parochial records. P 29/7/1, 9, f. 24v.)

11 Chester. 1619 vis. EDV 1/22, f. 27v.

12 Chester. 1622 vis. EDV 1/24, f. 10v.

13 Chester. Consistory Court papers. EDC 5, 1637. Miscellaneous.

14 On the other hand, no evidence has been found either in the ecclesiastical records or in the sermon literature to suggest that the use of the ring in marriage was an important issue amongst the puritans of the diocese of Chester. (Cf. Richard Baxter, *Autobiography*, Everyman edition, 17: 'The ring in marriage I made no scruple about.')

Nicholas Helme, the puritan vicar of Kirkham, Lancashire, was one who certainly took this view. He was charged in the 1598 visitation with having preached

> against the sign of the cross in baptism or otherwise, and said that whosoever did maintain or allow the same to be made is a traitor to God, and commits as great an offence against the second commandment as if he had committed the sin of whoredom or theft, and said if there be any that can prove out of the word of God that it is not suspicion to make the sign of the cross, tie him to a stake and burn him.[15]

The views of Ralph Kirk, curate in the parish of Manchester, were similar. In 1604 in the Consistory Court the charge had been made against him:

> that in baptism he does not observe the Book of Common Prayer in signing with the sign of the cross, and if any of the parties that come with the child to be baptised or any other request him to make the sign of the cross, he asks them whether they will have a black, a red, a blue or a headless cross and such other contemptuous words.[16]

But in areas of established puritanism, laymen—as will be shown in a later section of this book—were sometimes even more insistent opponents of the sign of the cross than their ministers. Where the hold of puritanism was precarious, however, the lead in this matter, as in others, was taken by the clergy, often in direct opposition to the wishes of their parishioners. In 1604, for example, Peter White, vicar of Poulton in the Fylde, was presented in the visitation for not having 'baptised with the sign of the cross, which caused many to be baptised out of the parish'.[17] Earlier in 1590 James Hawksworth, vicar of Middleton Tyas in Richmond deanery, had been charged with refusing to baptise a child since the parents had insisted on the full official ceremony.[18] A strong anti-puritan group in the Cheshire parish of Tarporley complained to the J.P.'s in 1642 that their minister and curate:

> do utterly refuse to execute the holy orders of the Church in ... baptising ... insomuch one William Johnson's child upon Sunday last was forced to be carried to another church two miles from Tarporley to be

---

15 Chester. 1598 vis. EDV 1/12, f. 116.
16 Chester. Consistory Court papers. EDC 5, 1604. Miscellaneous.
17 Chester. 1604 vis. EDV 1/13, f. 198v.
18 York. 1590 vis. RVIA 11, f. 24v.

baptised according to the lawful rites and ceremonies of the Church of England . . .[19]

Puritan ministers, intent on undermining the superstitious belief that the sign of the cross was an integral part of baptism, were equally obstinate in attacking the view that the ceremony of baptism itself was essential to the salvation of the child. Richard Rowe, for example, the puritan vicar of Bunbury, Cheshire, was presented in 1611 'for not using the sign of the cross in baptism [and that he] refuses to baptise any but on the Sabbath or holy day although it be in danger of death'.[20] Similarly, John Swan, a later minister in the same living, was charged in 1626:

> that you have . . . divers times or at least once . . . refused to baptise one or more child or children being in danger of death although you had notice before of the same, insomuch that they have died without that holy sacrament of baptism from you.[21]

But to Swan and others like him this was not a catastrophe. Even if a child's death was imminent, private baptism by either minister or midwife ought not to be allowed. The ceremony ought always to take place in church before the congregation. In itself it was not a grant of grace; its main significance, puritans held, was that it marked the admission of the child to the flock of Christ.

The opposition sometimes shown by puritan ministers to the use of the font in baptism was largely based on this same determination to break with Catholic tradition. And so the substitution of a basin or dish for the font in baptism emphasised puritan dissociation from the pre-Reformation past. The practice, writes Professor Collinson, was 'an implicit denial that their church was in any way the successor of the Popish congregation which had earlier made use of the same building'.[22]

In 1611, for example, Thomas Elcock, rector of Bartomley, Cheshire, was charged with having 'christened two children in a pewter basin in the chancel'.[23] And John Gee, curate of Newton in Winwick parish, took the baptism of his own child as an opportunity to set an example. The charge was that 'his child [had been]

---

19 Chester. Quarter sessions. QSF 4/24. 1642. The two clergymen in question were Nathaniel Lancaster, who had been vicar since 1638, and his curate, John Jones.
20 Chester. 1611 vis. EDV 1/17, f. 54.
21 Chester. 1622 vis. EDV 1/24, f. 165v.
22 Collinson, *Puritan Movement*, 370.
23 Chester. 1611 vis. EDV 1/17, f. 53.

christened in a basin of pewter and not in the font'.[24] The tradition was evidently continued at Newton, for in 1633 William Thompson, curate, was charged with 'baptising children in basins of pewter or wood in the chapel . . . and for omitting to use the sign of the cross'.[25] Thompson, significantly, was also charged with dispensing with godparents when he administered the sacrament of baptism.

The opinions of puritan divines about godparents were to some extent divided. Commenting on the evidence which the preachers had set before him, Bishop Morton wrote that 'some will have godfathers and godmothers and witnesses and some will be content only with the natural father'.[26] For those ministers, however, who opposed the practice of having godparents, their stand was based above all on puritan reluctance to allow an individual to take a solemn oath on behalf of others. At the baptism only the father could confidently make a promise concerning the upbringing of his child—a position which was perfectly in accord with the general emphasis in puritanism on the authority of heads of households.[27] Also, as puritan ministers recognised, the practice of having godparents had through much abuse been brought into discredit. At Gawsworth, for example, in 1578 the curate had been charged with having 'admitted Edward Fytton, son and heir of Mr Fytton, to answer as godfather, being but six years of age'.[28] Scandals such as this, the puritans argued, ought not to be allowed to occur.

Accordingly, some ministers, such as Ralph Kirk of Manchester, dispensed with godparents altogether. Similar to the charge made against Kirk was that against William Thompson of Newton. In addition to the charges already noted, he was also presented in the 1633 visitation as 'a great nonconformist and does not christen children unless the father be godfather'.[29]

24 Chester. 1622 vis. EDV 1/24, f. 136.
25 York. 1633 vis. RVIA 23, f. 366.
26 Morton, *A Defence of the Innocencie of the Three Ceremonies of the Church of England* . . . , 24.
27 Puritan opposition to godparents receives some attention in H. Davies, *The Worship of the English Puritans*, 1948, 151, 217, 219. The 1644 directory emphasised the role of the father in the baptismal ceremony. I am indebted to Dr C. Hill for his helpful comments on this point.
28 York. 1578 vis. RVIA 7, f. 5.
29 York. 1633 vis. RVIA 23, f. 378. It seems unlikely that laymen also were uninterested in this question. Taking an instance from another area, one can note that the Essex minister Ralph Josselin recorded in his diary on

While on the subject of puritan attitudes to the ceremonies, some mention ought perhaps to be made of funerals. The resistance shown by puritan ministers to superstitious practices at burials will be discussed at a later more appropriate stage in the book. What can usefully be considered at this point are the provisions concerning their own funerals which ministers sometimes made in their wills.

In the funeral service, as in all others, the puritan required that the accent should always be on simplicity. Richard Rothwell, for example, who spent a part of his ministry in the diocese of Chester, laid down in his will, proved in 1631, 'that I be buried in the church-yard without singing or ringing or any such solemnity which is now commonly used'.[30] William Leigh, parson of Standish, Lancashire, who died in 1639, also desired that his funeral should be conducted without show, disorder or unseemly conduct. Although he made bequests to the poor in his will, he desired that no doles were to be given at his funeral, since he had 'observed at funerals [where doles were given] much disorder and great abuse together with super-stition in praying for the dead'.[31]

The available evidence relating to this question, however, is scanty in the extreme. But the puritan theory and practice of the com-munion service is much more fully documented. This is particularly true of the failure to kneel during the celebration of the sacrament.

As with the surplice and with the sign of the cross, genuflexion was opposed by clergy and laity alike because it had no scriptural foundation and because to them it implied an adoration of the elements:

That which is contrary to the example of Christ in the first institution [wrote the Cheshire divine William Hinde] and also to the example of the Apostles and primitive Church successively, and that which is against the intention of Christ, being in itself idolatrous, must needs be abolished

17 August 1644 that 'this day I baptised three children. John Read held his own child, the first that I ever baptised so'. (F. Hockliffe (ed.), *Diary of Ralph Josselin*, Camden Soc., third series, 15, 1908, 27.)

30 The will is amongst the probate records at the Lancashire Record Office, although at his death Rothwell was a minister at Mansfield, Notts. In similar vein, John Bruen, Esq., of Stapleford, had earlier declared that 'I will have no blacks . . . I love not any proud or pompous funerals, neither is there any cause of mourning, but of rejoicing rather . . .' (Hinde, *Life of John Bruen*, 225.)

31 Probate records, Preston. Mention is made of puritan funerals in Collinson, *Puritan Movement*, 370-1.

as unlawful. Such is the gesture of kneeling in the receiving of the Eucharist . . .[32]

Puritan ministers themselves were sometimes charged with failing to kneel at the communion. In 1622, for example, Humphrey Tylecote, curate at Stretford, was charged at nearby Stockport 'for sitting at the communion', while the curate there was presented for administering it to him in this manner.[33] Similarly, Thomas Case, a visiting clergyman from outside the diocese of Chester, was charged in the Consistory Court in 1638 that 'you yourself do not usually and constantly observe the ceremonies of the Church by kneeling at the receiving of the holy communion . . .'[34] The refusal of William Thompson, curate at Newton, to conform to the prescribed gesture at the communion was even more complete. He was presented in the 1633 visitation 'for receiving the sacrament of the Lord's Supper at Winwick church sitting and leaning'.[35]

Normally, however, the charge against puritan ministers was not that they themselves sat or stood when they received the communion but that they administered it to others who received it in this manner. In 1616, for example, Hugh Burrows, minister at Shotwick, Cheshire, was charged in the Consistory Court that he had:

admitted divers strangers who are not parishioners of Shotwick parish to receive the holy communion . . . and has administered to some of them . . . sitting and not kneeling as by law they are bound.[36]

Similarly, John Ley, vicar of Great Budworth, Cheshire, was presented three years later in the visitation on the charge that he had 'served some sitting at the communion'.[37] At Middlewich, Cheshire, in 1622, Robert Halliley, the vicar, was charged that he 'admits strangers to the communion and administers the same to them that sit'.[38]

32 Quoted in Morton, *A Defence* . . . , 244.
33 Chester. 1622 vis. EDV 1/24, f. 52.
34 Chester. Consistory Court papers, EDC 5, 1638. Miscellaneous.
35 York. 1633 vis. RVIA 23, f. 366.
36 Chester. Consistory Court papers. EDC 5, 1616. Miscellaneous.
37 Chester. 1619 vis. EDV 1/22, f. 52. John Ley was born in Warwick in 1583 and educated at Christ Church, Oxford. He was presented by his college to Great Budworth in 1616 and remained there until the 1640's. Ley was presented for his nonconformity on several occasions and came to be recognised as the leading puritan divine in Cheshire at this time. He was later a member of the Assembly of Divines and was the author of numerous publications.   38 Chester. 1622 vis. EDV 1/24, f. 32.

Far more explicit was the case of John Swan, of Bunbury, Cheshire, heard by the Consistory Court in 1626. Amongst a host of other charges, Swan was presented on the charge that he had:

> to strangers and others administered the holy communion sitting and to some standing and suffer them to use what gesture they please contrary to the canon in that behalf provided.[39]

But revealing though the charge was against the vicar, it also makes clear that it is in the context of lay rather than clerical puritanism that the question of failing to kneel properly belongs. Failing to kneel at the communion was by far the most common expression of lay puritanism—a point which will be explored in detail in the next chapter.

Little else is known of the manner in which the clergy administered the sacrament of the communion. In 1598, however, Nicholas Helme, vicar of Kirkham, was presented on the charge that he 'has ministered the wine as the same came from the cellar without any prayers . . .'[40] And so distinctive was the way in which Joseph Midgley, vicar of Rochdale, conducted the communion service that it was singled out for mention at the Hampton Court conference in 1604. Midgley's method, apparently, 'consisted chiefly in this, that the minister suffered . . . each man to put his hand into the basket and take his own part of the bread'.[41]

Relatively little is known of the frequency with which the communion was celebrated by puritan divines in the diocese of Chester. There are occasional references to the subject in the printed sermon literature but they are not sufficiently numerous to permit generalisation. Samuel Clarke, the martyrologist, for example, recalled how in his ministry at Shotwick, Cheshire, in the 1630's he 'set up monthly sacraments, and we enjoyed much sweet liberty and communion in the same'.[42] Samuel Torshell, preacher at Bunbury, had

---

39 Chester. Consistory Court papers. EDC 5, 1626. Miscellaneous.
40 Chester. 1598 vis. EDV 1/12, f. 116.
41 Ley, *A Case of Conscience* . . ., 1641, 9. Possibly Midgley's method owed something to his experience at Cambridge—he was there in the early 1580's. A contemporary noted that at Emmanuel College 'they receive that holy sacrament sitting upon forms about the communion and do pull the loaf one from the other after the minister has begun . . .' (Baker MSS, VI, 85–6, quoted in J. B. Mullinger, *The University of Cambridge*, Cambridge, 1884, II, 314.)
42 Clarke, *Lives of Sundry Eminent Persons*, 1683, 4.

rather more to say about this subject.[43] He opposed infrequent communion as a sign of hypocrisy.

> I have observed this [he wrote] in many good churchmen and women, as they call themselves, that is such as scarce ever omit a day or an opportunity of hearing who are yet so stiff in the custom of receiving but once in the year and that at Easter that nothing will persuade and invite them to more frequency. This deformity [he went on] argues some unsoundness at the root.

Torshell proceeded to sketch the process by which the number of communions celebrated had declined.

> The old christians [he wrote] communicated as oft as they heard, then afterwards weekly, after that monthly, after that twice in the year, which is that at which our Church canon sticks . . . and at last it came to once a year.[44]

The trend, Torshell argued, ought to be reversed. Like Clarke, he favoured a monthly celebration.

The failure of puritan ministers to conform to the gestures prescribed by the Book of Common Prayer was not confined only to the communion service. For basically the same reasons as they used to oppose genuflexion, puritan divines preached against standing at the reading of the Gospel and against bowing at the name of Jesus. Significantly, the most explicit evidence of this defiance comes from parishes in predominantly Catholic areas where puritan ministers struggled for ascendancy.

In 1616, for example, a case was heard in the Consistory Court concerning Hugh Burrows, incumbent at Shotwick in the Wirral.

43 Samuel Torshell (1604–50), born in London and educated at Christ's College, Cambridge, was appointed by the London Haberdashers' Company to the living of Bunbury early in the 1630's. Torshell was a prolific writer, and several of his works will be referred to in the course of this study.

44 Torshell, *The Hypocrite discovered and cured*, 1644, 49–50. The subject is mentioned in H. Davies, *Worship of the English Puritans*, 212. Sometimes economics or friction between minister and parish explain the infrequency with which the communion was celebrated. For example, when the vicar of Burton in Richmond deanery was presented in the visitation of 1590 for having only one communion service in the year, he explained that the parish refused to provide bread and wine for other occasions. (York. 1590 vis. RVIA 11, f. 31.) Perhaps the principal reason for a parish's opposition to a puritan minister's admitting strangers to the communion was that they resented the additional expense involved.

Amongst the evidence offered, a deponent in the case declared that
Burrows had preached in a sermon that:

> it was not lawful for any man to rise and stand upon their feet at the
> public reading of the Gospel in time of divine service or to bow the knee
> or body at the repeating or nominating of the name of Jesus and that
> whosoever did so did bow his body or knee unto the devil, or words to
> the like effect.[45]

A case involving similar charges was heard in 1638 in the Consistory
Court, a case which concerned Edward Fleetwood, vicar of Kirkham.
Rather than preach against these superstitious practices, Fleetwood
had simply 'omitted to read the Epistle and Gospel . . . lest the
people should stand up thereat'. He was also charged with having
'likewise omitted to read the name of our saviour Jesus on purpose
to prevent the people from bowing or bending the knee at the
naming thereof'.[46]

But the puritan divines were not invariably inflexible in matters
of this kind. Robert Nicholls, of Wrenbury, Cheshire, was one who
argued that 'the use of ceremonies ought to be free'.[47] And William
Hinde agreed. 'It is our christian liberty,' he wrote, 'to use ceremonies as things indifferent.'[48] When in 1590 Edward Fleetwood
of Wigan had written to his former Oxford friend, Humfrey Fen,
for advice on the ceremonies, he was told that many of those whose
views Fen had sought regarded the wearing of the surplice 'as an
indifferent thing [and] do refer the consideration of the inconveni-
ences to yourselves, who know the country better'.[49] Much later in

45 Chester. Consistory Court papers, EDC 5, 1616. Miscellaneous.
46 Chester. Consistory Court papers. EDC 5, 1638.
47 Nicholls, *Of Kneeling in the Act of Receiving the Sacramental Bread and
    Wine*, in J. Cotton (ed.), *Some Treasure fetched out of Rubbish*, 1660, 73.
    This short treatise was Nicholls' defence of puritan opposition to kneeling
    which he submitted to Bishop Morton of Chester.
48 Quoted in Morton, *A Defence . . .*, 175.
49 Queen's College, Oxford. MS 280, ff. 173v–5 (letters of Fen and Rainolds
    to Fleetwood of Wigan). I am indebted to Professor Collinson for drawing
    my attention to these letters.
       Edward Fleetwood (*c.* 1534–*c.* 1600) was rector of Wigan from 1570 and
    was without a doubt the most active and prominent of the puritan divines
    in Elizabethan Lancashire. Professor Collinson has described him as 'the
    government's Protestant conscience in Lancashire'. ('The puritan classical
    movement in the reign of Elizabeth I', Ph.D. thesis, University of London,
    1957, 1081.) Certainly he deserves the title. It was partly from Fleetwood's

1638 Thomas Case was charged that in a sermon on the text 'Be not over righteous':

> you thence concluded all those to be in a damnable state who made more sin than God had made, under which case you concluded all those to be who made things indifferent to be necessary thereby condemning the governors of the Church of England for forcing divers ceremonies of the Church to be observed as necessary being otherwise in their own nature indifferent . . .[50]

But puritan opinion on the ceremonies was to some extent divided. It was perfectly possible—especially when the authorities were taking a firm line on the question—for a puritan minister to combine a fundamental puritanism with conformity to the prescribed ceremonies. John Rainolds, in his reply to Fleetwood's request for advice on this subject, urged the Lancashire ministers to conform. He recognised, however, that for some amongst them this might be unacceptable counsel.

> As for them who have taught in former time against it, yea, have suffered for it, stood constant and won credit thereby, I know not what to say if they be still so minded but to pray God to give them favour in the eyes of such as press them thereunto that for their consciences' sake they will forbear them.[51]

Similarly, in the following century John Ley of Great Budworth spoke of the 'latitude of liberty allowed by Christ' in the matter of the ceremonies, and gave his full approval to the conformity of puritan laymen.[52] Interesting light is thrown on Ley's attitude

---

detailed reports that the Privy Council was made aware of the religious condition of the county. He played a central part in the scheme of preaching Exercises set up in the diocese of Chester in the 1580s.

50 Chester. Consistory Court papers. EDC 5, 1638.

51 Queen's College, Oxford. MS 280, f. 174v.

52 Ley, *A Patterne of Pietie*, 1640, 145. Richard Baxter gives a particularly explicit account of his early attitude to the ceremonies. As in the case of John Ley, Baxter's willingness to conform in many respects is at once apparent. 'Kneeling I thought lawful,' Baxter declared, 'and all mere circumstances determined by the magistrate . . . The surplice I more doubted of, but more inclined to think it lawful; and though I purposed while I doubted to forbear it till necessity lay upon me, yet could I not have justified the forsaking of my ministry for it . . . The cross in baptism,' Baxter went on, 'I thought Dr Ames proved unlawful, never used it to this day . . . Subscription I began to judge unlawful . . . So that subscription, and the cross in baptism and the promiscuous giving of the Lord's Supper to all

to the ceremonies in the Consistory Court book for 1634. Ley was obliged to defend himself in this year, since:

> there was bruited and spread abroad an aspersion against him, the said Mr Ley, that although he . . . had publicly convinced and persuaded . . . Mr Hopwood[53] of the lawfulness of his conformity to the ceremonies of the Church of England, yet afterwards and at other times in secret and privately he should persuade him otherwise not to conform to the same.

Ley denied the charges, and in this he was corroborated by Hopwood. The latter:

> being so sworn, did affirm and acknowledge that the said Mr Ley in public and open conference had convinced his judgement and conscience of the lawfulness of yielding to conformity, and divers and several times in private he had conferred with him to that purpose yet never uttered or used any words to his knowledge which might tend to the dissuading or withdrawing him from his conformity and yielding obedience to the ceremonies of the Church of England.[54]

But although there were conformists as well as nonconformists amongst the puritan clergy of the diocese of Chester, the historian is obliged to give most attention to the latter. Inevitably, information relating to conforming clergymen is meagre since the ecclesiastical records, upon which the historian largely relies, are in the main silent about them. It was the extremists who drew attention to themselves.

Such, for example, were those clergymen who took the lead in the organisation of conventicles. Discussion of devotional meetings of this kind, however, belongs most properly to the next chapter, since in areas of established puritanism the holding of conventicles was generally an expression of lay initiative, the role of the clergy being quite secondary in importance. But where puritanism was newly introduced and where its hold was exceptionally precarious, its momentum was still primarily provided by the clergy.

---

dunkards, swearers, fornicators, scorners at godliness, etc, that are not excommunicated by a bishop or chancellor that is out of their acquaintance —these three were all that I now became a nonconformist to.' (*Autobiography*, Everyman edition, 16–17.)

53 Hopwood was curate at Whittle, Cheshire, and had been charged in the 1630 visitation with administering the communion to people who were sitting. (York. 1630 vis. RVIA 22, f. 149v.)

54 Chester. Consistory Court books. EDC 1/52, 7 June 1634.

For example, at Ormskirk, Lancashire—a parish still largely dominated by the old religion—the vicar, John Broxopp, was presented in the 1630 visitation 'for keeping conventicles in his house upon Sabbath and other festival days in night'. Twelve of his congregation were involved, and they appeared in court and declared that:

> they hope they are not within the compass of conventicles, for they only were present at Mr Broxopp's house when he did to his children and servants by way of repetition of the heads of his own sermon which that day he had delivered only for the better information and instruction of his family in the way of godliness and to no other end, neither intending any faction.[55]

On this occasion Broxopp and his lay supporters were dismissed with a warning, but it was one which clearly went unheeded. In 1637 the charges against them were repeated and a case was opened in the Consistory Court. Richard Rose, one of those called to give evidence, deponed that:

> there was a common speech and report that divers persons of divers and several families did upon Sundays and other times in the evening resort unto the house of the said Mr Broxopp and there remained until daylight . . . having prayers and expounding of scripture.

This and other depositions, then, fully substantiated the main charge against Broxopp, that he had admitted to the vicarage of Ormskirk:

> about the hours of nine or ten of the clock in the night, and at other times, divers and sundry people of several families . . . And then and there you, the said John Broxopp, did in the presence and amongst the said persons pray conceived or other prayers and did preach or rehearse sermons unto them.[56]

Similar charges were made in the same year against William Ellison, curate of Areholme in the Lonsdale parish of Melling. In this parish, as in the case of Ormskirk, the hold of puritanism was weak, and Ellison, like Broxopp, faced with a largely hostile or indifferent congregation, found it expedient to retreat to the smaller unit of the conventicle. He was charged with having:

> used and kept conventicles both in your own and other houses with strange and several families and consulted upon some matter or course

---

55 York. 1630 vis. RVIA 22, f. 108v.
56 Chester. Consistory Court papers. EDC 5, 1637. Miscellaneous.

which did or may tend to the impeaching or depraving of the doctrine of the Church of England or of the Book of Common Prayer.[57]

Another aspect of clerical nonconformity which attracted official attention was the failure to catechise, and it is this which will now be considered. The catechism—the basis of all religious education—laid down the principles governing the beliefs and practices of the Church, and it was enjoined in the canons of 1604 that:

> every parson, vicar or curate, upon every Sunday and holy day before evening prayer shall for half an hour or more examine and instruct the youth and ignorant persons of his parish in the ten commandments, the articles of the belief and in the Lord's Prayer, and shall diligently hear, instruct and teach them the catechism set forth in the Book of Common Prayer.[58]

It is not surprising, therefore, that puritan clergymen, deviating from many of the official standpoints of the Church, should have expressed their own beliefs in catechisms which at least supplemented, and often rivalled, the official catechism of the Church of England. The main problem, then, which confronted the ecclesiastical authorities in this connection was not negligence in catechising—this was a common charge against ministers but was nothing new—but the puritan use of unauthorised catechisms.[59]

For example, in 1611 the notoriously puritan clergy of Bunbury, Cheshire, were presented on the charge that 'they are ready to catechise but not that is appointed by the Book of Common Prayer'.[60] In a court case heard in 1634 one of the articles alleged against John Swan of Bunbury was that at the time of the administration of the communion he did:

> usually molest and disturb the congregation then assembled and prepared with unusual, uncivil and unnecessary questions, at least questions

---

57 Chester. Consistory Court papers. EDC 5, 1637. Miscellaneous.
58 E. Cardwell, *Synodalia*, Oxford, 1842, I, 280. Canon 59.
59 About a hundred unofficial catechisms were published in Elizabeth's reign alone. (H. S. Bennett, *English Books and Readers, 1558–1603*, Cambridge, 1965, 147.) Further discussion of this subject is found in L. B. Wright, *Middle Class Culture in Elizabethan England*, 1964 impression, 239, 245, 246. H. C. White in *The Tudor Books of Private Devotion*, Madison, Wis., 1951, 169, mentions that Edward Dering's *Shorte Catechisme for Howsholders* . . . first published in 1582, had gone through fourteen editions by 1631.
60 Chester. 1611 vis. EDV 1/17, f. 53v.

though fit to be asked before yet not at that instant fit, to the disturbance, trouble, amazement of some or most then assembled.[61]

Earlier, in 1633, the incumbent of the Cheshire parish of Thornton-in-the-Moors was presented 'for teaching or suffering to be taught another catechism than that which is set down in the Book of Common Prayer'.[62] Also in 1633, Archbishop Neile's commissioners in the metropolitan visitation found that at Nantwich and Chester as many as four or five different catechisms were being taught in the churches.[63]

That there were other cases of this kind we may be sure, for Archbishop Neile wrote in his report of the 1633 visitation of the diocese of Chester that 'the catechism of the Book of Common Prayer has been in many places neglected and divers other new-fangled catechisms, no way authorised, brought into the Church'.[64] Nor was he able to reform the abuse. At Tarporley, for example, in 1642 the ultra-puritan clergyman Nathaniel Lancaster and his curate John Jones were presented for withholding the sacrament from members of their congregation 'unless they will be catechised by a catchism of their own invention not expressed in the Book of Common Prayer'.[65] The catechism, then, was of central importance in the organisation and practice of puritanism. It was a test of fitness to receive the sacrament, and as such differentiated the elect from the ungodly.

So varied and widespread was clerical nonconformity in the diocese of Chester that Archbishop Neile could write in 1633 that:

the Book of Common Prayer is so neglected and abused in most places by chopping, changing, altering, omitting and adding at the ministers' own pleasure, as if they are not bound to the form prescribed. In sundry places [he went on] the Book of Common Prayer was so unregarded that many knew not how to read the service according to the Book.[66]

---

61 Chester. Consistory Court papers. EDC 5, 1634. Article 3.
62 York. 1633 vis. RVIA 23, f. 430v.
63 Bradford MSS, 9/8. Bridgeman's copy of the 1633 visitation report, f. 5v. (The Bradford MSS from Weston Park, Shropshire, were consulted in the Cheshire Record Office. For this I am indebted to the county archivist, Mr B. C. Redwood.)
64 P.R.O. State Papers Domestic. SP 16/259/78. Adam Martindale tells how, early in the 1650's, 'multitudes of little catechisms we caused to be printed, designing one for every family in our parishes'. (*Life of Adam Martindale*, 122.)
65 Chester. Quarter sessions. QSF 4/24, 1642. Mention is made of this use of the catechism in Collinson, *Puritan Movement*, 349.
66 P.R.O. State Papers Domestic. SP 16/259/78.
D

Puritan ministers, at odds with the distribution of emphasis in the Prayer Book and with the 'dregs of Popery' it contained, were experimenting with new and, in their eyes, more satisfying forms and expressions of worship.

In 1595 the puritan rector of Wigan, Edward Fleetwood, and his curate were charged because 'they do not say service nor minister the sacraments as by the Book of Common Prayer is prescribed'.[67] One of the articles alleged against Ralph Kirk, the Manchester curate, in 1604 was that he 'says that the Book of Common Prayer is no scripture'.[68] At Rochdale in 1605 it was said that the vicar, Joseph Midgley, 'observes not the form of Common Prayer'.[69] While Samuel Eaton of West Kirby, Cheshire, was presented in 1630 'for delivering in his sermon upon Easter Tuesday last that the first and second lesson and the reading of the homilies was nothing available nor to be esteemed of'.[70] As a final example, it can be noted that at Richmond in 1633 the minister—Thomas Rokeby—was discovered:

> to add many words of his own, almost to every prayer, never to read full service, to leave out the Te Deum and Benedictus, etc, and always to sing two psalms for them; to alter, add and omit according to his fancy...[71]

2 Preaching and prayer

Some of the presentments involving deviations from the prescribed order of service make it clear that puritan ministers were not only altering the arrangement of the Prayer Book service but were deliberately abbreviating it. Perhaps the most common motive behind this practice was the desire to give more time and emphasis to the sermon. At Rochdale, for example, in the visitation of 1598, it was noted that there the 'service [was] shorter than the Book of Common Prayer allows by reason of sermons'.[72] And when

---

67 York. 1595 vis. RVIA 15, f. 8.
68 Chester. Consistory Court papers. EDC 5, 1604. Miscellaneous. Rather later —in 1642—John Jones, curate at Tarporley, was said to have declared 'that the Book of Common Prayer was made and ordained by the imps of the Devil'. (Chester. Quarter sessions. QSF 4/24. 1642.)
69 Chester. 1605 vis. EDV 1/14, f. 93.
70 York. 1630 vis. RVIA 22, f.206. For the puritan nothing less than a sermon would do—a point discussed in the present chapter and in the next.
71 Bradford mss, 9/8. 1633 vis. f. iv.
72 Chester. 1598 vis. EDV 1/12, f. 85v.

Ralph Kirk, the Manchester curate, was presented for his nonconformity in 1604 he freely confessed that he 'omitted divers parts of the service appointed to be said when there is a sermon'.[73] Similarly, a deponent in the Consistory Court case concerning Samuel Clarke of Thornton in 1623 declared that services there had been abbreviated 'at such times and upon such days wherein there have been sermons'.[74] But these are only examples of what was normal practice amongst puritan ministers. 'The public prayers of the Church', wrote Archbishop Neile in 1633, 'are generally neglected, as if all religion were but in a sermon.'[75]

The preaching of sermons, according to the puritan view, was of very great importance. Ralph Kirk, the Manchester curate whose nonconformity has already been repeatedly noted in the course of this chapter, was alleged to have gone so far as to say that 'no man was ever saved but by preaching'.[76] In this view he was supported by Nicholas Byfield, incumbent at St Peter's, Chester. 'Can any man be made a religious man without the Word?' asked Byfield. 'Can a man be saved and find the way to heaven without the preaching of the Gospel?'[77] Byfield was in no doubt that he could not. 'Preaching of the Gospel,' he went on in another work, 'is the means to make men actually of the Church and members of Christ and so to have [the] right to salvation.'[78]

Given the fact that the sermon was of fundamental importance to puritans, it is not surprising that much attention was given to preaching style. In a particularly frank passage in one of his published works Nicholas Byfield admitted that:

It requires a great deal of the spiritual policy and skill to win souls. A minister that would do it must sometimes be like a fox. It is written of the fox that when he is hungry after prey and can find none, he lies down and feigns himself to be a dead carcass and so the fowls fall upon him and he catches them. Even so a minister who hungers after the winning of his hearers must sometimes be driven to make a very carcass of himself

73 Chester. Consistory Court papers. EDC 5, 1604. Miscellaneous.
74 Chester. Consistory Court papers. EDC 5, 1623. Miscellaneous.
75 P.R.O. State Papers Domestic. SP 16/259/78.
76 Chester. Consistory Court papers. EDC 5, 1604. Miscellaneous.
77 Byfield, *Commentary upon the three first chapters of . . . St. Peter*, 1637, 584.
78 Byfield, *The Rule of Faith*, 1626, 559. Nicholas Byfield (1579–1622), born in Warwickshire and educated at Exeter College, Oxford, held the living of St Peter's, Chester, in the early part of James' reign. He was the author of numerous published works.

by denying himself and turning himself into all forms that his hearers may be enticed to flock to his doctrine . . .

Yes, sometimes a man [Byfield went on] to entice his people must deny his own profit . . . They will endure to hear such a man and so may be caught.[79]

Adam Martindale made basically the same point. 'Ministers who would do good in a country auditory,' he wrote, 'must not study to be copious orators but to stir up the people's affections with pithy matter and a warm delivery.'[80]

And so the sermons preached by puritan ministers were often directly intended to appeal to the emotions. In Essex, for example, when John Rogers was minister at Dedham, it was a common saying, 'Come, let's to Dedham to get a little fire.' Nor were his hearers disappointed:

His taking hold with both hands at one time of the supporters of the canopy over the pulpit [we are informed], and roaring hideously to represent the torments of the damned, had an awakening force attending it.[81]

But, at least by the mid-seventeenth century, there were signs that unsophisticated, revivalist preaching of this type was falling out of favour in puritan circles at the same time as it gained ground with extremist groups such as the Quakers. The biographer of the Lancashire puritan divine John Angier, for example, took pains to point out that although Angier was an inspiring and effective preacher 'yet he was far from Enthusiasm'.[82]

Puritan ministers, however, still claimed that they preached in a style which was both plain and edifying.

Our preaching must be plain and lively [wrote the Cheshire divine Samuel Torshell], plain that Christ may be truly painted before us, lively that in the fresh knowledge of his death he may be crucified among us. They are bad preachers that paint themselves in their own colours [he went on] instead of Christ. While in our ordinary sermons we do unnecessarily tell you how many Fathers we have read, how much we are acquainted with the schoolmen, what critical linguists we are or the like. It is a wretched ostentation . . .

---

79 Byfield, *Commentary* . . ., 590–1.
80 *Life of Adam Martindale*, 185.
81 O. Heywood, *Life of John Angier*, Chet. Soc., new series, 97, Manchester, 1937, 50. Thomas Whately earned the title of 'Roaring Tom of Banbury'. (M. M. Knappen, *Tudor Puritanism*, second impression, Chicago, 1965, 390.)
82 Heywood, *Life of John Angier*, 76.

We preach with most authority [Torshell concluded] when we deny ourselves.[83]

But plainness of style was a relative concept and did not preclude the careful preparation of sermons. 'He took great pains in studying his sermons,' Angier's biographer wrote, 'and they were elaborate, full fraught with spiritual marrow, very exact, no waste words or repetitions, but went on smoothly, pertinently, sententiously.' Heywood, however, went on to point out that Angier 'studied matter rather than words and never used notes in all his life, but took pains to commit his sermon to memory which he had before diligently penned . . .'[84] The methodical way with which William Bourne, Fellow of the Manchester College, presented his sermons was noted by his contemporary Richard Hollingworth:

> His preaching was plain yet profitable to the conversion and edification of many souls [the latter wrote] . . . He seldom varied . . . the method of preaching, which after explication of his text was doctrine, proof of it by scripture [and] by reason, answering one or more objections and then the uses: (1) of information, (2) of confutation of Popery in this or that, (3) reprehension, (4) examination, (5) exhortation. And lastly consolation.[85]

Similarly, the biographer of Richard Mather of Toxteth noted that although 'his way of preaching was plain and zealous it was moreover substantial and very judicious'.[86]

'Substantial and very judicious . . .' The phrase is a reminder that in puritan preaching the intellect was appealed to as well as the

83 Torshell, *Three Questions of Free Justification, Christian Liberty, the Use of the Law*, 1632, 104–5, 106.
84 Heywood, *Life of John Angier*, 71. John Angier (1605–77) was born in Dedham, Essex, a great nursery of Elizabethan puritanism, and was educated at Emmanuel College, Cambridge. He was much influenced by John Rogers, minister at Dedham, and later by John Cotton of Boston in Lincolnshire. It was from Boston in 1629 that Angier came to Ringley chapel, Lancashire. After his suspension there in the early 1630's he moved to Denton, in the parish of Manchester, where he attracted large congregations.
85 Hollingworth, *Mancuniensis*, Manchester, 1839, 105.
86 Increase Mather, *The Life and Death of . . . Richard Mather*, Cambridge, Mass., 1670, 31. Richard Mather (1596–1669) was educated at Winwick Grammar School and for a short time at Brasenose College, Oxford. He was the first master of the school at Toxteth, Liverpool, and became minister at the chapel there in 1618. Mather was twice suspended for his nonconformity and felt obliged to emigrate to New England in 1635. He ministered at Dorchester, Mass., until his death in 1669.

emotions. As Perry Miller has contended, it is a mistake to view 'the puritan ideal [as] simply an impassioned harangue, the sort of emotional evangelism familiar to eighteenth- and nineteenth-century revivals'.[87] Although puritan ministers preached for maximum effect, the arrangement of the sermon, as well as its delivery, was important. Logic, then, quite definitely had a part to play in the art of preaching, and in this connection it is important to observe how puritan divines were influenced by Ramist dialectic.[88]

Ramus's logic established itself at the universities, though its hold at Oxford was weaker than at Cambridge.[89] In their student days, therefore, the puritan ministers of the diocese of Chester would be introduced to the new teaching. Direct references to the fact, however, are not numerous. But something is known of the reading matter recommended by his tutor to Richard Mather, who went up to Brasenose College, Oxford, in 1618. 'Amongst other things,' wrote Mather's biographer, 'he advised [him] to read the works of Peter Ramus, which counsel he followed and saw no cause to repent of his so doing.'[90]

The sermon, then, logically planned and preached for maximum effect, held an important place in the puritan order of worship. But Archbishop Neile was mistaken in 1633 if he thought that every puritan believed that 'all religion were but in a sermon'. The Cheshire divine Samuel Torshell, for one, was well aware first of all of the way preaching could be abused. The possibility of pulpit rivalries, for example, was a real one, but one that ought at all costs to be avoided. 'It is well if one pulpit envy not another,' wrote

87 Miller, *The New England Mind: the Seventeenth Centrury*, New York, 1939, 301.

88 Perry Miller argued (in *ibid.*, 116) that 'while Augustine and Calvin have been widely recognised as the sources of puritanism, upon New England puritans the logic of Petrus Ramus exerted fully as great an influence as did either of the theologians'. The subject is also examined in W. S. Howell, *Logic and Rhetoric in England, 1500–1700*, Princeton, 1956, and in H. Kearney, *Scholars and Gentlemen: Universities and Society in Pre-industrial Britain*, 1970.

89 Christ's College, Cambridge, was the real seminary of Ramist teaching in England from the late 1560's and early 1570's, when the Lancashire-born Laurence Chaderton had first expounded Ramus in his lectures. The first English edition of *The Logike* was published under the editorship of Roland McIlmaine in 1574.

90 *Life and Death of . . . Richard Mather*, 7. The library of John Assheton, rector of Middleton from 1559 to 1584, contained a copy of Ramus's *Logic*. Chetham's Library, Manchester. Assheton MSS A3 91, vol. II, unpaginated.)

Torshell, 'and lecture be not preached against lecture out of contention and to win the crowd . . . A sincere preacher may be followed
by the people, but if he be popular I doubt whether he be sincere.'[91]

Torshell, in fact, was in fundamental disagreement with those who
placed an undue and disproportionate emphasis upon the sermon.

> It is hypocrisy [he roundly declared] that makes men all for hearing,
> which is to some the easy duty, while they know not how to frame their
> spirits to prayer, which requires the labour of the soul, the exercise of
> humiliation and brokenness of spirit.[92]

Torshell's argument reminds us of a fact which is often overlooked, namely that prayer was of vital importance to the puritan
and one of the main aspects of the appeal of puritanism itself. For
the puritan, in everyday life as well as in emergencies, nothing was
more powerful than prayer. In a sermon preached in Manchester
in July 1640, Richard Heyricke, Warden of the Collegiate Church,
proclaimed that 'an army of men cannot stand against a man of
prayer, much less against an army of prayers; surely, my brethren,
it is the prayers of the Church that have kept off judgements to this
day'. Heyricke, in short, believed that:

> the more prayers the more power . . . Get what stock of prayers you
> can [he went on], pray for yourselves, call in others to pray. Let the
> husband pray with the wife, the wife with her maids, the parent with
> his children. Let one neighbour provoke another. An army of men [he
> repeated] cannot stand against an army of prayers; one praying town
> can overcome a fighting kingdom. Make your party strong by prayers.

Nor did Heyricke cease here in his assertion that fervent prayer
would bring results.

> I cannot foretell you of certainty [he went on] what this day may
> bring forth [and] what answer we shall have of our prayers, but I
> can say this confidently and promise you in the name of the Lord:
> they that pray for the peace of Jerusalem, they shall prosper.[93]

---

91 Torshell, *The Hypocrite Discovered and Cured,* 1644, 56–8.
92 *Ibid.*, 49.
93 Heyricke, *Three Sermons preached at the Collegiate Church in Manchester . . .*, 1641, 47–8, 50. Richard Heyricke, born in London in 1600,
  was educated at St John's College, Oxford, graduating B.A. in 1619 and
  M.A. in 1622. He became Warden of the Manchester College in 1635 and
  quickly assumed a leading role in Lancashire puritanism. He was the author
  of several published works and was later a member of the Assembly of
  Divines.

It was part of the Covenant that God should hear and grant the prayers of the godly.

When puritan divines like Heyricke spoke of prayer, it was usually extemporary prayer which they had in mind, for there was considerable opposition to set forms. Horton Davies, in his study of *The Worship of the English Puritans* (1948), suggests that this antipathy may have been based on five main considerations. First, puritans believed that prescribed prayers stifled religious initiative. Set forms of prayer and service were resisted in the belief also that they could not meet the varying needs of different congregations: the Prayer Book was ordered for national use and therefore could not help but be impersonal. Third, the regular use of set forms promoted the view that worship could not be conducted in any other way. Set forms, too, could encourage hypocrisy. Lastly, set forms came to be resisted since their imposition had involved persecution.[94]

This puritan preference for extemporary prayers can be illustrated by the case heard in the Consistory Court in 1631 against Ralph Hulme, a minister from outside the diocese. Hulme was charged with having preached at Harthill, Cheshire, that:

> every man ought to kneel at all prayers as well as at the Lord's Prayer, for that prayer was no more holy than others and any minister might make as good a prayer as the Lord's Prayer was. And you gave this reason that the prayer made by Christ and other men came from one spirit and therefore every prayer was as pleasing and acceptable to God as that was . . .[95]

A similar attitude was shown by Edward Fleetwood, vicar of Kirkham, Lancashire. Fleetwood was charged in 1638 with having 'said prayers of your own invention and usually refused to follow the form prescribed . . .'[96]

But puritan ministers were not completely opposed to the use of set prayers. Their argument quite often was simply that there ought to be room for ministerial—and lay—initiative and improvisation within the prescribed framework. William Hinde, for example, the leading puritan divine in early seventeenth-century Cheshire, contended that set forms could be useful to a man 'if he bring new

---

94 Davies, *The Worship of the English Puritans,* 104.
95 Chester. Consistory Court papers. EDC 5, 1631.
96 Chester. Consistory Court papers. EDC 5, 1638. Miscellaneous.

affections to renewed petitions and set his heart a work to seek more
seriously for the best things such as the godly labours of good men
have in print set before him'. But in themselves set prayers were not
enough. 'If any man will rest in his book prayers,' Hinde went on,
'and never strive to speak unto God out of his own heart, such a
man in my opinion comes far short of the power and practice,
comfort and fruit of true prayer . . .'[97]

3 *The godly discipline*

The puritan divines of the diocese took a leading part in the struggle
to achieve 'reformation' and to set up the 'godly discipline'—distinct yet at the same time simultaneous processes.[98] This discipline,
of course, was intended for the godly themselves, and it was a willing and unswerving submission to its yoke which most of all distinguished the elect from the reprobate. But although God was on
the side of the righteous, worthiness of salvation, the divines argued,
had to be continually proved. Nicholas Byfield, for example, in his
popular treatise on *The Marrow of the Oracles of God*, declared
that:

> Our life is like a race. Now in a race it is not enough that a man run
> now and then, though he run fiercely for the time; he must not trifle
> and look behind and stand still at his pleasure and then run again,
> but he must be always running. So ought it to be with us [Byfield
> went on] in the race of godliness. It will not serve the turn to be good
> by fits.[99]

However, although the godly discipline was primarily designed for
puritans themselves, the aim—for social as well as religious reasons—
was to make 'reformation' more generally operative. If all would
not espouse puritanism and willingly accept its high standards of
behaviour—and not even the most optimistic preacher expected this
—then they must be forcibly reformed if possible, or at least held in
check to prevent their being a nuisance to the godly.

97 Hinde, *Life of John Bruen*, 1641, 70. Cf. Baxter's attitude to this question.
'A form of prayer and liturgy,' he declared, 'I judged to be lawful and in
some cases lawfully imposed; our liturgy in particular I judged to have
much disorder and defectiveness in it, but nothing which should make the
use of it in the ordinary public worship to be unlawful to them that have not
liberty to do better . . .' (*Autobiography*, Everyman edition, 17.)
98 The role of the laity in this connection will be discussed in the next chapter.
99 Seventh edition, 1630, 481.

Besides discussing these matters in their published work, the puritan clergymen of the diocese used their ministries as a means of putting into effect what they preached. It was normal practice, for example, for puritan divines to direct private warnings and pulpit admonitions against known offenders in their parishes. One of the charges against John Bowen of Goostrey, Cheshire, for instance, in 1616 was that he did:

> particularly inveigh and preach against particular persons in [his] sermons, and namely against one Richard Parker of the said chapelry of Goostrey, saying that he was worthy to have or wear chains about his legs and a rope about his neck.[100]

Similarly, John Angier's biographer tells that:

> if he heard of the breaking out of sin in any of his hearers, he faithfully admonished them privately and sometimes publicly, sometimes sending for the persons and pleading with them with much gravity, humility and bowels of compassion. Ordinarily [Heywood went on], when strangers came to settle under his ministry, he sent for them, discoursed with them, counselled, instructed, exhorted them.[101]

It was also the custom of John Fletcher, minister of the Cheshire parish of Siddington, to 'speak against any notorious sinners in his sermon, as namely drunkards, whoremongers and such like'.[102]

Equally normal was the tendency of puritan divines to exercise their right to exclude ungodly parishioners from the communion. In 1626, for example, John Swan of Bunbury was said to 'have caused sundry men that come prepared to the communion to depart thence without any at all'.[103] While in 1638, Edward Fleetwood of Kirkham was charged with having 'repelled Roger Threlfall . . . being duly prepared and ready amongst other communicants to be partaker of the Lord's Table from receiving the same to his great disgrace . . .'[104]

Samuel Clarke's experiences provide a good illustration of the role of the clergy in this connection. Clarke, it will be remembered, had at one time served as a preacher in Cheshire, but it is his later ministry at Alcester in Warwickshire which concerns us here. When first he came to the living, he tells us in his autobiography, 'the inhabitants of the town were much given to swearing, drunkenness and profana-

---

100 Chester. Consistory Court books. EDC 5, 1616. Article 7.
101 Heywood, *Life of John Angier*, 77.
102 Chester. Quarter sessions. QFS 2/152, 1624.
103 Chester. Consistory Court papers. EDC 5, 1626.
104 Chester. Consistory Court papers. EDC 5, 1638.

tion of the Sabbath, opening of their shops and selling wares, especially meat, publicly'. But a notable reformation was achieved in the nine years he remained there. His people 'were edified and built up in their faith, and the town which before was called *drunken Alcester* was now exemplary and eminent for religion all over the country'.[105]

Even fuller information concerning the lead taken by the clergy in the work of 'reformation' and in the imposition of the 'godly discipline' is provided by the anonymous biography of John Murcot. Having briefly ministered for a time in the Cheshire parishes of Astbury and Eastham, Murcot (1625–54) removed to West Kirby in the Wirral late in the 1640's. Almost immediately, his biographer tells us, this young and relatively inexperienced minister actively began to set up the godly discipline in his parish. Although he had:

> no other sword to fight withal save that of the spirit, yet such was his integrity, gravity, austerity and his activity in informing and exciting magistrates to punish offenders impartially that the people round about him had an awe and dread of him and dared not lash out into public, extravagant, scandalous courses . . .[106]

On one occasion, for example, we are told that Murcot and a godly neighbour secured the assistance of the constables in dispersing a crowd of revellers at a wakes. Only one of this 'rabble rout' dared defy the minister, but Murcot's triumph, in this matter at least, was made complete when his remaining opponent fell victim to the plague shortly afterwards and died. The moral was obvious, and Murcot hammered the point home by preaching a sermon on 'the dreadfulness of wrath deserved'.[107]

105 Clarke, introduction to *Lives of Sundry Eminent Persons*, 1683, 6–7. Baxter gave a similar account of his Kidderminster ministry. 'When I came thither first,' he wrote, 'there was about one family in a street that worshipped God and called on his name, and when I came away there were some streets where there was not passed one family in the side of a street that did not so.' (*Autobiography*, Everyman edition, 79.) Clearly, both Clarke and Baxter attributed too much to their own efforts.

106 *Moses in the Mount . . . the Life and Death of Mr. John Murcot written by a friend* in *Several Works of John Murcot*, 1657, 8.

107 *Moses in the Mount*, 9. It was common practice for puritan writers to strengthen their standpoint on the godly discipline by giving details of divine judgements falling on the reprobate. Edward Burghall, puritan vicar of Acton, Cheshire, for example, recalled how in 1634 'a woman in Chester, going upon the walls to get plums on the Lord's day, fell down and broke her neck'; while in 1639 'one Lawrence Smith of Peckforton, a proud and profane man, and a hater of good men, especially Mr Hinde

But Murcot did not confine his surveillance to his parishioners alone. Visitors to West Kirby were equally bound by the discipline.[108] For example, his biographer tells how an Irish gentleman temporarily resident in the parish caused great offence by swearing excessively. He was dealt with by the same method as before. A warrant was obtained from the magistrates and the support of the constables enlisted.

> This exemplary act of justice, procured and prosecuted by Mr Murcot's zeal, so daunted and overawed his lordship that during his abode there he held his tongue and mouth as it were with bit and bridle.[109]

One of the most prominent features of the clergy's strivings towards reformation and the godly discipline was their resistance to Sunday work and amusements. Certainly by the seventeenth century the divines of the diocese are known to have been giving the fourth commandment a literal interpretation—a position which the Cheshire minister John Ley amply justified in his treatise *Sunday a Sabbath* in 1641.[110]

John Angier, pastor at Denton, Lancashire, in his *Helpe to Better Hearts* was one who emphasised that Sunday ought to be kept free from work of any kind. He attacked:

> that allowance only of the forenoon on the Lord's day to the worship of God and the reservation of the afternoon by some, which is a clipping of the King's coin of heaven. For the Sabbath is the Lord's day in a special respect.

He also fulminated against those who behaved 'as if the Sabbath were a market day, a day of bargaining, paying, receiving rather than for worshipping of God or seeking the good of the soul of men'.[111]

[the puritan minister of Bunbury], having been at an alehouse near Malpas and staying late till he was drunk, [as he journeyed home] fell off his horse and dashed out his brains on a stepping stone'. (Burghall, *Providence Improved*, in *Memorials of the Civil War*, Rec. Soc. Lancs. and Ches., 19, 1889, 10, 14.)

108 West Kirby was a port of minor importance.

109 *Moses in the Mount . . .*, 8. Despite these successes, however, Murcot found that he and the godly element supporting him fought a losing battle. The opposition was too great, and so he felt obliged to quit the parish.

110 On this subject there is the useful collection by R. Cox, *The Literature of the Sabbath Question*, Edinburgh, 1865, and W. B. Whitaker, *Sunday in Tudor and Stuart Times*, 1933. Most recently, Professor Collinson has written on 'The beginnings of English Sabbatarianism' in C. W. Dugmore and C. Duggan (eds.), *Studies in Church History*, 1964.

111 Angier, *op. cit.*, 373, 375.

Given this stress on the central importance of the Sabbath, it followed on naturally that it required thorough spiritual preparation. Richard Midgley, the puritan vicar of Rochdale, once rebuked the young Richard Rothwell for playing bowls on a Saturday when he should have been thinking of the day's worship which was to follow.[112] Similarly, John Angier contended that:

> the godly that use our Saturday markets do exceedingly fail in that they come home so late, not through necessity of business, but carelessness; much time is spent on that day which they can give no account of when they come to recollect themselves. Nothing but sleep parts the Lord's day and their days with them beside ordinary duties.[113]

Angier's argument rested on the belief that a man's calling ought always to be kept in check, and earlier in the century Nicholas Byfield had given much the same advice to his readers. 'You must not make a vocation of recreation,' he wrote. 'You must spend only your own time upon them, not the Lord's.'[114]

Byfield had in fact been involved in a controversy on this very subject with Edward Brerewood, professor at Gresham College. The debate originated in the advice about Sunday observance given by Byfield to Brerewood's nephew while the latter was in Chester. Young Brerewood was an apprentice, and his master had occasionally required him to work on Sundays. Influenced by Byfield's sabbatarianism, the apprentice came to believe that 'he sinned against God in yielding obedience to every such commandment of his master's that day, which by the precept of almighty God was wholly, precisely consecrated to rest and the service of God'.[115]

Edward Brerewood, on the other hand, interpreted Byfield's advice to his nephew as an incitement to disobedience. Although he granted that masters ought ideally to respect the Sabbath, he contended that the matter of observance rested with them and not with their servants, whose first duty was always to obey. 'If servants by their master's command do any work on the Sabbath,' he wrote, 'the sin is

---

112 S. Gower, *Life of Richard Rothwell*, Bolton, 1787, 170. It was by Midgley's preaching that Rothwell—who later ministered in Lancashire, Yorkshire and Nottinghamshire—was converted.

113 Angier, *op. cit.*, 281. The Massachusetts Bay Company insisted that all labour should cease at 3 p.m. on Saturdays and that the remainder of the day should be devoted to spiritual preparation for Sabbath worship. (C. Hill, *Society and Puritanism in Pre-revolutionary England*, 1964, 166.)

114 Byfield, *A Commentary . . .*, 1637, 56.

115 Brerewood, *A Learned Treatise of the Sabaoth*, Oxford, 1630, 3.

not theirs, who as touching their bodily labour are merely subject to their master's power, but it is their master's sin.'[116]

The debate, however, was largely one-sided, since Byfield refused to elaborate his position. He considered that the Gresham professor was clearly in error and that 'it is no point of discretion to make the settled doctrine of God questionable'.[117]

As well as opposing Sabbath-breaking, puritan divines took every opportunity to attack the sin of drunkenness.[118] In an account which they gave of the state of Lancashire in 1590 the puritan divines of the county denounced not only heavy drinking but also its accompanying evil of 'seditious and mutinous talking upon the ale-bench and openly in their street assemblies, tending to the depraving of religion and the ministry now established'.[119]

In similar vein Christopher Hudson, lecturer at Preston, in 1631 thundered against:

the multitude of alehouses, which are nests of Satan where the owls of impiety lurk and where all evil is hatched and the bellows of intemperance and incontinence blown up to the provocation of God's wrath in the subversion of a kingdom.[120]

His sermon was preached at the Lancaster assizes, and there in the following year he continued the same theme:

Oh that I could blow the coals of your zeal against drunkenness [he declared] and the innumerable multitude of alehouses[121] . . . You often complain of bastards, sheep stealers, etc [he went on], and would cure these. Surely these assemble together in the foresaid houses as humours into the stomach before the fit of an ague. Expel them hence [Hudson concluded] and in that one work you shall heal infinite distempers . . .[122]

---

116 Brerewood, *A learned Treatise of the Sabaoth*, Oxford, 1630, 11.
117 *Mr. Byfields Answere, with Mr. Brerewoods Reply*, Oxford, 1630, 95.
118 Unlike nineteenth-century temperance reformers, however, puritans limited their opposition to excessive drinking and its consequences, and did not attack the demon drink itself.
119 F. R. Raines (ed.), *A Description of the State Civil and Ecclesiastical of the County of Lancaster about the year 1590* in *Miscellany, vol. V,* Chet. Soc., old series, 96, Manchester, 1875, 12.
120 Preston. Hudson's MS sermons. DP 353, f. 46.
121 According to Hudson, there were well over 1,400 alehouses in the county.
122 Preston. Hudson's MS sermons. DP 353, f. 53.

John Ford, vicar of the Cheshire parish of Over, took up the same
subject in a petition he sent to the J.P.'s in 1645:

> Among all the means whereby the kingdom of Satan is advanced and
> sin promoted [he declared] one of the chiefest is the toleration of a
> needless multitude and vain superfluity of alehouses. Sir, we cannot
> but grieve [he continued] to see the Sabbath profaned, the good
> creatures of God so abused and the Lord so provoked to a just occasion
> of further judgements.[123]

4 Preachers from outside the diocese

The efforts of the puritan clergy of the diocese of Chester were
sometimes reinforced by visiting preachers. For example, geographical proximity encouraged links between puritanism in Lancashire and Yorkshire. It was not unusual for a minister's career
to be divided between the two counties. To take an instance, Roger
Brearley, born at Rochdale in 1586, spent most of his ministry in
Yorkshire and there was proceeded against as the founder of the
Grindletonian sect. But his last years —1631–37—were spent in
Lancashire ministering at Burnley.[124] Earlier, Richard Midgley had
returned to his native Halifax after the close of his ministry in
Rochdale. His son, Joseph Midgley, later did the same.[125] For a
time in the 1640's the Yorkshire divine John Shaw preached in
Manchester and in parts of Cheshire, and by invitation even went
evangelising in the remote area of Cartmel in north Lancashire.[126]
Oliver Heywood was equally at home as a minister in Lancashire
or Yorkshire, as was Nathaniel Rathband, who was at Sowerby,
Yorkshire, in the 1630's and 1640's and at Prestwich, Lancashire,
in the following decade.[127] Rather later the Lancashire divine Isaac
Ambrose was to dedicate one part of a theological work to a group
of aldermen and merchants of the city of York and he took the

123 Chester. Quarter sessions. QSF 3/110. 1645.
124 Marchant, *Puritans and the Church Courts in the Diocese of York*, 233–4.
125 The will of Joseph Midgley of Halifax was proved at York in 1637.
126 *Life of Master John Shaw*, 138–9.
127 Conversely, the divines of the diocese of Chester contributed to the develop-
    ment of puritanism in Yorkshire. The system of Exercises set up in the
    West Riding in the 1580's was probably inspired by the Lancashire
    precedent. At least two of the Lancashire preachers—Gosnell and Rathband
    —preached at these Yorkshire meetings. (Newton, 'Puritanism in the diocese
    of York', 220–2.)

opportunity to thank them for their generosity to him and his children.[128]

But it was not only from Yorkshire that assistance of this kind came. In 1631, for example, a case was heard in the Consistory Court concerning Ralph Hulme, a clergyman from the diocese of Coventry, who had preached at Harthill in the Malpas deanery of Cheshire.[129] In his sermon Hulme spoke in favour of extemporary prayers. He also took occasion to criticise the assembling together of large numbers of clergymen in cathedrals—an unjustifiable policy, he thought, while large tracts of country were still without a preacher.[130]

Later in the 1630's Thomas Case, who was later to be a prominent member of the Assembly of Divines, came from the diocese of Norwich at the invitation of Richard Heyricke to preach in the Manchester area. Exactly when Case arrived in Manchester is uncertain, although it was probably some time during 1636. A manuscript copy of the sermon he delivered at the Collegiate Church, Manchester, on Easter day 1637 has survived, however, and unmistakably reveals the preacher's puritanism.

Case urged his hearers to recognise the great value of private conferences and conventicles and emphasised that all, not only the most educated laymen, could take part. Private doubts about the meaning of parts of scripture ought, Case argued, to be discussed with others so that their help could be obtained. 'This were profitable,' Case argued, 'not only for weak but strong Christians.'[131]

The full range and significance of Case's preaching in Manchester is made clear in the records of the proceedings against him in the Consistory Court in 1638–39. Case was first of all charged that in the previous two years he had:

> delivered many dangerous and unsound doctrines and uttered many passages both privately in conscience and publicly in your sermons within the parish of Manchester . . . and other places thereabouts, thereby manifesting your great dislike of the government and discipline established in this our Church of England.

---

128 Ambrose, *Three Great Ordinances of Jesus Christ,* 1662, sixth section.
129 Hulme was from Betley, Staffordshire, a parish just outside the diocese.
130 Chester. Consistory Court papers. EDC 5, 1631. Hulme was also charged with not wearing the surplice and with omitting the sign of the cross in baptism.
131 Manchester Central Library. Worsley MSS, M 35/5/3/7. Unpaginated. 'Sermon preached by Mr Case at Manchester, Easter day, 9 April 1637.'

For example, in a sermon preached in Manchester on the previous Christmas day Case was said to have spoken of persecution taking place at that time in Europe:

> And you said there were many others which were likewise in persecution which you would not name. Under which 'many others' divers of your auditors conceived that you meant the kingdom of Scotland for one, as indeed you did.[132]

Case was also charged (article 7) with having consorted with known nonconformists. Article 9 charged him with giving encouragement to the laity's practice of leaving their own churches and chapels in order to hear him preach. He was alleged also to have been present:

> at divers conventicles where there have been private preachings, prayers, repetitions and exhortations in private men's houses, both in the day and night time, and where there were congregated divers persons of several families to the number of ten or above. [Article 10]

Moreover, Case was said to have in his possession 'scandalous and offensive books' which opposed the imposition of the Prayer Book on Scotland. Finally, it can be noted that another of the charges against him concerned a service he had taken at Didsbury chapel.

> In your prayer [so the article ran] you suddenly stayed and desired the people to pray for a sick member of the Church, and when the people gazed and expected to hear the name, you said it was sick and dying England, the Church of England, which was sick and ready to die, or in words to the like effect. [Article 14]

The contribution of visiting preachers to the development of puritanism in the diocese of Chester is further illustrated by a case heard in the Consistory Court in 1639 concerning the puritans of the parish of Holt in Cheshire. The churchwardens there were charged that:

> upon or about the first of September last past [they] procured or at least permitted one Oliver Thomas, a stranger who lives in another

---

132 Chester. Consistory Court papers. EDC 5, 1638. News of this or a similar sermon had by the following year come to Archbishop Laud. Accordingly the primate wrote to Bishop Bridgeman about the matter on 10 March 1638/9, warning him about Case and requesting that action be taken against him. (G. V. O. Bridgeman (ed.), *History of the Church and Manor of Wigan*, II, Chet. Soc., new series, 16, Manchester, 1888, 419–20.)

E

diocese and is suspended for his nonconformity and one that had no licence to preach within this diocese, to preach and make a sermon in your church at Holt.

Perhaps nothing further would have been heard of the matter had not Thomas preached in his sermon that:

all subordinate magistrates had their authority only from the Devil. And that he and you with others of that congregation had endured the yoke of them a good while but now you were in a fair way to be freed, or words to the same and like effect.[133]

5 *The educational background of the preachers*

An examination of the work of visiting preachers in the diocese reminds us that the growth of puritanism in this region was not entirely separate and self-contained; the puritan ministers did not work in complete isolation.[134] Nor, of course, were their religious ideas conceived independently or in a vacuum. In this connection it is important to give some attention to the available evidence concerning the books which these clergymen are known to have possessed.

Take, for example, the case of John Buckley, preacher at the Collegiate Church, Manchester, who in 1590 had been charged with omitting to wear the surplice and with departing from the prescribed order of service. Buckley died in 1593, and his impressive library along with his other goods was then listed for probate purposes. The inventory contains a list of eighty-four named books of the total value of £13 4s 10d. Buckley's collection contained a large number of the standard theological works of the Church Fathers and of the leaders of the Reformation,[135] but it is his choice of more recent English works which is particularly interesting. He possessed, for example, a copy of Foxe's *Book of Martyrs* and two titles by the

133 Chester. Consistory Court papers. EDC 5, 1639. Miscellaneous. In the absence of further information Oliver Thomas, the preacher, cannot be precisely identified. Two of this name—both of Pembrokeshire–are listed in J. Foster, *Alumni Oxonienses*, four vols., Oxford, 1891–92.

134 The advice about the ceremonies which Edward Fleetwood, rector of Wigan, sought and obtained from his two Oxford friends John Rainolds and Humfrey Fen in 1590 has already been mentioned earlier in the present chapter.

135 These included copies of Calvin's *Commentary on the Psalms* and his *Institutes of Religion*, and the Geneva Bible in English.

Lancashire-born Dean of St Paul's, Alexander Nowell.[136] Most interesting of all, however, for the historian of puritanism is that Buckley owned a copy of Thomas Cartwright's *Second Reply* to Archbishop Whitgift.[137]

Certain book titles are mentioned in the will of Joseph Midgley, formerly vicar of Rochdale, proved in 1637. After his deprivation in 1606 Midgley returned to the Halifax area, from which his family originated, and it was here that he died. To his son Midgley bequeathed 'two bookes in folio of Mr Perkins' works in English', while to his daughter, Rebecca, went his 'English Bible in folio printed at Geneva which was my father's'. She was also given 'a book by Mr Dyke of the deceitfulness of the heart and another of the same author of repentance, also a book called *The Practice of Christianity*, being an epitome of Mr Rogers' seven treatises'.[138] To another daughter, Dorothy, Midgley bequeathed 'a book written by Mr Crooke called *A Guide to True Blessedness*'.[139]

Also interesting from the point of view of the book titles it contained is the will of John Conney, incumbent of St Oswald's, Chester, which was proved in 1642. Conney had in his collection the complete works of William Perkins in three folio volumes.[140] He also had a copy of William Gouge's influential treatise *Of Domesticall Duties* and one of Thomas Goodwin's *Child of Light Walking in Darkness*.[141] His library also included 'two books of Mr Byfield on the first chapter of the first epistle of St Peter'.[142]

Most frequently, however, all that is known about clergymen's libraries is the value of the whole collection; it was unusual for executors to go to the trouble of itemising all the books in a library. So all that we know about the books belonging to John Caldwell of Mobberley, for example, is that he had a very large collection; the

136 These were (1) *Reproofe . . . of a booke entitled A Proofe of certain Articles in Religion denied by Mr. Well, set forth by T. Dorman*, 1565, (2) *Reproofe of Mr. Dorman his proofe of certaine articles in religion, etc* continued by A. Nowell, 1577.
137 Cartwright's *Second Reply* was published in London in 1577.
138 D. Dyke, *Deceitfulnes of the Harte*, 1615. Editions of the work by Rogers were published in 1618, 1623 and 1629.
139 S. Crooke, *Guide unto True Blessednesse*, second edition, 1614.
140 Complete editions of Perkins' *Works* were published at Cambridge in 1609 and at London in 1612 and 1613.
141 Gouge's work was first published in 1622, Goodwin's in 1636.
142 These would be Nicholas Byfield's *Sermons upon the first chapter of the first Epistle generall of St. Peter*, 1626, and his *Commentary on the three first chapters of the first Epistle of St. Peter*, ed. William Gouge, 1637.

inventory of 1595 mentions books to the value of £40.[143] The inventory of James Langley of Leyland (1650) shows that he had a library valued at £32 13s 2d—almost a quarter of his total wealth. John Broxopp, the notorious nonconformist vicar of Ormskirk, also had a library of considerable size. The inventory, which was drawn up in 1643 and lists goods to the total value of nearly £400, mentions books worth £25 6s 8d. Lastly we may note that the Cheshire divine William Hinde possessed a huge library, its total value at the time of his death being no less than £101 4s 0d.

Of the actual titles in Hinde's collection the inventory unfortunately says not a word, but some indication of the theological works which most influenced him and those which he most admired is given by the works of other divines which he prepared for publication. In 1603, for example, Hinde brought out an edition of *The Prophecie of Obediah* by John Rainolds. He had obviously been impressed by the work and admitted to having 'sometimes lighted my candle at his torch [and] stored myself of his treasure . . .' In the following year, Hinde published another work by the same author. This was Rainolds' *Discovery of the Man of Sinne* and again Hinde acknowledged his indebtedness. The title page of the work makes clear that its substance had first been preached as sermons in Oxford, and it was here—as a student at Queen's College, where Rainolds lectured—that Hinde had become acquainted with Rainolds' teaching.[144]

The available evidence concerning clergymen's books serves as a reminder, then, that puritanism in the diocese of Chester was not intellectually isolated. But the point is emphasised still more when the university background of the preachers is considered.

Of the 160 known puritan ministers, at least ninety-five (60 per cent) had attended either Oxford or Cambridge. Of this group, the great majority are known to have graduated. Fifty-nine of them proceeded to take the M.A. degree[145] and ten graduated with the degree of B.D.

143 The total value of Caldwell's goods was £314 18s 6d. As well as being rector of Mobberley, Caldwell also held the rich rectory of Winwick in Lancashire.
     The financial position of the clergy in Lancashire is discussed in D. Lambert, 'The lower clergy . . . in Lancashire, 1558–1642', M.A. thesis, University of Liverpool, 1964.
144 Both the works by Rainolds which Hinde edited were published in Oxford.
145 Some discussion of the M.A. degree of this period is found in M. H. Curtis, *Oxford and Cambridge in Transition*, Oxford, 1959, 91–2.

That the educational qualifications of the clergy as a whole in the diocese of Chester underwent an improvement in the course of the sixty years before the Civil War seems fairly clear.[146] The complaint was made in 1580 that 'the curates throughout the whole diocese of Chester for the most part are utterly unlearned'.[147] By 1642 there had been considerable changes in the situation and the same sweeping complaint could not have been made. Generalisations on this score are difficult, but it would seem that by this date it was becoming increasingly hard for a young puritan minister to succeed if he was not a university man. Adam Martindale was one who certainly recognised the fact. 'Because the name of a mere country scholar might be some prejudice to me,' he wrote, 'I was resolved, when I could get an opportunity, to enter my name in some college in Oxford or Cambridge.' When, despite his lack of academic honours, he received his first invitation to preach he admitted that 'it was so grievous to me to think of running like a lapwing with the shell on my head so raw in university learning . . .'[148]

Of the ninety-five university-trained puritan divines in the diocese, fifty-three had been to Cambridge and thirty-nine to Oxford.[149] The second total provides further evidence that, despite the 1581 matriculation statute requiring subscription to the thirty-nine articles, Oxford clearly raised a good many puritan sons.[150] One can agree, therefore, with Professor Curtis's contention that 'although Cambridge . . . was without a doubt the chief academic centre for the puritan movement, both universities contributed to the cause and furnished England with ardent puritans'.[151]

The collegiate background of the fifty-three ministers educated

146 The improvement, however, was not general throughout the diocese; in this, as in other respects, the northern deaneries lagged far behind.

147 P.R.O. State Papers Domestic. SP 15/27/94. An anonymous report.

148 *Life of Adam Martindale*, 53, 58. Richard Baxter was equally conscious of the difficulties facing a non-graduate minister. 'I knew,' he wrote, 'that the want of academical honours and degrees was like to make me contemptible with the most and consequently hinder the success of my endeavours.' (*Autobiography*, Everyman edition, 15.)

149 In the case of three clergymen—Thomas Hunt, William Langley and Samuel Eaton—it has not been possible to establish with certainty which of the universities they attended.

150 At Cambridge, subscription to the articles was not finally enjoined until 1616. (Curtis, *op. cit.*, 170.)

151 Curtis, *op. cit.*, 191. Conversely, Curtis shows that 'High Church' theology had roots in Cambridge as well as in Oxford, with which it is more commonly associated.

at Cambridge is summarised in table 1.[152] The importance of
Emmanuel and Christ's colleges as training grounds for the puritan
clergy was not, of course, accidental. In Elizabeth's reign Christ's
College numbered the puritans Chaderton, Dering and Perkins

Table 1

College	Number of ministers there	College	Number of ministers there
Emmanuel	9	Corpus [Christi]	1
Christ's	9	Pembroke	1
Trinity	6	Caius	1
Queen's	6	King's	1
St John's	6	Peterhouse	1
Magdalene	4	Clare	1
Jesus	2	Sidney Sussex	1
		Trinity Hall	1

among its great teachers and was the main centre at the university
for the study of Ramist logic.[153] Emmanuel College also from the
days of its first Master—the Lancashire-born Laurence Chaderton—
was noted as a puritan stronghold. Samuel Clarke, the martyrologist,
told how his father entered him at Cambridge 'in Emmanuel
College, which was the puritan college'.[154] And generalising on the
same subject, Cotton Mather wrote that 'if New England has been
in some respect Emmanuel's land, it is well. But this I am sure of,
Emmanuel College contributed more than a little to make it so.'[155]

152 It is uncertain which colleges Alexander Horrocks of Deane, John Buckley
   of Manchester and Alexander Clark of Eccleston, Cheshire, attended, but
   they are known to have been Cambridge men.
153 Collinson, *Puritan Movement*, 128; Howell, *Logic and Rhetoric in England*,
   211. The nine ministers in the diocese of Chester who had been educated
   at Christ's College were John Jackson of Melsonby, William Bourne of
   Manchester, Arthur Storer of Stockport, Robert Whittle of Tarporley,
   Richard Redmaine of Kirkby (Liverpool), Matthew Clayton of Witton,
   Cheshire, Thomas Shaw of Aldingham, William Curwen of Over Kellet and
   Samuel Torshell of Bunbury.
154 Clarke, introduction to *Lives of Sundry Eminent Persons*, 3.
155 Mather, *Ecclesiastical History of New England*, III, 217. Quoted in
   Mullinger, *University of Cambridge*, II, 213. Those ministers in the diocese
   of Chester who had attended Emmanuel were William Harrison, one of the

Thirty-nine of the puritan clergymen in the diocese of Chester are known to have been educated at Oxford, and their distribution amongst the constituent colleges of the university is summarised in table 2.[156] As the table shows, by far the largest number went to

Table 2

College	Number of ministers there	College	Number of ministers there
Brasenose	14	St John's	2
Christ Church	7	New	1
Exeter	4	Balliol	1
Lincoln	2	All Souls	1
Queen's	2	St Mary Hall	1

Brasenose. No other college—at either Oxford or Cambridge—produced so many of the diocese's puritan divines. This was not a fortuitous result, however, for of all university colleges Brasenose had the closest links with the North-west.[157]

Brasenose College had been re-founded early in the sixteenth century by William Smyth, Bishop of Lincoln, a native of Prescot, Lancashire, and by Sir Richard Sutton, who had been born in the Cheshire parish of Prestbury.[158] From the first the college reflected the local origin and interests of its founders. (Lancashire and Cheshire students and candidates for fellowships were always to be given preference.) But Brasenose's links with the North-west,

Queen's Preachers in Lancashire, Richard Rowe of Bunbury, John Broxopp of Ormskirk, Ralph Stirrup of Ashton-on-Mersey, Robert Parke of Bolton, John Breres of Rivington, John Angier of Denton, John Harrison of Ashton and Jeremiah Horrocks of Hoole.

156 Edward Fleetwood of Wigan, William Brownall of Gawsworth, John Nutter of Sefton and Robert Osbaldeston of Whalley were Oxford men, but there is no record of the college they attended. These figures relating to university attendance are based mainly on information in J. and J. A. Venn, *Alumni Cantabrigienses*, Cambridge, 1922–7, and in J. Foster, *Alumni Oxonienses*, Oxford, 1891–92.

157 Significantly, the majority of those ministers who attended Brasenose had been born in the diocese to which they later returned to preach.

158 F. Madan (ed.), *Brasenose College Quatercentenary Monographs*, two vols., Oxford, 1909–10, II, Pt. 1, 4–7.

and with Lancashire particularly, were made stronger by the college's association with some of the sixteenth-century grammar schools in the area. Bishop Smyth himself had in 1507 endowed Farnworth Grammar School with the sum of £10 a year.[159] Later in 1569 when Robert Nowell, a prominent London lawyer, died, he left a substantial amount of money to enable his brother and executor, Alexander Nowell, Dean of St Paul's, to set about the re-founding of the school at Middleton, where they had both been educated. It was Nowell's wish that the school should be directly linked with Brasenose from the outset, and after Alexander's death the college was to be given complete control of its affairs.[160] Moreover, scholarships to Brasenose were endowed by Nowell, to be taken up by Lancashire youths from the County's grammar schools.[161]

A high proportion of Lancashire and Cheshire entrants to Brasenose was maintained throughout the seventeenth, eighteenth and early nineteenth centuries. Of those young men who went up to Oxford from Cheshire in the course of the eighteenth century, the majority went to Brasenose, many of them *via* Manchester Grammar School.[162] Even in the early nineteenth century almost a third of the college's intake was still drawn from Lancashire and Cheshire.[163] Not until the foundation of open scholarships to Oxford, the establishment of the Lancashire universities and the reduction in the number of ties with the county families of the region did Brasenose begin to lose something of its original Northern flavour. But even in the second half of the nineteenth century the college still had some links with the North, a situation demonstrated by the foundation in 1869 of the Brasenose Club in Manchester.[164]

Of the fourteen puritan divines of the diocese who attended Brasenose, the earliest—in the 1540's—was Christopher Goodman, a Marian exile, author of the controversial tract on *How Superior*

159 *V.C.H. Lancs.*, II, 589.
160 R. S. Paul and W. J. Smith, *A History of Middleton Grammar School*, Middleton, 1965.
161 *Ibid.*, 9. Small additional sums from the Nowell bequest were to be given to actual or would-be scholars of Brasenose. (A. B. Grosart (ed.), *The Spending of the Money of Robert Nowell*, privately printed, 1877.)
162 D. Robson, *Aspects of Education in Cheshire in the Eighteenth Century*, Chet. Soc., third series, 13, Manchester, 1966.
163 Madan, *op. cit.*, II, Pt. II, 35.
164 Cf. A. Darbyshire, *Chronicle of the Brasenose Club, Manchester*, Manchester, 1892.

Powers ought to be obeyed[165] and later a minister in Chester and
Archdeacon of Richmond. In the later sixteenth century Anthony Calcott of Astbury, Cheshire, William Leigh of Standish,
Lancashire, Christopher Harvey of Bunbury, Robert Eaton of
Mobberley and Nicholas Hulme of Kirkham had all studied at
Brasenose. In 1618 Richard Mather of Toxteth was admitted to the
college, and according to his biographer 'it was a joy to him to
find many there who had been his quondam scholars' in his school
at Toxteth.[166] Mather did not remain at Brasenose long enough to
graduate—he was recalled to be pastor of the Toxteth congregation
—but he may have been there long enough to have become
acquainted with Timothy Aspinwall, later curate at Knutsford,
Cheshire, who matriculated from the college in 1620. Other
ministers in the diocese of Chester who attended Brasenose about
this time were William Gregg of Bolton, Isaac Ambrose of Preston,
Adam Bolton of Blackburn, Richard Holker of Guilden Sutton
and Edward Gee of Eccleston. Finally, we may note that James
Bradshaw of Wigan was a student at Brasenose early in the 1630's.[167]

6 *The brotherhood of the preachers*

Over half the puritan clergy of the diocese of Chester had this
important common ground: they had attended either Oxford or
Cambridge. But the significance of the fact is not only that the
diocese came to contain a relatively high proportion of well educated
puritan clergy. As Professor Collinson reminds us:

> Clerical puritanism, as a cohesive, national movement, was created in
> the universities. It was here [he continues] that the various regional
> and social origins of the Elizabethan preachers were submerged in a
> common brotherhood.[168]

College and university contemporaries frequently found themselves
reunited as ministerial colleagues in the diocese of Chester. The most
convenient way of showing these associations is in a table, and four of

165 The work was published in Geneva in 1558 and spoke in Knox-like terms of
'that monster in nature and disorder amongst men which is the empire
and government of a woman'.
166 *Life and Death of Richard Mather*, 8.
167 Details of the degrees which these and other clergymen obtained are given
in the appendix.
168 Collinson, *Puritan Movement*, 127. The point is also made in W. Haller,
The Rise of Puritanism, New York, 1957, 52, 54, and in the same author's
Liberty and Reformation in the Puritan Revolution, New York, 1963, 11–12.

these—one for each university in the Elizabethan and early Stuart periods—are placed together in the appendix.

Occasionally the links between preachers even went back to their schooldays. As a notable example, it can be observed that Richard Heyricke and Thomas Case were at Merchant Taylors' School at the same time and went up to Oxford together, though to different colleges. Their subsequent careers continued to be closely associated. When, in 1626, Heyricke secured his first preferment to the rectory of North Repps in Norfolk, Case became his curate. And when in the 1630's Heyricke was Warden of the Collegiate Church, Case accepted his invitation to come and preach in Manchester.

Other factors, however, promoted this brotherhood of the puritan clergy. Some of the puritan clergy whose activities have been discussed in this chapter were local men—men who already knew the area, the dialect and the people with whom they had to deal in their ministries. Of the university-trained preachers, about a third were in this category. Nine of the sixteen Lancashire clergymen who drew up a detailed description of the county in 1590 were men of local origin.[169]

Some of the preachers strengthened their ties with the areas in which they served and with their ministerial colleagues through marriage. Edward Tacey, chaplain at the Manchester College, came by his marriage to be linked with the Nugents, a puritan family of Manchester merchants. In 1637 Thomas Case married Anne, daughter of Oswald Mosley, of Ancoats. John Angier also came by marriage to be connected with the same family, since his second wife was Margaret Mosley.[170]

169 The Lancashire-born preachers among them were Peter Shaw, William Langley, John Buckley, Leonard Shaw, Miles Aspinall, Peter White, Edward Walsh, Robert Osbaldeston and Edward Assheton. (Biographical details of these preachers are given in F. R. Raines (ed.), *Miscellany*, vol. V, Chet. Soc., old series, 96, Manchester, 1875.)

The advantages conferred by a Northern background could often be considerable. In 1602/3, for example, Bishop Vaughan of Chester recommended a Mr Duckett, Fellow of Trinity College, Cambridge, as a particularly suitable candidate for one of the Queen's Preacherships in Lancashire, he being: 'a man sufficiently qualified both for learning and staidness, who being born in these parts and well acquainted with the nature and manners of the people, is most likely to prevail with them in cases relating to their souls and consciences'. *Salisbury Mss*, H.M.C., xii, 606–7.)

170 Heywood, *Life of John Angier*, 62. Angier's first wife was also a native of Lancashire and was a niece of the puritan divine John Cotton of Boston, Lincolnshire. (*D.N.B.*)

Mr Walzer contends that partly because of the changing social character

The establishment of preaching Exercises throughout the diocese of Chester in the 1580's helped to strengthen the bonds uniting the preachers and to put puritanism itself on a more organised footing. But the real purpose of the scheme was to win over the people from Popery and to improve the educational standards of the lower clergy. So before moving on to discuss the attendant results of the Exercises, their educational purpose deserves some mention here.

The Exercises in the diocese of Chester, as has already been briefly noted, originated in an arrangement made in 1582 for three synods a year to be held at the central and easily accessible market town of Preston. It involved only the Lancashire clergy, all of whom were required to attend. The synods or prophesyings were held at Easter, midsummer and Michaelmas and were primarily gatherings of the clergy rather than of the laity. Only at the end of the meeting were the laity to be admitted to hear a sermon preached by one of the moderators.[171]

For the synods to function properly, disciplinary powers might have to be invoked. Accordingly it was laid down that any minister who failed to attend or refused to be guided by the moderators might—since the scheme was officially sponsored—be dealt with by the bishop.

The 1584 scheme of Exercises retained this educational purpose. All clergymen and schoolmasters were required to attend monthly at the Exercise in their own deanery. The procedure was for:

the learned sort [to] speak publicly in the said Exercise; the mean sort to write upon such matter as shall be proposed unto them by the moderators by the way of examination; so many of each sort to speak, write and answer as by the moderators shall be thought convenient.

The synods set up in 1582, as has been said, were designed only for Lancashire ministers, and the moderators were all drawn from the two most puritan deaneries of Manchester and Warrington. The later scheme of 1584, however, established with the full support of the Bishop of Chester and of the Privy Council, was for a

of the puritan clergy it was easier for them to marry well in the seventeenth than in the sixteenth century. (*The Revolution of the Saints*, 1966, 135-7.)

171 The moderators were Oliver Carter of Manchester, Edward Fleetwood of Wigan, Simon Harwood of Warrington and Richard Midgley of Rochdale. Full details of the 1582 scheme and of the later Exercises are found in Gonville and Caius MS 197, ff. 175-85.

system of monthly Exercises throughout the whole diocese.[172] In all, there were fourteen centres for the holding of the Exercises, and at each there were usually four moderators.[173]

Fifty-three moderators in all were involved in the Exercises of the 1580's, and of these twenty-three were puritans. But in the archdeaconry of Chester the moderators were overwhelmingly puritan. Since they numbered twenty-two out of a total of thirty-one, they were able to dominate the scheme from the start. This being the case, the Exercises, by regularly bringing them together and associating them in a common enterprise, must undoubtedly have promoted unity within the ranks of the puritan clergy.

Although the network of Exercises as a whole had probably ceased to exist by the early 1590's, there is considerable evidence to show that in the puritan areas of the diocese Exercises continued to be held right up to the Civil War. In these areas at least, the

172 No Exercises, however, took place in the three coldest months of November, December and January.
173 In Cheshire the Exercises were held at four towns—Chester, Macclesfield, Nantwich and Northwich. At *Chester* the moderators were Christopher Goodman, William Wright of Waverton, the Chancellor of the diocese and Mr Litchens, Reader in Divinity. At *Macclesfield* Mr Rogers, Archdeacon of Chester, Richard Gerard of Stockport, John Caldwell of Mobberley and Edward Hollinshead were the moderators. Those who led the Exercise at Nantwich, on the other hand, were Thomas Coller of Swettenham, William Lawton, Anthony Calcott of Astbury and Matthew Wood of Wybunbury. At *Northwich* the moderators were John Caldwell of Mobberley, Robert Eaton of Grappenhall, Mr Warburton of Warburton and William Brownall of Rostherne.

In Lancashire the Exercises were held at five centres—Prescot, Bury, Padiham, Preston and Ulverston. At *Prescot* the moderators were John Nutter of Sefton, Edward Fleetwood of Wigan, Thomas Meade of Prescot. (The fourth is not named in the MS.) At *Bury* Oliver Carter of Manchester, Peter Shaw of Bury, Thomas Williamson of Eccles and William Langley of Prestwich were the moderators. At *Padiham* the Exercises were led by Edward Assheton of Middleton, Robert Osbaldeston of Whalley, Leonard Shaw of Radcliffe and Richard Midgley of Rochdale. The *Preston* Exercise was led by William Leigh of Standish, Edward Walsh of Blackburn, Henry Porter of Lancaster and William Sawrey of Preston. The moderators for *Ulverston* were Robert Parkinson (Commissary of the archdeaconry of Richmond), Mr Gilpin of Aldingham, Mr Magson, preacher at Hawkshead, and Mr Lindall of Urswick.

In the northern deaneries of the diocese Exercises were held at five centres, namely at Richmond, Beedal, Knaresborough, Egremond and Kendal. Only one of the moderators involved, it should be noted, was a puritan. (This was John Jackson of Melsonby.)

mid-seventeenth-century Presbyterian experiment was not a completely new departure—as such it would be largely inexplicable—
but the climax of previous developments.

That there were Exercises of a kind in Manchester, for example,
in the early seventeenth century is fairly certain. Hollingworth, in
his *Mancuniensis*, has it that William Bourne, Fellow of the Collegiate Church, and other clergymen of the parish, such as John Gee,
Thomas Paget and William Rathband, 'often met in a kind of
consultative classis'.[174] In 1630 Christopher Hudson, lecturer at
Preston, is known to have preached a sermon at 'Blackburn Exercise',[175] while in the 1633 visitation it was observed that at Blackrod
chapel, Lancashire, 'there is a monthly Exercise of two sermons'.[176]
At Kirkham also in the following year at least one Exercise is known
to have taken place.[177]

At irregular intervals preaching Exercises are also known to
have been taking place at this time in the Cheshire market town
of Congleton. The earliest reference in the account books of the
corporation relating to the Exercises occurs in 1632, when the
following entry appears:

> Paid to Alderman Rode of the 'Swan' in discharge of a note for dinners,
> wine and beer, etc, bestowed on ministers that have preached here on
> Exercise days: 10s 4d.

A further sum was paid in the fourth quarter of the same year
to the same innkeeper 'in discharge of a note for the clerk of the
market and preachers' dinners upon Exercise days: 14s 4d'. In
the second quarter of 1633 the sum of twenty pence was 'bestowed
upon two preachers two Exercise days in wine and beer'. For some
reason there are no further entries relating to these Exercises until
1641, when the following payment is recorded:

> At three Exercises bestowed upon the ministers in wine and meat for the
> quarter: 19s 8d.[178]

---

174 Hollingworth, *op. cit.*, 106.
175 Preston. Hudson's MS sermons. DP 353, f. 55v.
176 York. 1633 vis. RVIA 23, f. 565v.
177 The churchwardens' accounts record a payment of 4s 3d being made 'for
   the Exercise in the old churchwardens' time and for the moderators and
   the preachers'. (R. C. Shaw (ed.), *Records of the Thirty Men of the Parish
   of Kirkham*, Kendal, 1930, 22.) Edward Fleetwood, a staunch puritan, had
   been vicar of Kirkham from 1630.
178 Transcripts of the borough accounts, Congleton. I am indebted to Dr
   R. W. Dunning of the *Victoria County History* for these references. See

At Frodsham, Cheshire, preaching Exercises of this kind were also being held at least by 1640. The churchwardens' accounts for that year record a payment of nine shillings being made to one Ellen Pyke 'for the ministers' dinners who preached at our Exercise'.[179] And by the following year a Cheshire letter writer could declare that:

> the greatest news we have is that all our country churches are full of Exercises for thanksgiving . . .
> This last week there was one at Little Budworth. This week there was one at Barrow and Thornton. The next week at Tarvin.[180]

The holding of regular preaching Exercises, besides tending to promote further unity amongst the puritan clergy who participated, also provided them with an opportunity for taking concerted action if and when the need arose.

Such was clearly the case in 1640–41 at the Warrington Exercise.[181] It was here that the assembled puritan divines and their lay supporters discussed the recently announced sixth canon of 1640, which enjoined an oath for the preventing of all innovations in doctrine and church discipline. The leading Cheshire divine John Ley has left a full account of the proceedings. He tells how at a previous Exercise held at Warrington on 18 August 1640 the moderators were Charles Herle, rector of Winwick,[182] and himself, and

also the section on 'Religion in Congleton'—to which Dr Dunning contributed—in W. B. Stephens (ed.), *A History of Congleton*, Manchester, 1970, 211.

179 Chester. Parochial records. P8/13/1. Vol. II, f. 72.

180 Thomas Moreton to Sir Thomas Smith, August 1641. P.R.O. State Papers Domestic. SP 16/483/20.

181 The origins of the Warrington Exercise are to some extent obscure. John Ley, however, has it that it was established with the approval of James I as a thank-offering after the discovery of the Gunpowder Plot. (Ley, *Defensive Doubts, Hopes and Reasons for Refusall of the Oath imposed by the late synod*, 1641, epistle dedicatory.) The Exercise, which continued throughout the 1640's and into the 1650's, was held on the third Tuesday of each month. (J. E. Bailey, *Life of a Lancashire Rector in the Civil War*, Manchester, 1877, 9.)

182 Charles Herle M.A. (1598–1659) was born in Cornwall and educated at Exeter College, Oxford. He was presented to the wealthy rectory of Winwick in 1626 and published numerous works. Herle was to preach before the House of Commons in the 1640's and was a member of the Assembly of Divines. His close contacts with the Earl of Derby, to whom he was indebted for his presentation to Winwick, will be discussed in chapter four.

that the subject for the day's discussion was 'Peace and charity'. Ley goes on to describe how:

> Our sermons ended, and some of us invited to a place of convenient repose, the rest of our tribe, who were a part of that congregation resorted unto us, every man accompanying his acquaintance, and so making as it were a whole chain of many links; and withal it is not unlike but that the most that there met in person met also in perplexity of mind by reason of the late canonical oath and in their desire to be resolved of their doubts.

All were asked whether they thought the oath was of doubtful validity and they agreed unanimously that it was. Discussion quickly moved to the question of what action could be taken, and it was finally agreed that the doubts of the assembled puritan company about the oath should be communicated to the Bishop of Chester. Ley was chosen to express these doubts in writing.

This he did, and duly presented the document for the consideration of his ministerial colleagues—his 'brethren of the Presbytery', as he significantly terms them—at the next Exercise. There he received their full approval.[183]

But this was not the first time that puritan preachers in the diocese of Chester had united in action. It will be remembered that in 1590 sixteen Lancashire divines had combined to draw up their description of the religious condition of the county.[184] And when in the same year a number of the same preachers—mainly those of Manchester deanery—had been censured by the Archbishop of York they had united in presenting a common defence.[185]

Co-operation, then, did exist amongst the puritan divines of the diocese. In addition to the evidence already presented it can be noted that wills sometimes provide a further indication of the fact. A good example is that of John Buckley, a preacher at the Collegiate Church in Manchester. The will, which was proved in 1593, shows first of all that Buckley was on close terms with his immediate

183 Ley, *op. cit.*, epistle dedicatory.
184 Those ministers who collaborated in the 1590 Description were Oliver Carter of Manchester, Peter Shaw of Bury, William Langley of Prestwich, John Buckley of Manchester, Leonard Shaw of Radcliffe, Miles Aspinall of Blackburn, James Gosnell of Bolton, Peter White of Poulton, Edward Walsh of Blackburn, Edward Fleetwood of Wigan, John Caldwell of Winwick, Robert Osbaldeston of Whalley, Edward Assheton of Middleton, James Smith of Kirkham, Richard Midgley of Rochdale, John Ashworth of Warrington and the Cheshire minister Henry Sumner of Disley.
185 F. R. Raines (ed.), *Miscellany, vol. V*, Chet. Soc., 9–14.

ministerial colleagues. To Oliver Carter, his fellow preacher, Buckley bequeathed his Latin Tremellius Bible, while to Robert Barber—also of the Collegiate Church—he gave his large Geneva Bible in English. Volumes by Alexander Nowell, Dean of St Paul's, were bequeathed to Robert Leigh, 'one of the four clerks of the same college'.

But the gifts of books which Buckley made in his will were not only to clergymen of the parish church. To John Morris, preacher at Ashton-under-Lyne, he gave a copy of Luther's *Commentaries*. The curates at Littleborough, Blackley, Denton and Blackburn all received books under the terms of Buckley's will.[186]

The close association of puritan teachers is also reflected in the sermon literature. John Ley's treatise *Sunday a Sabbath* (1641) can be cited as an example. The preface of the work consists of a letter sent to Ley by fourteen of his ministerial colleagues[187] urging him to make an authoritative statement on Sabbatarianism. Ley in turn partly dedicated another work—*Defensive Doubts, Hopes and Reasons* (1641)—to his 'brethren of the diocese of Chester' such as Richard Heyricke and Charles Herle. Rather later—in 1662—Isaac Ambrose, then vicar of Garstang, dedicated the second part of his work on *The Three Great Ordinances of Jesus Christ* to his 'dear brethren in the ministry of the Gospel, Mr John Angier, Mr Edward Gee, Mr John Harrison, Mr John Tildesley'.

7 The clergy and the 'puritan movement'

In trying to reach a conclusion about the nature and extent of the role of the clergy in puritanism, it may be useful first of all to

186 It was common practice, too, for puritan ministers to lend books to each other. Cf. Henry Newcome: 'Although I had so few books of my own, yet I had such a supply from others, and that by this course I had such profitable use of those books I borrowed, that a greater library could not have been a greater advantage to me.' (*Autobiography*, I, 12.)

187 These ministers, who subscribed themselves 'your very respective Friends and Brethren in the ministry', were William Moston of Christleton, Andrew Wood, perhaps curate at Knutsford, John Conney of Chester, Samuel Clarke, formerly of Shotwick, Matthew Clayton of Witton, William Shenton of Rostherne, Richard Holker of Guilden Sutton, Robert Whittle of Tarporley, Charles Herle of Winwick, Nathaniel Lancaster of Tarporley, Richard Wilson of Chester, Alexander Clark of Eccleston, John Glendole of Chester and Thomas Holford of Plemondstall.

But the very fact that an appeal of this kind was made to Ley reminds us that the existence of the Presbyterian idea of clerical brotherhood did not exclude the possibility of the emergence of ministerial leaders such as Ley, Heyricke, Bourne, Hinde and Fleetwood.

consider what the clergy themselves thought about the subject. Generally they took a lofty view. For example, in a sermon preached in Manchester in 1637 Richard Heyricke proclaimed that:

> Heaven itself cannot show forth a more excellent creature than a faithful preacher . . . Yea, heaven itself is not more glorious than a small village having a Peter, a Paul, to preach in it. The great bishop of our souls, Christ Jesus himself, he has the faithful preachers of the Church as stars in his right hand, not only to defend them from the tyranny and malice of the wicked, but he holds them forth to show their glory. We are ambassadors of God.[188]

Views such as this—and it is only one example of many—remind us that much of our knowledge of puritanism is derived from accounts by the clergy, who, writing always from their own particular standpoint, naturally tended to over-emphasise their own importance. Sources of this kind, therefore, present a picture of puritanism which is to some extent distorted. This distortion was, moreover, increased by contemporary observers of the political scene, such as Hobbes and Clarendon, who took the view that it was the puritan clergy who were the main agents through whom rebellion had been fomented.[189]

But such views of the role of the clergy also remind us that, partial and incomplete though this interpretation of puritanism is,

188 Central Library, Manchester. Worsley MSS. M 35/5/3/7. Unpaginated.
189 In 1688 Hobbes asked whether it 'had not been much better that these seditious ministers, which were not perhaps 1000, had all been killed before they had preached? It had been, I confess, a great massacre, but the killing of 100,000 (in the Civil War) is a greater one.' (*Behemoth* in *English Works*, ed. Molesworth, 1839–45, v 1, 282.

Clarendon similarly contended that 'this strange wild fire among the people was not so much and so furiously kindled by the breath of the Parliament as of the clergy, who both administered fuel and blowed the coals in the house too . . .' (*History of the Rebellion*, ed. W. D. Macray, Oxford, 1887, 11, 319.) But, of course, he needed a scapegoat.

Charges of this kind were made before the seventeenth century and after. In his famous sermon on 'Covetousness' in 1550 Latimer noted that 'some say that the preaching nowadays is the cause of all sedition and rebellion . . . Here was preaching against covetousness all the last year in Lent, and the next summer followed rebellion . . .' (*Select Sermons and Letters of Hugh Latimer*, Religious Tract Society, n.d., 79–80.) Much later it was rumoured that Popish priests and Methodist preachers had helped to incite those who took part in the disturbances of 1830–31. (G. Rudé, 'English rural and urban disturbances on the eve of the first Reform Bill, 1830–31', *Past and Present*, 37, 1967, 99.)

F

it is one which has greatly influenced past historians of the subject. To Benjamin Brook, for instance, whose *Lives of the Puritans* was published in 1813, the term 'puritan' meant puritan minister.

A view similar to this was taken by the American scholar R. G. Usher in his work on *The Reconstruction of the English Church* (New York, 1910) and in an earlier article on 'The people and the puritan movement' (*Church Quarterly Review*, LVIII, 1904). Like Brook's Usher's contention was that puritanism was primarily clerical.

> The strength of the puritan movement [he declared] must have lain entirely in its clergy. It was a movement of the ministers and for the ministers, who heeded little the desires of their congregations. The people were to be ruled and obey the word of God as delivered by the lawful interpreters thereof and it was not their place to give suggestions of their own . . .[190]

Even allowing for the fact that Usher concentrated upon the reign of Elizabeth, when the clerical contribution was greater than it was in succeeding decades, his argument seems to be no more than partially acceptable. His so-called definition of puritanism, quoted above, is in fact no more than a description of the views which Presbyterian clergymen such as Heyricke were putting forward. Usher assumed that the clergy always had a captive audience—that the congregation was obliged to listen to whatever might be preached. It was also his assumption that there was always an immense intellectual gulf separating clergy and laity, and that in consequence a clergyman's opinions could never be challenged by a member of his flock.

We may wonder whether puritanism was ever so entirely centred upon the clergy as these views suggest. The role of the puritan divines in the diocese of Chester was varied and important, as this present chapter has shown, but it ought not to be exaggerated by being viewed in isolation. Clerical puritanism was, after all, only an aspect of puritanism as a whole, albeit often the most conspicuous. It seems generally true that the role of the clergy was greatest in the initial stages of the development of puritanism, for it was then that the challenge facing them was strongest and then that there was least competition from puritan laymen. Consequently, in predominantly Catholic areas the puritan clergy in the seventeenth century continued to play a role which elsewhere they had begun

190 Usher, *Reconstruction*, I, 268.

to share with the laity. But in order to prosper, puritanism required active lay support and participation—a fact which the puritan clergy recognised and tried to bring about. Ironically, of course, in so doing they undermined their own position.

Organised puritanism, then, involved a partnership between the puritan layman and clergyman, a state of affairs which was well described by Thomas Case in a sermon he preached in Manchester in 1637.

> My brethren, [he declared to the congregation], if you will share with ministers in their work you will share with them in their wages. Ministers are the chief workers [he went on], the master builders, but you are God's labourers; they are the beginners, overseers of the work, but you must bring materials and lay them one upon another. Ministers must labour and beget men into Christ, you must labour to preserve one another. You do not know [he continued] what you may do with a word. God may make you spiritual fathers and spiritual mothers one to another . . .[191]

Seventeenth-century puritanism in the diocese of Chester, as elsewhere, was by no means wholly clerical in character. The role of the puritan layman was considerable, and it is this which must now be explored.

191 Central Library, Manchester. Worsley MSS, M 35/5/3/7. Unpaginated.

Chapter Three

The role of the laity

I was never acquainted with more understanding Christians in all my life, though the best of them went but in russet coats and followed husbandry.

Samuel Clarke in the introduction to his *Lives of Sundry Eminent Persons*, 1683, 4

1 *The forms of lay nonconformity in worship*

'It is the multitude and people,' wrote John Field, the Elizabethan Presbyterian propagandist, 'that must bring the discipline to pass which we desire.'[1] Constitutional means failing to further Reformation, this might b the only way open. For puritanism—contemporaries recognised, even if historians such as R. G. Usher did not— was by no means entirely restricted to the clergy, and it is only when placed in the context of the society in which it originated that it becomes meaningful. As Tawney long ago pointed out, 'Puritanism helped to mould the social order, but it was also increasingly moulded by it.'[2] More recently Professor Collinson has reminded us of 'the inner momentum' of puritanism and stated that:

> the popular protestant element in Elizabethan society was not subordinate to the preachers, but possessed of a mind and a will of its own to which the conduct of the puritan minister, including his own nonconformity, was partly a response.[3]

Members of the congregation were quite capable of exerting themselves and expressing their independence in thought and action.

Even in the matter of the ministerial use of the surplice, lay attitudes were expressed. For it is a mistake to view the Vestarian controversy as an academic contest in which only the clergy participated. Such a view unwarrantably isolates the clergy from their social

---

1 P. Collinson, 'The godly: aspects of popular Protestantism in Elizabethan England', *Past and Present Conference Papers*, 1966, 4–5.
2 Tawney, *Religion and the Rise of Capitalism*, xiii.
3 Collinson, *op. cit.*, 15, 3.

setting and wrongfully assumes that the laity were uninterested in the matter.

> On few issues [Professor Collinson has written] did lay prejudice find such forceful expression as in the rejection of the surplice and the square cap. All the indications are that, contrary to the impression of some historians, the scandal of the 'Popish rag' was felt more strongly by the godly than by their ministers . . . For simple gospellers . . . the symbols themselves were a concrete visible offence . . . When a nonconformist baulked at the surplice, it was often not so much his own scruples which deterred him as fear of the catastrophe which might overtake his ministry if he were to appear before his people in the offensive garment.[4]

Such was certainly the case in Essex, a county much used by Professor Collinson in his researches.[5] But it was not only in this advanced puritan county that such opposition was expressed. Several instances of this phenomenon have been found for the diocese of Chester. At Rochdale, for example, in the 1590 metropolitan visitation, Richard Midgley, the vicar, was charged for consistently evading the use of the surplice over a period of twenty years. 'They had none all that time,' it was said. 'Mr Midgley does not refuse to wear the surplice but refers himself to unity seeking the quiet of the Church.'[6] Although Midgley's own nonconformity was not caused by his congregation's views, clearly the latter were playing an important part in the expression and organisation of puritanism in Rochdale. John Rainolds of Oxford recognised the strength of the laity's views on this subject in a letter he wrote to Edward Fleetwood of Wigan in this same year. Although he advised the Lancashire divines to conform and to wear the surplice rather than risk deprivation for suspension, he admitted that 'the godly would dislike thereof and would depart, divers of them, from their [i.e. the preachers'] public ministration'.[7]

4 Collinson, *Elizabethan Puritan Movement*, 94–6.
5 Disturbances amongst Essex clothworkers in 1566 were said to be partly caused by 'the regulations with regard to the ministers wearing a decent clerical habit as formerly and also as to wearing surplices in churches'. (De Silva to the King of Spain, August 1566. *Cal. S.P.Spanish*, 1,571.(Quoted in Collinson, 'The puritan classical movement', 45.) Lay opposition to the wearing of the surplice in Essex continued to be expressed, especially as a reaction against the declared policy of Laud's visitation of 1636. (For examples see T. W. Davids, *Annals of Evangelical Nonconformity in Essex*, 1863.)
6 York. 1590 vis. RVIA 12, f. 68.
7 Queen's College, Oxford. MS 280, f. 174v.

A further instance of opposition to the wearing of the surplice was noted at Deane, Lancashire, in the visitation of 1619. In that year a group of laymen were charged on several counts of non-conformity. Two of them were accused of failing to receive the communion and one of these—John Tildesley—so the churchwarden deposed, 'does not receive that he can see and the reason is, as he believes, because the vicar ministers in the surplice'.[8] Thomas Constable—a puritan of advanced views from Winwick parish—declared in 1641 concerning 'the surplice and other ceremonies that all men that have the use of reason do tread them underfoot'.[9]

Easily the most common and conspicuous expression of lay puritanism, however, was the failure to kneel at the prescribed times in Church services, particularly at the receiving of the communion.

Archbishop Neile of York believed that this aspect of lay non-conformity was mainly attributable to the influence of the puritan clergy:

> The disrespect that the ministers have shown of public prayers of the church [he declared in 1633] has bred such irreverence in the people that it is a rare thing in many places to see any upon their knees [as and when required].[10]

The Archbishop's explanation of non-kneeling, however, was—as will be shown—by no means wholly accurate or complete. But certainly his observations on the extent of the practice were well founded.

At Oldham in the 1605 visitation the inhabitants were collectively charged with not kneeling at the receiving of the communion.[11] At nearby Middleton in 1622 it was observed that 'none bow the knee', while at Astbury, Cheshire, a similar discovery was made in 1633 that 'it is a general default that the people do not kneel at prayers'.[12] From the authorities' point of view the situation was almost as bad at Richmond in that year. 'Upon Sunday the fore-noon,' Neile's commissioners wrote in 1633, 'we could not observe six persons [there] that kneel at prayers . . .'[13]

There seems little doubt that this expression of dissent was a

8 Chester. 1619 vis. EDV 1/21, f. 67.
9 Preston. Quarter sessions records. QSB 1/246/31. 1641.
10 P.R.O. State Papers Domestic. SP 16/259/78.
11 Chester 1605 vis. EDV 1/14, f. 92v.
12 Chester. 1622 vis. EDV 1/24, f. 105v; York. 1633 vis. RVIA 23, f. 475v.
13 Bradford MSS, Weston Park, Salop, 9/8. Bridgeman's copy of the visitation report, f. 1.

purposeful action. On numerous occasions the presentments make clear that the deviation was not a casual departure from the prescribed form but that it was deliberate policy. At Manchester, for example, in 1622, twenty-four of the congregation were presented not just for failing but for refusing to kneel at the communion.[14] In 1633 twenty were similarly charged at Bolton.[15] At Middlewich, Cheshire, in 1605, a group of eight laymen, including the schoolmaster, were presented on the charge that they 'refused to receive the communion because they might not have it standing or sitting'.[16]

Puritans' determination in this respect is also witnessed by the fact that on numerous occasions the charge of failing to kneel was repeated over the years against the same individuals. Many examples of this kind—as might be expected—occur in the visitation records relating to Manchester. One Edward Briddocke, for example, was first presented for his failure to kneel in 1622. The charge was repeated in 1625, but eight years later he was still refusing to conform in this matter.[17] Thomas Nield, tailor, was presented on this charge in 1622, five years after he had first been presented for this offence.[18]

But it was not only in the ultra-puritan deanery of Manchester that examples of this type occur in the visitation records. At Warrington, for instance, William Fallows and his wife, Jeremy Smith and Richard West were reported as nonconformists in this regard in 1625 and again in 1628.[19] At Grappenhall, in Frodsham deanery, one William Morris was charged in 1619 for failing to kneel. The charge was repeated in 1622, but in 1633 his name again appeared in the visitation records 'for not receiving the communion at Easter last because he refuses to take the same kneeling'.[20]

Fuller details concerning opposition to kneeling are available in the records of a case heard by the Consistory Court in 1607. The accused persons were Richard Fryer, Junior, of Witton, Cheshire, and John Broody of Lostock Gralam in the same county. Both—

14 Chester. 1622 vis. EDV 1/24, f. 126v.
15 York. 1633 vis. RVIA 23, ff. 561–61v.
16 Chester. 1605 vis. EDV 1/14, f. 71v.
17 Chester. 1622 vis. EDV 1/24, f. 126v; Chester. 1625 vis. EDV 1/26, f. 98v; York. 1633 vis. RVIA 23, f. 601.
18 Chester. 1614 vis. EDV 1/19, f. 163. Cases; Chester 1622 vis. EDV 1/24, f. 126v.
19 Chester. 1625 vis. EDV 1/26, f. 129v; Chester. 1628 vis. EDV 1/29, f. 28v.
20 Chester. 1619 vis. EDV 1/22, f. 48v; Chester. 1622 vis. EDV 1/24, f. 43; York. 1633 vis. RVIA 23, f. 399.

so the records say—had previously been presented for their failure to kneel at the communion, but they had obstinately continued to be nonconformists in this respect. Broody was charged with having come:

> into the church or chapel of Witton . . . with an intent to have received the holy communion, but being not permitted to receive the same sitting, as formerly you have done, you, the said John Broody, did utterly refuse to receive the sacrament kneeling and did contemptuously and irreverently depart from the said holy communion, to the great danger of your own soul and most wicked example of others.

One of the articles against Fryer was that he:

> did in most irreverent manner receive the blessed sacrament of the Lord's Supper sitting and did not kneel down to receive the same, contrary to the form prescribed.

Admonition followed, but again with little effect.

> Not withstanding the said admonition and injunctions [we learn in another document connected with the case] and since the same you do not only refrain yourself from receiving the said holy communion kneeling but do dissuade others as much as in you lies to abstain and refrain themselves from receiving thereof, and do continue your said perverse and lewd opinions.[21]

The case is interesting not only as an illustration of the purposeful nature of failing to kneel but also for the light it throws upon the competence of laymen to be proselytisers in their own right. It emphasises once again that lay puritans had definite views on matters of this kind, views which could develop without the assistance or prompting of the clergy. But the case is significant in date as well as in substance, for it represents the first recorded expression of puritanism—either lay or clerical—in this chapelry.

Perhaps the most explicit local illustration, however, of this determination amongst puritans to worship in the way they felt was right comes from Acton parish, Cheshire, in the 1625 visitation. The wheelwright, Thomas Constable, and his wife were charged on this occasion with not receiving the communion. Constable was ordered to rectify the omission, but in making this injunction the court had not reckoned on the tenacity of the man with whom it was dealing. ' "I will never kneel at the communion while I live," Constable

21 Chester. Consistory Court papers. EDC 5, 1607. Miscellaneous

proclaimed, "and if I be torn in pieces with horses." This he spoke publicly in court.'[22]

Constable meant what he said. Sixteen years later this resolute nonconformist was still defying the authorities. By this time he had removed to Winwick, Lancashire, and it was the churchwardens from that parish who deposed in 1641 that they had heard Constable:

> utter and give out speeches . . . that he did not value or care for any presentment that could be made against him by any of the churchwardens or sworn men, for that for space of twenty years past he had stood in the chancellor's teeth in defiance of his authority, and for all the bishops [he went on] they are as they have proved themselves—the very scum of our country.[23]

While still on the subject of the receiving of the communion, the case of Robert Dorning of Winwick parish should be cited. Dorning's method of communicating was sufficiently individualistic and extreme to attract special notice. He was charged in the 1620's 'for receiving the cup sitting and refused the bread, and took the cup out of another man's hand and not at the minister's'.[24] This was not the only occasion, as will be shown, on which the Reformation attack on the professionalism of the clergy was carried to an extreme conclusion.

Within the context of lay puritanism some discussion of the ceremony of baptism is essential, for this undoubtedly afforded to godly laymen the opportunity—if they chose to take it—of expressing their opposition to the established rite. Above all, it was the use of the sign of the cross in baptism—a hated relic of Popery—which often aroused the animosity of puritan parents.

In 1605, for example, one Samuel Lyon of Prescot was presented in the visitation for having 'caused his children to be christened in another parish because the minister offered to baptise them with the sign of the cross',[25] while at Haslingden, Lancashire, resistance to the ceremony was openly expressed, one Alice Cundcliffe being charged that she 'would not suffer the minister to sign a child in

22 Chester. 1625 vis. EDV 1/26, f. 40v.
23 Preston. Quarter sessions records. QSB 1/246/30. 1641.
24 Chester. EDV 1/23, f. 157v. Cases. 7 January 1623/4.
25 Chester. 1605 vis. EDV 1/14, f. 120v. In seventeenth-century Kent the puritans of Brenchley in the Weald were prepared to walk seven miles to East Peckham to have their children baptised in the manner they preferred. (A. M. Everitt, *The Community of Kent and the Great Rebellion*, Leicester, 1966, 225.)

baptism but pulled off the minister's hand'.[26] A similar demonstration occurred at Oliver Heywood's baptism. He describes how:

> the day of my baptism, Mistress Andrew of Little Lever being the person that held me when I was baptised, when Mr Gregg, the vicar there, had said those words (I baptise you in the name of the Father, Son and Holy Ghost) she stepped back off from the steps and so prevented my being signed with the sign of the cross. She did it purposely to prevent it, which I am glad of, since I heard it related that I was not signed with that addition, which I look on as not grounded on the word of God, and it may be was a providential presage of my proving a n.c. minister.[27]

At Stoke in Wirral deanery one Ralph Hickock, yeoman, was presented in the 1625 visitation 'for interrupting the minister at the baptising of his child in bidding the minister not to use the sign of the cross and calling him doting fool and unmannerly fellow'.[28]

In addition to these expressions of puritanism there is also some evidence to suggest that amongst puritans, as later amongst the Quakers, the practice of keeping the hat on in church can be viewed as an expression of dissent. For men to act in this way was directly opposed to the eighteenth canon of 1604, which required that 'no man shall cover his head in the church or chapel in the time of divine service except he have some infirmity'.[29] To remove the hat in church was to show respect for the place and occasion, but it could be interpreted by puritans as an exaggerated display of reverence for the church building. This was certainly the motive behind the Quakers' action but, as will be shown, the practice did not originate with them.[30]

At Middleton, near Manchester, in 1617 William Widowson and John Allance were charged with 'sitting in the church with their hats on and going from their own parish church to others', their puritanism being further indicated by the charge that they had received the communion sitting at Bolton parish church;[31] while at Bolton in 1617 one Daniel Barnet was charged with 'not receiving

26 Chester. 1619 vis. EDV 1/22, f. 106.
27 Diaries, etc, of the Rev. Oliver Heywood, III, 281.
28 Chester. 1625 vis. EDV 1/26, f. 35v.
29 E. Cardwell, Synodalia, Oxford, 1842, I, 255.
30 Some discussion of the Quakers' attitude to the question is found in H. N. Brailsford, The Levellers and the English Revolution, 1961, 42–46.
31 Chester. 1614 vis. EDV 1/19, f. 199v.

the holy and blessed communion kneeling and wearing his hat in time of divine service'.[32]

One of the charges made against Ralph Kirk, the Manchester curate, in 1604 had been that he 'did minister the sacrament to one sitting with his hat upon his head'.[33] Also at Manchester, in the 1633 visitation, no fewer than sixteen members of the congregation were charged with 'sitting in the church with their hats on their heads in the time of divine service'.[34] Although the charge is less explicit than the previous examples, it would seem probable that this too was a demonstration of puritan opposition. Such a view is strengthened by the fact that three of this group were also presented for their failure to kneel at the receiving of the communion.

The significance to be attached to the practice of remaining covered in church is made clearer when—as in nearly all those instances so far cited—the same individuals were presented on other, distinctly puritan, charges. However, where a presentment of this kind is not supported by any corroborative evidence of puritanism it would be unwise to make too much of the keeping on of hats in church. Some of these cases, clearly, were quite unconnected with puritanism. In 1619, for example, one John Rhodes of Blackburn was charged as 'a common and ordinary sleeper in the church at prayer and sermon and for having his hat on his head unreverently in time of service and sermon'.[35]

Caution, then, is needed in interpreting this type of case; it does not automatically follow that a layman presented for keeping his hat on in church was a puritan. A variety of motives could inspire this action. The main significance of some of these cases is probably only that they illustrate the extreme informality and unsophisticated manner in which worship was conducted.[36] So although this type of evidence can provide a further indication of puritanism, it cannot in itself be taken as a sure sign that a given individual was a puritan.

32 *Ibid.*, f. 202v. Cases.
33 Chester Consistory Court papers. EDC 5, 1604. Miscellaneous.
34 York. 1633 vis. RVIA 23, ff. 610–610v. Three of the sixteen later conformed.
35 Chester. 1619 vis. EDV 1/21, f. 74. Cases.
36 It is possible that men disliked removing their hats for fear of having them soiled or crumpled in the football-crowd atmosphere of seventeenth-century churches. Such was certainly the case in the nineteenth century, when the possibility of 'hat-spoiling' was reckoned as a cause of men's non-attendance at church and of the preponderance of women in congregations. (K. S. Inglis, *Churches and the Working Classes in Victorian England*, 1963, 333.)

In point of fact, few aspects of puritanism are uncomplicated and straightforward. It was even possible—especially in the 1630's, when a stiffer attitude was being shown by the authorities—for a layman to reconcile his puritanism with conformity to the ceremonies. This can best be illustrated, perhaps, by reference to the changing outlook of a single individual, and fortunately a spiritual biography exists which permits us to do this.

We are told by John Ley in his life of Mistress Ratcliffe of Chester[37] that in the early days after her 'conversion':

> while she was thus straitened by her ignorance of the lawful use of the gesture enjoined by the Church, and of the latitude of her liberty allowed by Christ, she took their example for a rule who thought they could not be good and sound Protestants unless they showed themselves zealous detestants of whatsoever had been abused by Popish superstitions.

Her attitude began to change, however, 'considering that [as in her present condition] she was liable to complaint upon oath and upon complaint to censure of suspension from the sacrament'. Rather, therefore, than invite this sentence she determined to examine afresh her position as regards the ceremonies.

> She betook herself [Ley tells us], with a discreet and impartial indifference, to search into the lawfulness of that gesture, and by reading of some of the chief books of controversy concerning it and conference with those divines and other good christians whose knowledge might inform her and their godly conversation confirm her in the truth, she received good resolution that she might safely receive the sacrament upon her knees, and so she did, and so continued without change of mind or scruple of conscience or alteration of practice as long as she lived in this city.

Although prompted by necessity in the first instance, this was clearly a reasoned change in attitude on the part of Mistress Ratcliffe:

> She did not rashly yield to conformity at first [Ley continues] but as I have said was very studious and deliberate to make such a resolution of her practice as that she might persist in it without perplexity or change.[38]

It was not, then, mere expediency which modified her outlook on this question, and there is no evidence that she later repented.

37 Jane Ratcliffe was a niece of Edward Brerewood, the puritan professor at Gresham College, and was married to a leading brewer in Chester.
38 Ley, A Patterne of Pietie . . .' 1640, 145–9.

These details are of the greatest interest on several counts. They demonstrate the flexibility and moderation which so often characterise puritanism, as opposed to sectarianism.[39] They emphasise also how impossible it is to use the numbers of those laymen presented for nonconformity as an accurate indication of the strength of puritanism. Conforming puritans such as Mistress Ratcliffe could have a faith which was unshakeable, yet they would not find their way into the ecclesiastical records. From the information given about the discussions which preceded Mistress Ratcliffe's decision to accept the gesture of kneeling, it seems possible that this conformity may have become fairly general amongst the puritan element in Chester. If this were indeed the case, then it would do much to explain the absence of visitation presentments against the puritans of Chester and the consequent paucity of information concerning them.

The conforming puritan is an elusive figure unless—as in Mistress Ratcliffe's case—he can be studied from non-official sources. But, as a rule, all the historian can do is to observe the expression of nonconforming puritanism in the church records. In so doing, of course, the danger is that of anachronistically equating pre-1642 puritanism with later Nonconformity. The two are closely connected, but there are differences between them as well as similarities. The caution should always be borne in mind that there were conforming as well as non-conforming puritans.

2 *The enthusiasm for preaching*

To the puritan layman the sermon was the main element in the Church service; without it, the religious exercise almost lost its purpose. For example, when Humphrey Booth, a puritan clothier, of Manchester, founded and endowed Salford chapel in the 1630's he was careful to make adequate provision 'for the maintenance of a preaching minister there, without which the building of a chapel would little profit'.[40]

An accusation sometimes made against godly laymen was that they did not attend the whole service but arrived at church only in time to hear the sermon. The charge was made, for example,

---

39 Interesting also is the obvious approval of Mistress Ratcliffe's conformity shown by the clergyman–author.

40 Preston. Probate records. The will was proved in 1635. Richard Yawling, a puritan of Woodham Mortimer, Essex, declared in 1584 that a Church service was 'no service unless there be a sermon'. (Quoted in Collinson, 'The godly', *Past and Present Conference Papers*, 11.)

against the wheelwright Thomas Constable in Winwick parish in 1641. Despite the fact that he had been excommunicated for his nonconformity and was therefore banned from attending church, Constable, it was said, 'at time of sermon only does come and sit down in the church among the congregation'.[41]

Given this puritan view of the central importance of preaching, it is not surprising that godly laymen, if deprived of the Word in their own parishes, should have disregarded their statutory obligation to attend their own church and instead looked elsewhere for spiritual refreshment. 'Gadding to sermons' became, in fact, a common feature in the religious life of puritan laymen. George Walker, a Lancashire-born London preacher, described in vivid language how the people of his native county:

> are ready and willing to run many miles to hear sermons when they have them not at home, and lay aside all care of profit, leaving their labour and work on weekdays to frequent public meetings for prophecy and expounding of God's word, and hardly can a preacher travel through their towns and lodge there on any day in the week but they will by importunity obtain a public sermon from him and in great troups suddenly and upon short warning assembled they will gladly and cheerfully hear him with all reverence and attention.[42]

The accuracy of Walker's observation is confirmed by cases in the ecclesiastical records. At Wilmslow, Cheshire, for example, in 1619 one Hugh Worthington was charged 'for leaving his own parish church and going to others', his explanation being that 'sometimes in the afternoon upon the Sabbath day he goes to Ringey chapel to hear a sermon'.[43] A similar case was noted at Brigmel, in Richmond deanery, in the same year. On this occasion a group of four of the congregation, William Hamby, Bartle and George Poulson and Anne Pareman, were presented by the wardens on the charge that 'in the absence of their vicar, notwithstanding that there were in their own parish church both divine service and sermon yet left they [their] own church and prayer and followed another preacher'.[44]

The desertion of the parish church by this group seems to have happened regularly, for they were all presented on exactly the same

41 Preston. Quarter sessions. QSB 1/246/30.
42 Walker, *An Exhortation* . . ., 18.
43 Chester. 1619 vis. EDV 1/22, f. 64.
44 Leeds. Archdeaconry of Richmond records. Churchwardens' presentments. RD CB/8/6/34.

charge in 1621.[45] Again, in the episcopal visitation of 1623 two of their number—Hamby and George Poulson—were once more charged that they 'leave their own church and follow other ministers'.[46]

Similar presentments involving the practice of 'gadding to sermons' were made in the visitation of 1622. At Over Peover, Cheshire, for example, a group of seven of the congregation were said to 'leave their own church and follow other ministers and did not communicate at their own parish church at Easter last'.[47] At Holt, in Chester deanery, two groups—one of them a family—were similarly charged in this year.[48]

Puritanism was well established in the parish of Holt by the 1620's. Further light is thrown on the situation there in the records of a case heard by the Consistory Court in the following decade. This concerned Alexander Powell, who was charged in 1638 with absenting himself 'either in the aforenoon or afternoon or both from your own chapel[49] and parish church and have gone to other churches to hear sermons and to receive the communion sitting'. Moreover, the ministers at whose heels he followed were:

> suspended for their excess and nonconformity and did not wear the surplice nor read public prayers according to the Book of Common Prayer at such time as you so heard them pray, preach or expound. And therefore you the rather did desire to follow . . . them.[50]

The logical—though by no means invariable—culmination of 'gadding to sermons' was open separatism. This seems to have been happening at Lowe chapel in Lancashire, for in 1618 eight laymen were charged that they 'will not come to their parish church to hear divine service and are termed puritans',[51] while at Burton-in-Kendal in 1633 Elizabeth Thomson, Henrietta Lucas and William Chambers were presented 'for separating themselves from the congregation and running after a schismatical minister at Barwick called Richard Fletcher'.[52]

45 Leeds. Archdeacon's act book. RD/A6, f. 62.
46 Chester. 1623 vis. EDV 1/25, f. 59v. Poulson was a tailor by trade.
47 Chester. 1622 vis. EDV 1/24, f. 33v.
48 *Ibid.*, f. 12.
49 Powell was from Iscroyd chapelry within the parish of Holt.
50 Chester. Consistory Court papers. EDC 5, 1638. Miscellaneous.
51 Chester. 1614 vis. EDV 1/19, f. 212, Cases. 25 September 1618. Those charged were Richard Sharrock, Seth Longton, George Eastham, Thomas Sharrock, John Cowpe, James Sharrock and Edmund Euxton.
52 York. 1633 vis. RVIA 23, f. 111v.

3 *Conventicles and household devotions*

Although complete and deliberate separatism seems to have been uncommon in this period among the puritans of the diocese of Chester, nonetheless godly laymen were capable of organising themselves if or when the need arose. In practice it must have arisen frequently, for the typical form of puritan organisation seems to have been that of the cell within the larger unit of the parish or, indeed, of the chapelry—itself an ecclesiastical subdivision. The godly were always a minority, though a growing one in the decades before the Civil War. Given this numerical disadvantage, a closely knit organisation of puritan sympathisers was desirable if their own identity and also the conviction and continuity of their devotional life was to be maintained. Conventicles, then, provide one of the surest indications of the existence of organised lay puritanism.

No sixteenth-century examples of these meetings of the godly have been found in the diocese of Chester, although it is known that conventicles were being held elsewhere in the country at this time.[53] To some extent this absence of information about sixteenth-century puritanism in the diocese of Chester may be merely a reflection of the leniency of the bishops. But even if allowance is made for this, it would still suggest that puritanism developed later in the North than in the South. Clearly, the regional variations in the chronology of puritanism were significant and it is unwise to speak of a single monolithic and national puritan movement.

In the diocese of Chester the earliest case which has come to light concerning conventicles was in 1605. At Middlewich, Cheshire, a vocal puritan element was developing by the beginning of the seventeenth century and it was here that Robert Watts was charged on this occasion 'for keeping a private fast upon Xmas day last in the house of Waring Croxton'.[54] The latter and his wife were presented in this connection, as were eleven others. Those charged

---

53 In Essex, for example, conventicles are known to have been taking place as early as the 1570's. At Strethall, for instance, in 1574, regular devotional meetings were being held. At Aythorp Roding ten years later puritans resorted to the house of one Davies, where the assembled company then 'conferred together of such profitable lessons as they had learned that day at a public catechising'. Foxe's *Book of Martyrs* was read in the course of the proceedings. (Collinson, *Puritan Movement*, 379.)

54 Chester. 1605 vis. EDV 1/14, f. 72. There was a preacher by the name of Watts in the parish at this time but it is not clear whether he can be identified with the Robert Watts of the presentment.

were Thomas Yates, Senior, John Beckett, Charles Dresser, James Wright, Katherine, wife of Francis Hollis, Isabella Swinton, Elizabeth Trevett, Edmund Harrison and his wife, Thomas Street and William Cooke, the schoolmaster.[55] In Wigan in the same year eleven of the congregation were presented for holding conventicles in the house of one John Hamson, but they were subsequently dismissed 'because the judge finds no fault in them'.[56]

But similar charges made in 1607 against a small ultra-puritan group within the congregation at Oldham were not dismissed; their case was in fact heard in the Consistory Court. The document listing the articles against them, unfortunately—like many of the series— is severely damaged. Enough remains, however, to indicate the nature of the case against them.

The case involved Thomas Milnes and John Butterworth of Oldham and Abraham Dawson of Rochdale, who were charged with having 'assembled and met in divers houses' for religious purposes. These meetings, the charge went on, were 'held or taken [to be] tending to the impeaching and depraving of the doctrine of the Church of England and of the Book of Common Prayer'. The members of the group were additionally charged with refusing to kneel at the communion. Indeed, they had clearly moved in the direction of separatism, for they were also presented for having:

> refused to come unto your parish church of Oldham aforesaid and Rochdale on Sundays and other festival days to hear divine service and to join with the rest of the congregation there assembled in prayers prescribed and appointed by the said Book of Common Prayer and that you do not use the said prayers but do neglect and refuse the same, contrary to the said canons.[57]

Thomas Hunt was the curate at Oldham at this juncture but, though a puritan, his views were clearly too moderate for at least some members of his congregation.

The holding of conventicles at Alderley in Macclesfield deanery was noted by the Church authorities in 1613. In that year one Edward Oldham was charged 'for having a private meeting at his house of men and women but not known to what end'. Oldham's

55 Many of these were also presented for their failure to kneel at the communion.
56 Chester. 1605 vis. EDV 1/14, f. 135.
57 Chester. Consistory Court papers. EDC 5, 1607. Miscellaneous.

deposition made clear that these meetings were indeed conventicles, but he refused to give the names of those who had been present.[58]

In the 1619 visitation conventicles were discovered at Acton, Cheshire,[59] and at Deane in Lancashire. At Deane, William Pendlebury, Adam Mollineux and John Tildesley were charged—among other things—'for having private meetings in their houses'. Pendlebury, when questioned, did not hesitate to admit the charge and saw no reason why these meetings should be discontinued. Five others from Deane—James and Adam Pendlebury, Ralph Chaddock and his son William, and Lawrence Mollineux—were separately charged on this occasion 'for going to conventicles'.[60]

Further instances of the holding of conventicles were discovered in the Archbishop of York's metropolitan visitation of 1630. At Great Budworth, for example, John Jackson and John Minshall were presented 'for having private meetings of ministers and other people at their houses tending to conventicles',[61] while at Liverpool in the same year one James Chambers was charged 'for repeating sermons in his house and entertaining people to hear him, the same being held to be conventicles'.[62] In 1633 at Winwick parish John Robleson was charged on the same count, and at Burton-in-Kendal Edward Preston, an unlicensed schoolmaster, was 'suspected to draw together and make unlawful assemblies and conventicles'.[63]

An interesting case involving conventicles was heard by the Consistory Court in 1639. It concerned Robert Shenton of Coppenhall, Cheshire, and shows that meetings of this kind were sometimes held in places other than private houses. The charge against Shenton was that he had attended conventicles held in the parish church of Coppenhall:

with ten other persons of several families, the doors of the said church being shut, and there stayed from service and sermon in the forenoon until service and sermon in the afternoon or most part thereof, and did there pray together and sing together and used there exercises of religion

---

58 Chester. 1611 vis. EDV 1/17, f. 200v. Cases. 4 May 1613.
59 Chester. 1619 vis. EDV 1/22, f. 31v.
60 Chester. 1619 vis. EDV 1/21, f. 67.
61 York. 1630 vis. RVIA 22, f. 150. Jackson, a yeoman, died in 1632 and nothing further is known of his nonconformity. Minshall, also a yeoman, was presented in the 1633 visitation for his failure to kneel at the communion. (York. 1633 vis. RVIA 23, f. 388.) He died in 1639.
62 York. 1630 vis. RVIA 22, f. 102v. Nothing further is known of Chambers, unless he was the felt-maker of this name whose will was proved in 1634.
63 York. 1633 vis. RVIA 23, f. 321v.

after a private manner, contrary to the canons of the Church of England.[64]

A similar situation existed at Tarvin, Cheshire, earlier in the century, since it was the practice of John Bruen and his family to remain in church for the interval between the two Sunday services.[65]

But conventicles usually, if not invariably, took place in the home. For example, the holding of meetings of this type was a normal practice in early seventeenth-century Bolton. Oliver Heywood, the preacher, described how his father:

> associated himself with God's people, promoted days of fasting and of prayer, conference and other christian exercises. In my childhood I can remember many days of that nature and the apparitor searching them out and one appointed in the entry to deafen the noise of such as were praying in the parlour.[66]
>
> Many days of prayer [Heywood went on] have I known my father keep among God's people; I remember a whole night wherein he, Dr Bradshaw, Adam Fearnshaw, Thomas Crompton and several more excellent men did all pray all night in a parlour at Ralph Whitall's, as I remember, upon occasion of King Charles the First demanding the five Members of the House of Commons. Such a night of prayers, tears and groans I was never present at in all my life.[67]

In Blackburn parish—particularly in Darwen chapelry—conventicles were a common feature of the organised religious life of the godly element in the congregation. Official attention was given to their existence in 1636 when no fewer than twenty-nine were charged with attending these clandestine meetings.[68] The charges varied slightly against individuals in this large group. Some were presented 'for using and frequenting conventicles' or being 'present at several private meetings and conventicles contrary to the laws'. But against three of the accused—John Harward, William Berry and William Ellison—the charges were more detailed. It was alleged that they:

> did meet together in private houses to hear preachings or repetition of sermons and also to pray, sing psalms and perform other duties of

64 Chester. Consistory Court papers. EDC 5, 1639. Miscellaneous.
65 Hinde, *Life of John Bruen*, 211.
66 Heywood, *Autobiography, Diaries,* etc, 1, 77.
67 Hunter, *Life of Oliver Heywood*, 1842, 33.
68 Chester. Court book. EDC 1/52. 2 September and 3 November 1636. Consistory Court papers. EDC 5, 1636. Miscellaneous.

religion and divine worship and the same offices and religious duties you and every of you did perform and were present at with the assistance of a minister in holy orders in that behalf procured.

The final section of the charge is most significant of all. In circumstances such as these, where lay initiative and ascendancy were established facts, the role of the clergymen was limited in the extreme. He could be merely the assistant.

As many of these cases suggest, the holding of conventicles was often a continuation of the puritan emphasis on household religion; the one could naturally develop out of the other. This was made clear at Alderley in 1613, for example, when Edward Oldham was charged with holding conventicles. He explained that 'he had a meeting in his house and that half a dozen of his friends were there besides his family and they sang psalms, read chapters and praised God in his house in the day time'.[69] Normal family devotional meetings became conventicles merely through the presence of a few neighbours. Thomas Benson, a brewer, of Chester, when questioned in the Consistory Court in 1611 about the religious life of the household of his master John Bruen, declared that:

he has prayers with his family morning and evening and if a stranger chanced to lodge at his house all night they have been present at evening prayer or other prayers and if any other of this respondent's acquaintance came by chance at prayer time they would sometimes stay with this respondent.[70]

Thomas Paget, the Lancashire divine, in his *Demonstration of Family Duties* (1643), justified the enlargement of the family religious exercise into a conventicle:

It is not only lawful and expedient [he wrote] but also useful and necessary that the governor of a family sometimes, as extraordinary occasions require and opportunities serve thereunto, do call for and crave the company and assistance of some godly brethren and christian neighbours, for the more solemn performance of religious duties together.[71]

The household was in fact the basis of puritan organisation, and its importance was repeatedly stressed in sermons and devotional

69 Chester. 1611 vis. EDV 1/17, f. 200v. Cases.
70 Chester. Consistory Court papers. EDC 5, 1611. Miscellaneous. This was Bruen's house in Chester.
71 Paget, *op. cit.*, 82.

literature.[72] William Hinde, for example, considered that 'family exercises were the very goads and spurs unto godliness, the life and sinews of grace and religion, the bonds and cords of love, drawing or leading to perfection'.[73] John Angier, the puritan pastor of Denton, Lancashire, was later to declare that 'the more we worship God in secret, the fitter shall we be for family worship, and the more we worship God in our families, the fitter shall we be for public worship'.[74] Nicholas Byfield, preacher in Chester in the early seventeenth century, was equally convinced of the value of family-based religion and emphasised its instructional use:

> Parents [he argued] should carefully set up the worship of God in the family that from their cradles [children] may see the practice of piety ... The family [Byfield went on] is the seminary both of Church and commonwealth ... [75]

The logical culmination of this emphasis on family religion was, of course, Independency, and the clergy by their constant advocacy of household devotions were unconsciously, but in a very real way nonetheless, tending to undermine their own position.[76] 'Family prayers and family catechising,' Dr Hill has observed, 'offered an alternative to public worship, especially when the worship itself left so much to be desired as that of the Laudian Church.'[77]

The importance attached to family religion by the puritan laity can be well illustrated by Hinde's biography of John Bruen, of Stapleford, Cheshire.

> It was his ordinary course [wrote Hinde of Bruen] to rise very early in the morning before the rest of his family, betwixt three and four of the

---

72 The point is made and illustrated at length, for example, in the chapter on 'The spiritualization of the household' in C. Hill, *Society and Puritanism*. The subject is also explored in L. L. Schücking, *The Puritan Family: a Study from the Literary Sources*, English trans. 1969.

73 Hinde, *Life of John Bruen*, 66.

74 Angier, *Helpe to Better Hearts for Better Times* . . ., 1641, 445.

75 Byfield, *Commentary upon the Three First Chapters of the First Epistle Generall of St. Peter*, 1637, 142. 'Good members of a family are like to make good members of Church and commonwealth,' declared William Gouge in his influential treatise on *Domesticall Duties*, 1622, epistle dedicatory.

76 In New England, as E. S. Morgan has argued, the culmination of the stress on family religion was that puritanism retreated to the household so completely that all missionary purpose was stifled. Puritanism became totally introspective and in so doing lost its grip upon society and government. (E. S. Morgan, *The Puritan Family*, Boston, Mass., 1944.)

77 Hill, *Society and Puritanism*, 454.

clock in summer and at or before five in the winter, so that by his vigilancy and industry he gained the liberty and opportunity most commonly of an hour or two before he rung the bell to awaken the rest of the family.

After his own personal preparation the household devotions could begin. It was Bruen's practice in these exercises to open with a short set prayer. Then psalms were sung, a chapter of the Bible was read and prayers were offered.

Bruen's enthusiasm for household devotions went with him to the home of his second wife's family, where:

> my mother-in-law . . . then giving me table for a year there and then we set up the exercise of religion morning and evening. In which time [Bruen went on] I trust through God's grace my mother-in-law there got true saving grace and my sister-in-law, now Mistress Hinde, and another half-sister of hers and their brothers Master William and Master Thomas Foxe, and a servant or two, and some neighbours which joined with us in the evening.[78]

Household devotions, as this last extract suggests, could involve not only the immediate family circle but also the servants.[79] Bruen, as we know from Hinde's biography, took good care that his servants shared in the religious life of his home. They had all in any case been hand-picked by their master; only the godly might have a place in his household. 'In a short time,' Hinde tells us, 'he was so well provided and furnished with honest and faithful, godly and gracious servants, both men and women, that he had now . . . a Church in his house.'[80] Hinde was well aware of what he was saying and recognised the need to justify the nature of the role which Bruen had assumed. 'Some may mistake him and me in this business,' he wrote, 'as imagining that by his private expounding of the scriptures he did usurp too much and trench too near upon the office of the ministry.' Such was not the case, Hinde argued. Bruen's care for family religion was not 'raised or grounded upon his own private conceit or fancy . . . I would to God,' Hinde went on, 'that all masters of families were such ministers in their families . . .'[81]

'A Church in his house', 'Ministers in their families' . . . Such

78 Hinde, *op. cit.*, 67, 70–71, 112.
79 The place of servants in seventeenth-century households is discussed in P. Laslett, *The World We Have Lost*, 1965.
80 Hinde, *op. cit.*, 55.
81 *Ibid.*, 76–7.

significant phrases indicate the extent to which the stress on family-based religion could be carried. But the practice of household devotions was, to state the obvious, dependent upon a concept of a unified family which was not general throughout society. For the poor—who probably numbered over a third of the population—family life was hardly permitted to exist in view of the great social and economic disabilities to which they were subject. For example, the indulgent attitude of the upper and middle classes towards children and the privileges which they allowed them were luxuries which the poorest of families could not afford.[82]

Household religious devotions, then, though they themselves did much to foster family unity, demanded a degree of existing solidarity as the prerequisite of their establishment. The point is implied in many of the works of puritan divines. Thomas Paget, for example, urged forward his scheme of household devotions:

> because the members of the same family do usually and for the most part share and partake more or less both in the welfare and in the miseries of one another mutually. And therefore they ought to use the means that God has sanctified and ordained for the mutual good and benefit of one another.

Like other writers on this subject, he argued that religious exercises should take place morning and evening:

> because God has ordered the condition of families for the most part in such sort that there is convenient opportunity for the members of them to be present together morning and evening every day, albeit in other parts of the day their affairs may call them to be abroad and severed one from another.[83]

Conditions such as these, however, as has already been said, were by no means general in sixteenth- and seventeenth-century England. But it was not only class distinctions which affected the develop-

82 In her review article on 'The family' (*Past and Present*, 27, 1964) Dr Thirsk has commented on class distinctions in the sizes of households, in educational opportunities and in available leisure.

83 Paget, *op. cit.*, 56–9. The architectural expression of this movement towards greater family unity and domestic privacy has been discussed in W. G. Hoskins, 'The rebuilding of rural England, 1570–1640', in *Provincial England*, 1963.
   Considerable research has been done in recent years, particularly in France, on the history of the family. See, for example, the study by P. Ariès, *Centuries of Childhood*, 1962, and most recent of all A. Macfarlane's book on *The Family Life of Ralph Josselin, a Seventeenth Century Clergyman*, Cambridge, 1970.

ment of family unity. Nor was family unity only possible in urban 'middle-class' households. For there were really two kinds of family unity. In the towns it was largely self-imposed. In the countryside, however, the general economic background against which the family existed could help induce domestic cohesion. Family unity, it has been argued, tended to be strongest in weakly manorialised pasture-farming regions where partible inheritance was practised and where the typical economic unit was the farmhouse rather than the village, and where in consequence the family was more closely integrated and inward-looking. Conversely, it meant little in highly manorial-ised areas, where primogeniture was followed and where decisions about farming methods and practice were the responsibility of the village rather than of the family.[84] Here, then, is a further argument to strengthen the theory advanced by Dr Thirsk in the *Agrarian History* that it was in pastoral and woodland areas that puritanism found its most conducive background. For, as this present regional study shows, puritanism—the organisation of which was based on the godly household—was strongest in the eastern, pastoral areas of Lancashire and Cheshire. All three of these elements—the pastoral background, family solidarity and puritanism—were interconnected.

Family groups often occur in the presentments of lay puritans made in the visitations. For example, two generations of the Yates family were charged as nonconformists at Middlewich, Cheshire, in 1605; Thomas Yates was presented, as were his son and his wife.[85] Amongst those puritans from Blackburn parish who appeared before the Consistory Court in the 1630's, two families seem to predominate —the Yates and the Astleys. In all, nine individuals with the sur-name Yate were presented. There were Ellen Yate, widow, and William, George, Robert and John Yate and their wives. In addi-tion, seven others bearing the name Astley were charged. Ralph Astley and his three sons were among those who attended conven-ticles, as did Margaret, Mary and Elizabeth Astley.[86] Family ties, too, seem to have connected those puritans who were presented at Deane in the 1619 visitation. William, James and Adam Pendlebury were presented in that year, and also Adam and Lawrence Mollineux and Ralph Chaddock and his son William.[87]

84 Thirsk, 'The family', *Past and Present*, 27, 1964, 118.
85 Chester. 1605 vis. EDV 1/14, ff. 72–72v.
86 Chester. Consistory Court book. EDC 1/52. 3 November 1636.
87 Chester. 1619 vis. EDV 1/21, f. 67. This type of evidence, admittedly, must be put forward with caution. The precise relationship between many of

Given the fact that puritanism drew its strength from its family organisation and that the idea of the godly household was constantly extolled by the preachers, it seems hardly surprising that there was considerable intermarriage among puritans. 'Marry in the Lord' was the advice of the seventeenth-century Lancashire divine Isaac Ambrose, and in this he was by no means original or unique.[88] Domestic and religious harmony was recognised as the basis of household devotional life. Amongst the godly, therefore, intermarriage was held to be desirable, and writers stressed that godly parents should choose a suitable partner for their children.

How general intermarriage was amongst puritans it is impossible to say, but the existence of the practice can be amply illustrated by examples. John Bruen, for example, took for his second wife—his first had been chosen for him by his father—Anne Foxe, a member of an undoubtedly puritan family. One of her sisters married William Hinde, the preacher at Bunbury. A brother John Foxe made an equally puritan match. Both he and his wife Judith were charged at Manchester in 1608 with not receiving the communion kneeling.[89] Later, in 1622, Judith Foxe—a widow now, her husband having died in that year—was again presented on the same charge.[90] When she herself died in the following year she made a will which was unmistakably puritan in content—a will, also, in which her clergyman brother-in-law William Hinde was twice mentioned.

Bruen's wife died after a weary life of child-bearing, and so her husband married for a third time. His new wife, Margaret, was also a puritan—an inclination which survived her husband's death. Bruen died in 1625; in 1630 Margaret Bruen, widow, was charged at Nantwich with failing to kneel at the communion.[91]

Bruen's sister, Katherine, was—as will be shown in a later chapter —a devout puritan, and it was surely no accident that she married William Brettergh, a Lancashire gentleman, 'one that likewise

these individuals has not been established, but in small communities such as these it is not unreasonable to assume that identity of surname implies a family connection. Several similar cases have been found in Manchester parish, but here, clearly, the possibility of quite unconnected families sharing the same name is much greater.

88 Ambrose, *Works*, 125. The literature relating to this subject is discussed in W. and M. Haller, 'The puritan art of love', *Huntington Library Quarterly*, 5, 1941–42.
89 Chester. 1608 vis. EDV 1/15, f. 134.
90 Chester. 1622/3 vis. EDV 1/24, f. 126v.
91 York. 1630 vis. RVIA 22, f. 177.

embraced religion sincerely and for the same endured many grievances at the hands of Papists'.[92]

Family ties, too, seem to have connected many of the puritans of Bolton. William Gregg, puritan vicar in the town in the 1630's, married Alice, daughter of James Crompton of Brightmet in Bolton. Now the Cromptons were staunch puritans. A Laurence Crompton was charged at Bolton with failing to kneel in 1614, while in 1633 the same charge was made against Joan Crompton and Robert Crompton's wife.[93] Thomas Crompton of Brightmet in his will of 1628 made bequests to the Bolton lecturer, to the preacher at Cockey chapel and to Mr Horrocks, the puritan pastor of Deane.[94] A Thomas Crompton is mentioned by Oliver Heywood as attending the conventicles held at his father's home.[95]

James Crompton's other daughters, like Alice, seem to have made equally puritan matches. Mary married the puritan James Okey. Abigail, another of James Crompton's daughters, became the second wife of Oliver Heywood, the preacher. Sarah Crompton—again a daughter from the same family—married Richard Goodwin, who was later ejected from his vicarage and became the founder of organised Presbyterianism in Bolton.[96]

At Ringley chapel in Prestwich parish, on the other hand, the Seddon family occupied a prominent position amongst the puritan element, and this family once again was linked by marriage to others of similar religious views. Peter Seddon was the son of Raphe Seddon of Prestolee, yeoman, and of Mary, daughter of William Foxe of Rhodes in Middleton parish—that same family into which John Bruen married. Peter Seddon himself married his cousin Ellen Seddon. His sister Dorothy married William Hulton, puritan minister of Ringley chapel from 1635 to 1647, while his brother Thomas married into the equally puritan Walworth family. The Seddons and Walworths were also connected by marriage with the local puritan families of Parr and Wilson.[97]

It was the usual practice for puritan ministers to 'marry in the Lord', but amongst the puritan laity also, as these examples suggest,

92 W. Harrison, *Life of Mistris Katherin Brettergh*, 1612, 5.
93 Chester. 1614 vis. EDV 1/19, f. 199v; York. 1633 vis. RVIA 23, ff. 561–61v.
94 J. P. Earwaker (ed.), *Lancashire and Cheshire Wills and Inventories*, Chet. Soc., new series, 28, Manchester, 1893, 36–8.
95 Hunter, *Life of Oliver Heywood*, 33.
96 J. C. Scholes, *History of Bolton*, Bolton, 1892, 261.
97 J. S. Fletcher (ed.), *The Correspondence of Nathan Walworth and Peter Seddon*, Chet. Soc., old series, 109, Manchester, 1880.

puritanism was often reinforced by the nexus of family relationships. As always, however, this evidence must be used with caution. There is no means of ascertaining how many of the marriages cited above were decided only from the religious angle. The businesslike approach to marriage could be shown by puritans as by others.

This is seen, for example, in the autobiography of Adam Martindale, the seventeenth-century divine who ministered in Lancashire and Cheshire. Martindale tells first of all how his eldest brother had aroused the opposition of his family by rejecting the offer of a well dowered wife in favour of a girl who was much less prosperous but more attractive. And this same attitude was shown by Martindale when his own son, Thomas, was looking for a wife.

> One young woman in London, that had five hundred pounds to her portion [Martindale lamented] he lost merely through a slighting humour. Another at Brainford, that had more than I think fit to speak of [he continued dolefully] was (as an honest gentleman told me) very fond of him; but because she was a little crooked (forsooth) he would not have her.[98]

In the end Thomas married a wife who brought no dowry, and Martindale could only helplessly denounce his reckless son and 'this foolish marriage'.

4 Lay independence; the layman as proselytiser

Godly laymen, trained in household religious exercises and in conventicles, were clearly capable of independent action. Puritanism at congregational level was to a considerable extent the expression of men's desire to control their own affairs and could involve opposition to the ecclesiastical authorities, to patrons and to parish clergy —to all, in fact, who claimed the right to impose upon congregations an unsatisfying religious settlement.

In this connection, it is important to stress that the clergy did not have a captive audience. As has been shown earlier in this chapter, laymen could express their dissatisfaction with a minister by 'gadding to sermons' elsewhere. So, in a very real sense, by this means laymen often chose their minister.

In some circumstances, however, congregations were in a position actually to nominate their pastor. This was especially the case in some of the chapelries which could be effectively controlled by

98 *Life of Adam Martindale*, 212.

congregations—or more probably by the 'better sort' of inhabitants within them—who were therefore in a position to secure the type of preaching they preferred. Darwen chapelry in Lancashire, where conventicles were being held in the 1630's, is a case in point. A deponent giving evidence before the Consistory Court in 1636 declared that Darwen chapel had been used:

> for the reading of divine service when it pleased the inhabitants and other neighbours for their ease to hire a reader, and of late sometimes there has been hired a minister that preached, *who continued at the pleasure of the inhabitants.*[99]

This congregational domination of the chapelry was stressed again in a further deposition made in 1637:

> When any such reader or curate did officiate at the said presented chapel [the deponent declared] his salary or wages was only a voluntary contribution and paid by such as hired or procured him or consented thereunto, who paid no certain sum or sums but sometimes more, sometimes less, according to their wills and pleasures or other particular promise or engagement.[100]

At Toxteth Park, also, the congregation chose its pastor. In 1618 Richard Mather was recalled by the inhabitants from his studies at Oxford to be their minister.[101] Having taken the initiative at this point, the congregation continued to play a positive role in the religious life of the chapelry. As Increase Mather later wrote in his biography of his father:

> The people, having had some taste of his gifts, were the more importunate in their desires that he might continue among them. And because that could not be without episcopal ordination they urged him to accept thereof.[102]

Similarly, John Angier was chosen by the congregation to be minister at Ringley, the whole body signing the petition which requested him to settle with them. Two members of the congregation even travelled to Lincolnshire to transport Angier, his family and their belongings to their new home.[103] And at Bolton in 1644 the congregation was sufficiently organised and sure of itself to

99 My italics.
100 Chester. Consistory Court papers. EDC 5, 1636, 1637. Miscellaneous.
101 Mather had previously been schoolmaster at Toxteth.
102 *Life and Death of Richard Mather*, 7.
103 Heywood, *Life of John Angier*, 8, 55–6.

depute Richard Heywood to go to Holland to negotiate the return of a popular preacher.[104]

Samuel Clarke, the martyrologist, came to minister at Shotwick, Cheshire, as a result of his being directly invited by the congregation there. In his autobiography he relates how:

> Some godly christians, inhabitants of Wirral, a peninsula beyond west Chester, which had been my frequent hearers at Thornton, meeting me at the fair, importuned my coming to Shotwick amongst them, and would receive no repulse till I had granted their desires.

Having settled amongst them, Clarke found that his:

> means of maintenance came by a voluntary contribution out of all those christians' purses; so all of them within six or seven miles' compass repaired to my ministry, both young and old, wet and dry, summer and winter, to their very great pains and labour.[105]

Less formal methods, however, could be used by individuals to introduce puritan ministers into their midst. At Astbury, Cheshire, for example, in 1608 one Thomas Rowe was obviously taking initiative of this kind, since he was charged with 'procuring one Mr Lightfoot to preach, who refuses to subscribe to the canons and is not licensed'.[106] Similarly, in 1618, one Richard Ramsbottom, of Bury, was presented 'for causing a Scotch fellow to go into the pulpit to preach and for ringing the bells'.[107]

Since such emphasis was placed by puritans upon the preaching of the Word, it not unnaturally followed that they were highly critical of those ministers who failed to satisfy them in this respect. In the visitation of 1605, for example, one Thomas Skillicorne was charged at Middlewich with saying that:

> Mr Mallory, parson of Davenham, preached false doctrine and spoke that in his sermon that he dare not speak again; called the vicar 'dumb dog', with many other opprobrious speeches against the vicar, the churchwardens and others, saying that his speeches would be maintained by better men than any he did speak against.[108]

At Tarporley, Cheshire, in 1611 the younger John Witter and his wife were presented on the charge that:

> they say a reading minister has not authority to minister the sacraments, neither do they baptise their children at Tarporley, the said John

---

104 Hunter, *Life of Oliver Heywood*, 37.
105 Clarke, *Lives of Sundry Eminent Persons*, 4.
106 Chester. 1608 vis. EDV 1/15, f. 93v.
107 Chester. 1614 vis. EDV 1/19, f. 207v. Cases. 1618.
108 Chester. 1605 vis. EDV 1/14, f. 73.

affirming that the curate at Tarporley is not able nor sufficient to minister the sacraments;[109]

while in 1619 at Ormskirk John Hayton was charged for 'not receiving the communion at Easter and uttering speeches against the vicar and curate, saying that they were dumb ministers and not fit to administer the sacraments'.[110]

Of considerable interest in this connection is the case of James Martin, vicar of Preston in the 1620's. For Martin claimed that he owed the deprivation of his living to 'the Puritans of Lancashire, who hated me for my conformity'. In a desperate effort to clear his name, Martin listed the chief of his opponents in Preston and proceeded at great length to describe their tactics. For example, Martin claimed that one of his adversaries in the town—Edmund Werden, a wealthy tradesman—was:

> a malapt censurer of my sermons, who, together with Inskip[111] most blasphemously endeavoured to maintain against me that the blessed Virgin was not the mother of God: having occasionally in a Christmas sermon touched on that point but briefly, and yet so fully as none but the puritans were unsatisfied, who repute themselves as good as she— as this Werden's mother did publicly profess herself.

This and other similar attacks made the unpopular Martin's position in Preston untenable, and he appealed to the Council to consider:

> whether this strange combination of the puritans against me—merely for my conformity to his Majesty's canons and opposition to their wild fancies—may not be drawn within the compass of a Star Chamber or High Commission censure, especially considering the tragical events thereof or thereby occasioned . . . Besides, the puritans prophesied I was not like to live long, wherein they said very true, having stript me of my tithes . . . the while I was prisoner.[112]

Many other instances of verbal—and sometimes physical—attacks upon ministers by members of their congregations have been found. Often, however, in the absence of further background information, it is difficult to know precisely what significance to attach to a particular case. Sometimes this criticism may have involved no more

109 Chester. 1611 vis. EDV 1/17, f. 33.
110 Chester. 1619 vis. EDV 1/22, f. 85v.
111 The clergyman, John Inskip, was the puritans' rival to Martin.
112 P.R.O. State Papers Domestic. SP 16/236/42, 1633. It ought perhaps to be pointed out that one of Martin's ministerial colleagues considered that he was 'reasonably qualified if [his] brain were settled'.

49234

than a negative anti-clericalism—and this, after all, was nothing new. But in those cases discussed above it is clear that it was not merely an opposition to the clergy which was expressed but a contempt for their inadequacies and intellectual weakness.

Puritanism in operation was to a considerable extent the expression of the initiative of an educated laity.[113] As Professor Haller, the doyen of historians of the subject, has observed:

> [The puritan laity], becoming more confident of salvation and more practised in the dialectic of faith . . . grew less dependent upon the preaching order, more critical of preachers . . . [They were] far from unread, uninformed, uncritical or inarticulate. Since moreover they had heard many sermons from many pulpits, they were not unprepared to take the measure of any preacher.[114]

Clearly, this is what puritanism had become by the seventeenth century. The Bible—which was at the heart of puritan preaching and whose authority was held to be irrefutable—was just as much studied and learned by laymen as by the clergy. For example, the young Henry Newcome, after his début as a preacher at Congleton, was told by an older and more experienced minister that his sermons contained too much history and were too carefully prepared. He was firmly reminded that 'the people came with Bibles and expected quotations of Scripture'.[115]

Adam Martindale, in the early days of his ministry at Gorton chapel, had encountered:

> an ancient professor that had formerly driven a great trade and after borne a considerable office as a soldier in the wars but at that time was out of all employment only gave himself much to reading and Christian converse. [This man, Martindale tells us, offered] to furnish me with

---

113 M. Spufford in her essay on 'The schooling of the peasantry in Cambridgeshire, 1575–1700' in J. Thirsk (ed.), *Land, Church and People: Essays presented to Professor H. P. R. Finberg*, 1970, offers evidence of the readily available educational facilities in her county and of the undoubted importance of literacy in facilitating the spread of new religious ideas in the late sixteenth and early seventeenth centuries.

114 W. Haller, *Liberty and Reformation in the Puritan Revolution*, New York, 1955, 163–4.

115 Newcome, *Autobiography*, I, 10. Trevor-Roper tells us of Comenius that 'everywhere he admired the signs of literacy and educational zeal. He watched the London congregations taking shorthand notes of sermons and admired the vast output of books'. ('Three foreigners: the philosophers of the puritan revolution', in *Religion, the Reformation and Social Change*, 1967, 268.)

any books he had or could procure for me [and] gave me a great deal of good advice.[116]

It is not surprising that Martindale found that 'divers belonging to Gorton leaned towards Independency before I came thither and others overwent me that way against my will . . .'[117]

Puritanism was related to the educational revolution which took place in the late sixteenth and early seventeenth centuries, the outlines of which have been mapped by Professor Stone and Mrs Simon.[118] But an intimate knowledge of the Bible was not restricted only to those laymen who could read. For example, Robert Pasfield, one of John Bruen's servants, was:

a man utterly unlearned, being unable to read a sentence or write a syllable, yet he was so taught of God that by his own industry and God's blessing upon his mind and memory he grew in grace as he did in years and became ripe in understanding and mighty in the Scriptures. He was so well acquainted with the history of the Bible, and the sum and substance of every book and chapter, that hardly could any ask him where such a saying or sentence were, but he would with very little ado tell them in what book and chapter they might find it. Insomuch that he became as a very profitable index to the family to call to mind what they had learned and to recover what they had lost by slip of memory, and not only so but a godly instructor and teacher of young professors also to acquaint them with the word and to exercise their hearts unto godliness.[119]

Pasfield, unschooled though he was, was clearly respected on account of his accumulated knowledge. William Hinde indeed went so far as to say:

Now if that which I have often heard be true, that . . . a good text-man is a good divine, then may old Robert in our country proceedings be allowed for a divine and a doctor also.

In this description of the servant, as well as in that of John Bruen himself, Hinde drew attention to the competence of the puritan layman; his role was manifestly important and ought not to be under-estimated. It was by no means impossible for the godly to

116 *Life of Adam Martindale*, 65.
117 *Ibid.*, 74.
118 L. Stone, 'The educational revolution in England, 1560–1640', *Past and Present*, 28, 1964; J. Simon, *Education and Society in Tudor England*, Cambridge, 1966.
119 Hinde, *Life of John Bruen*, 56–7.

assume a role similar to that officially allocated to the clergyman. For example, in cases concerning conventicles laymen were occasionally charged not only with meeting together to sing psalms, repeat sermons and the like, but with expounding doctrine. The 1607 case involving the puritans of Oldham is a good instance. They were charged with having 'read or expounded the Scriptures according to your own conceits or some one of you seemed meet not expressed in the Book of Common Prayer'.[120] At Preston it was alleged that one of the puritan opponents of James Martin, the ejected vicar, could be found 'interpreting the Scripture daily, as did also her sons and daughters by turns',[121] while at Burton-in-Kendal in 1633 one Edward Preston was charged 'for teaching without licence, for expounding and making of extemporary prayers being a layman and is suspected to draw together and make unlawful assemblies and conventicles'.[122]

The tendency for lay puritans to assume a quasi-ministerial function was eloquently expressed in the charges brought against George and Henry Seddon of Prestwich in 1612. It was said that on several occasions they had left their own parish for nearby Deane:

and then and there you, standing or sitting in some pew or stall within the same church, did with an audible and loud voice before and in the hearing of the congregation then assembled read, pronounce or repeat certain sermons, or some sermon before preached or printed or by yourselves or one of you or by some other penned or written from the mouth of some other preacher, or did expound some place of scripture so as you and either or one of you *did take upon you and execute in manner aforesaid the place or office of a minister of the Word of God, being thereunto no way lawfully called nor admitted.*[123]

The independence of the puritan laity, and especially the fact that they could be proselytisers in their own right, is well illustrated by the case of Thomas Benson, a Chester brewer. Benson had visited an acquaintance of his, one Thomas Marsland, who was recovering from an illness, and had taken the opportunity to denounce the latter's ungodly life. Marsland was first of all criticised for not allowing his wife to attend conventicles held by John Bruen in his house at Chester.[124] But this was only a beginning. Marsland

120 Chester. Consistory Court papers. EDC 5, 1607. Miscellaneous.
121 P.R.O. State Papers Domestic. SP 16/236/42.
122 York. 1633 vis. RVIA 23, f. 113.
123 My italics. Chester. Consistory Court papers. EDC 5, 1612. Miscellaneous.
124 Benson refers to Bruen as his master, and had apparently lived in the Chester home of the latter.

H

told the Consistory Court in 1612 how Benson had then declared that:

> he, this deponent, went all day tippling and drinking to get custom and said this deponent was as ill as any drunkard and would get custom thereby, and the devil and all, and said to this deponent—in regard of this deponent's sickness and weakness—that he this deponent had one foot in the grave and that he loved neither God nor his Word and therefore the judgements of God hung over this deponent.

Nor was this the end of Benson's moralising. 'Benson upon these speeches turned a book and did read to this deponent that though the children of Israel were as the sand of the sea, yet shall but a remnant be saved.'

In his answers to the articles alleged against him Benson made no attempt to deny the truth of Marsland's evidence. On the contrary, he admitted that he had told Marsland that:

> our time was but short and there was but a remnant should be saved, and showed him the text in his own testament [and] said it behoves you and I to look about us and to serve God that we may be of that remnant.

Clearly, the puritan layman could be confident not only of his own faith but also of his competence to evangelise and to uphold the godly discipline. A position such as this was the natural outcome of the independence gained through participation in household religious exercises.

In the struggle for the establishment of the godly discipline, then, puritan laymen themselves played—and were encouraged to play—an important part. And, as Benson's case reminds us, their influence in this connection was by no means restricted to their own domestic sphere. John Angier assured his congregation that 'God has . . . committed to us the care of our neighbours'. Laymen, he continued, ought not to refrain from criticising others for their ungodly behaviour merely on account of 'a base and unchristian fear that we shall anger them [and that] they will be displeased at us. Grant it be so. Shall we run upon God's displeasure to avoid men's?' Indeed, Angier even went so far as to give the assurance that 'God did never forbid you to help your betters to see their faults and to help them against them'.[125]

Similar advice to laymen was given about this time by the

125 Angier, *Helpe to Better Hearts for Better Times*, 516, 518, 522.

Cheshire divine Samuel Torshell in his *Helpe to Christian Fellow-ship*.[126] Torshell urged upon his readers the necessity of 'mutual serviceableness'. Laymen's competence in this field was clearly far-reaching, he argued, for it consisted not only in 'watching over one another' but also in 'admonishing and reproving those that fall, meekly and seasonably . . . in recovering those that are fallen through a spirit of weakness'. Their role in the furtherance of puritanism and of its godly discipline also involved 'stirring up the spirits and gifts of one another [and] raising, cheering and comforting the dejected' so that together they might all combine in a more effective witness for God.[127]

5 *The part played by women*

The basic unit of puritan organisation was the godly household, and another important consequence of the practice of family religion was that it enhanced the role of women within puritanism. The Lancashire divine Isaac Ambrose noted that it was the duty and privilege of a wife:

> that she may help her husband in erecting and establishing Christ's glorious kingdom in their house and especially in their own hearts. This is that one necessary thing without which their family is but Satan's seminary and a nursery for Hell.[128]

And the practice commonly coincided with the theory. It was the custom of Mistress Ratcliffe of Chester, for example, to catechise her children and servants,[129] and this arrangement seems to have been general in puritan households. The wife of Samuel Clarke, for example:

> would take all occasions and opportunities to manifest her love and care of their [i.e. her servants'] souls, by frequent dropping in good counsel and wholesome instructions, by catechising, enquiring them in what they remembered of the sermons they heard, reading her notes to them, encouraging them in what was good and with the spirit of meekness blaming them for what was evil.[130]

Although it was agreed that religious exercises in the home ought normally to be led by the master of the house, the role of the wife

126 The work was published in London in 1644.
127 Torshell, *op. cit.*, 12–13.
128 Ambrose, *Works*, 1839 edition, 133.
129 Ley, *A Patterne of Pietie*, 27.
130 Clarke, *Lives of Sundry Eminent Persons*, ii, 155.

in this context was often considerable, sometimes crucial. As Thomas Paget made clear in his *Demonstration of Family Duties* (1643), 'if the governor be remiss or indisposed hereunto, then his wife or some other ought to put the work forward'.[131] Samuel Torshell, preacher at Bunbury, continued the same argument in his treatise on *The Womans Glorie* (1645).

> Women [he wrote] may and must privately and familiarly exhort others; . . . where men are not present, women may speak—I mean, though others besides the maids and children of their own family be present . . . They may also privately admonish men and reprove them.[132]

The Chester minister Nicholas Byfield declared that the wife was not subject to the husband:

> in matters of her soul and religion when his will is contrary to God's will . . . The unbelieving husband must not compel the believing wife to change her religion or to neglect the means of her salvation. And again, she is not so subject but she may admonish and advise her husband with certain cautions, as [for instance] if she be sure the thing she speaks against be sinful and hurtful.[133]

Like other preachers, Byfield saw the very real possibility that the godly wife could win her husband over to religion.

Along with this stress on the religious role of women went an improvement in their recognised status. Samuel Torshell, for example, contended that:

> women are capable of the highest improvement and the greatest glory to which man may be advanced . . . As man and woman were equal in creation, so there is no difference between them in state of grace . . . The soul knows no difference of sex as neither do the angels and therefore it is that some learned men are of opinion that after the Resurrection in the state of glory there will be no more any distinction of male and female.[134]

The attitude of puritan preachers to women, however, was not completely removed from that taken by earlier writers such as

131 Preface. One of the questions discussed by the Dedham Classis was whether a woman should be permitted to pray in public worship, 'having a better gift than her husband'. (R. G. Usher (ed.), *The Presbyterian Movement in the reign of Queen Elizabeth*, Camden Soc., third series, 8, 1905, 35.)
132 Torshell, *op. cit.*, 160.
133 Byfield, *Commentary upon the three first chapters . . . of St. Peter*, 583.
134 Torshell, *The Womans Glorie*, 2, 10, 11.

Latimer, Knox and Goodman.[135] Women did enjoy an improved status within puritanism but it was with caution that writers approached the question. The spiritual equality of the sexes may have been conceded—but it remained spiritual. Byfield's liberal views on the status of women have been quoted already. But this was only one side of his argument. He also wrote that:

> God requires subjection of all wives, whether poor, rich, noble, wise, young or old, or of what state or quality soever. A queen has no more privilege than the poorest cottager's wife . . . A wife never carries herself with better grace, reputation or honour than when she shows most obedience and subjection to her husband. It is a wicked and senseless pride in women [continued Byfield] that they think it is baseness and dishonour to be at their husband's appointment and to be made to do what he lists. But these are utterly deceived . . . As man by obedience is God's image, so is the woman by obedience man's image.[136]

Torshell's attitude to women was also to some extent ambivalent. The first part of his book *The Womans Glorie*—extracts from which have already been quoted—stressed the spiritual and intellectual equality of men and women. But what he gave with one hand he almost took away with the other. 'As excellent as the woman sex is,' he wrote, 'yet it is in subjection to man . . .' Women were best to 'preserve and contain themselves quiet, undisturbed and impassionate'. He was ready to admit that women could play an important part in household religion 'but in the exercise of all these privileges let them have respect to the law of humility, without which they will never do anything becomingly'. As for the prospect of women evangelists, Torshell believed that it was 'against God's ordinance, against Church order and modesty for women publicly to preach'.[137]

Isaac Ambrose, like Byfield and Torshell, denied to the husband the authority of a tyrant, stressing instead that he should love, respect and provide for his wife. But the woman could in no sense be considered equal. The chief of the duties proper to the wife was that 'she should be in submission to her husband'. And the

135 Like Knox, Christopher Goodman, who ministered for much of his later life in Chester, believed that 'God . . . appointed the woman to be in subjection to her husband'. (*How Superior Powers ought to be obeyd*, 52.) In a sermon preached in 1550 Latimer had declared that women 'are underlings and must be obedient'. (*Select Letters and Sermons of Dr Hugh Latimer*, Religious Tract Soc., n.d., 82.)
136 Byfield, *op. cit.*, 580–81.
137 Torshell, *op. cit.*, 154, 160, 159.

submission—provided that the husband did not command her contrary to the laws of religion—ought to be complete.[138]

This view of the wife's subjection to the husband was one to which puritan women themselves generally subscribed. The wife whom Samuel Clarke, for example, married in 1625 was:

> singular and very exemplary in that reverence and obedience which she yielded to her husband both in words and deeds. She never rose from the table, even when they were alone, but she made curtsy. She never drank to him without bowing. His word was a law unto her.[139]

It was only among the religious extremists—where ideas of the equality of the sexes were not confined to the spiritual sphere—that the role of women was unrestrained.[140] Women were so numerous and conspicuous in the early Quaker movement, for example, that it was at first rumoured that the sect was confined to their sex.[141] And Thomas Edwards, the author of *Gangraena*, denounced the sectarian preachers for their activity:

> among the common people and especially the female sex, apt to be seduced, strong in their affections and loving too much Independency, but weak and easy in their understandings, not able to examine grounds and reasons nor to answer you.[142]

But admittedly, the puritan theory of the wife's subjection to the husband was to a considerable extent belied by practice. Elizabeth Symons of Nantwich, for example, was charged in 1611 because she 'does not come to church, nor will be drawn thither by her husband and does not absent herself as a recusant but of her wilful forwardness'.[143] Similarly, in the metropolitan visitation of 1633 it was noted

---

138 Ambrose, *op. cit.*, 133.
139 Clarke, *Lives of Sundry Eminent Persons*, ii, 154. Lucy Hutchinson was another who fully acquiesced in the inferior status of women. (C. H. Firth (ed.), *Memoirs of the Life of Colonel Hutchinson*, two vols., 1885, passim.)
140 The subject is examined in K. Thomas, 'Women and the Civil War sects' in T. Aston (ed.), *Crisis in Europe*, 1965, 317–40.
141 G. P. Gooch, *Political Thought in England from Bacon to Halifax*, 1914, 153.
142 A similar contrast between the main body of dissent and its more extreme offshoots existed in the nineteenth century. It was not in Methodism and in the Congregational Union but only in the newer and more democratic offshoots of nineteenth-century Nonconformity, such as Primitive Methodism and the Salvation Army, that women preachers were tolerated and indeed encouraged. (See the article by O. Anderson on 'Women preachers in mid-Victorian Britain: some reflections on feminism, popular religion and social change', *Historical Journal*, xii, 1969, 467–84.)
143 Chester, 1611 vis. EDV 1/17,, f. 58v.

that 'at Budworth there is a gentlewoman (one Mr Marbury, a Justice's wife) whom all the ministers there cannot persuade to kneel at the communion'.[144]

Variations in regional social conditions, too, could enhance the feminine contribution to puritanism and reduce a wife's dependence upon her husband. In this connection, for example, Professor Everitt has observed that since Northampton society tended to be matriarchal—in virtue of the fact that marriage to a widow conferred freeman's status on the new husband—women were able to exert a considerable influence on religious affairs.[145]

In practice, seventeenth-century women enjoyed a considerable degree of freedom in economic life. It was not unknown for ministers' wives, for example, to assume almost complete control over domestic and business affairs. Richard Mather was one who abdicated such authority in favour of his wife. The feeling of loss at her death, therefore, was:

> the more grievous in that she, being a woman of singular prudence for the management of affairs, had taken from her husband all secular cares so that he wholly devoted himself to his study and to sacred employment.[146]

The economic role of women, not only in household management but also in agriculture and domestic industry, was considerable. This situation, besides affecting the status of women in practice, also enlarged the opportunities available to them for participation in household devotions and for discussion of religious questions outside the home.[147]

Occasionally women predominated amongst the groups of puritans who were presented at the visitations. Such was the case at Ormskirk in 1637. On this occasion nineteen of the parishioners were charged with attending conventicles organised by John Broxopp, the vicar, and of these twelve were women. There were at least two widows amongst them—Margaret Walton and Grace

144 Weston Park, Salop. Bradford MSS 9/8. Visitation report. Interesting for comparative purposes is the case of Joseph Wood—a Yorkshireman—and his wife Grace Priestley. 'He was a very provident man,' we are told, 'of a quiet and peaceable temper, would seldom or never do anything but by the consent of his wife.' (*Priestley Memoirs*, Surtees Soc., 77, 1886, 14.)
145 'Social mobility: conference report', *Past and Present*, 32, 1965, 6.
146 Mather, *Life and Death of Richard Mather*, 25.
147 Cf. A. Clark, *The Working Life of Women in the Seventeenth Century*, 1919.

Cowp. Margaret Crossley and her maid were also regular attenders. Elizabeth Morecroft, too, frequented these meetings, as did Mary and Ellen Smith. Ann Wainwright went with her brother to the conventicles, while the wives of Robert Whitestones, Hugh Cowp and Richard Shaw attended with their husbands, who were also charged. The wife of Roland Furnace, however, was separately presented.[148]

Of these women, four—Elizabeth Cowp, Margaret Walton, Margaret Crossley and Ann Whitestones—had been previously charged for the same offence in 1630.[149] On this previous occasion another woman—Anna Wemming—was presented, but nothing further is known of her. The five women presented in 1630 were part of a group of twelve. In 1637, as has already been noted, women numbered twelve out of a total of nineteen. Thus in the years 1630–37 it can be seen that it was the recruitment of additional women supporters which swelled the size of the puritan element in Ormskirk.

This numerical strength of women in puritan groups was, however, in no sense general. In Manchester, for example, in 1617 thirty-six of the congregation were charged with failing to kneel at the communion. Fourteen of the accused were women, but with two exceptions they were all presented along with their husbands —a fact which may mean that they were following a lead rather than setting it.[150]

Although much more similar material could be presented, for the sake of brevity it is sufficient to note that the evidence on this point does not weigh decisively on either side. But on the whole it would seem that, numerically speaking, puritanism was not dominated by women. The great influence which women undoubtedly did exert over religious affairs was largely based, as has been shown, not on numbers but on their position in the household. It was in the home that women had the greatest scope not only for participating in, but for actually shaping, the religious life of the family.

Factors which influenced the adherence of women to puritanism can to some extent be analysed, but where the appeal of religion is concerned generalisations are difficult.[151] The reasons why women

148 Chester. Consistory Court papers. EDC 5, 1637. Miscellaneous.
149 York. 1630 vis. RVIA 22, f. 108v.
150 Chester. 1614 vis. EDV 1/19, f. 187. Cases. 23 September 1617.
151 It was not only in puritanism, of course, that women played an important part. Their role in survivalist Catholicism is discussed in J. Bossy, 'The

inclined to religion could be as varied as the women themselves. But although there was no one type of puritan woman, it seems likely that certain women, at least, were more willing than men to tolerate spiritual dependence upon a pastor. Discussing the role of women in the Reformation, Professor Collinson has written that 'these women belonged to a Church which had only recently abandoned the regular practice of spiritual direction . . . They leant on the preachers as a Catholic would lean on his confessor.'[152]

It is mainly in this light that Mistress Katherine Brettergh appears. She was the sister of John Bruen of Stapleford and carried to her husband's home in Childwall, Lancashire, that intensity in religion with which her own background had been associated. Her enthusiasm for sermons was almost boundless. According to William Leigh, the puritan pastor of Standish, who preached one of the sermons at her funeral in 1601, 'we preachers may mourn most for that we have lost an auditor who heard with reverence, felt with passion and followed with perseverance'.[153] William Harrison, who preached the sermon on the morning of the funeral, agreed and described Mistress Brettergh as one of his best hearers.

> She did most dutifully frequent the public exercises in the church, had a special care to sanctify the Sabbath and was greatly grieved if she might not hear one or two sermons on that day. Although she dwelt far from the church [Harrison continued] yet would she never be absent if she were able either to go or ride.[154]

It was Mistress Brettergh's habit, Harrison goes on to tell us, to read eight chapters of the Bible each day, and she was also much given to prayer.

Professor Stone has suggested that for women of the upper classes it was boredom and frustration which may have made them turn

character of Elizabethan recusancy' in *Crisis in Europe*. In an article on 'Women and the Counter-reformation in France', *Church Quarterly*, 1927, W. J. Payling Wright declared that 'it could be plausibly contended that the remarkable revival of Roman Catholicism in France at the end of the sixteenth and the beginning of the seventeenth centuries was largely the work of women and girls'. (115.)

152 Collinson, 'The role of women in the English Reformation', in C. W. Dugmore and C. Duggan (eds.), *Studies in Church History*, II, 1965, 260.
153 Leigh, *The Soules Solace against Sorrow*, 1612, 77.
154 Harrison, *Deaths Advantage Little Regarded*, 1612, 83, 80. For comparative purposes, D. M. Meads (ed.), *Diary of Lady Margaret Hoby*, 1930, is a useful source for the study of the religiosity of women.

in desperation to the comforts of religion.[155] But Richard Sibbes, the seventeenth-century puritan writer, drew attention to what was perhaps a more widely operative factor. It was his opinion that it was childbirth, above all, which made women psychologically receptive to religious ideas. 'Child-bearing women,' he wrote, 'bring others into this life with danger of their own; therefore they are forced to a nearer communion with God because so many children as they bring forth they are in peril of their lives.'[156]

The theory which he advanced can to some extent be supported by the local evidence at present under review. For example, it was the experience of childbirth and the loss of her first child which seems to have proved the decisive moment in the spiritual life of Mistress Jane Ratcliffe of Chester. John Ley, the author of her biography, contended that her 'conversion' came from:

> the immediate hand of God, who, having taken away her first child, which she took much to heart, made that an occasion to make her apparently his own child. For from that time the means of grace had a more kindly working on her, which made her to mind her Father in heaven [more] than afterwards she did any child she had upon earth when God for that one had given her many.

Personal sufferings, in fact, formed an almost continuous background to her religious life. Later in his narrative Ley tells how:

> she had endured more than death comes to, for she had of some her children long and very painful and perilous labour, above all that is ordinary in breeding women. But that which much exceeded all she sustained in female afflictions [Ley went on] was a long and sore sickness which required—at least, there was applied unto her—very rough and irksome remedies, so that her sufferings were doubled. She suffered first the anguish of her disease . . . and if it had been only pain and torment it had been more tolerable but it was accompanied with a strange both infirmity and deformity. So weak was she that, her jaw being fallen, she could not bring it up toward the upper part of her mouth. Her mouth was drawn away towards her ear, so that it was difficult not only for herself alone but with the help of another to conduct any nourishment by so crooked a passage to her throat.[157]

---

155 Stone, *Crisis of the Aristocracy*, Oxford, 1965, 738.
156 A. B. Grosart (ed.), *The Works of Richard Sibbes*, Edinburgh, 1863, VI, 520.
157 Ley, *A Patterne of Pietie*, 23–4, 118–19. This latter deformity, in fact, proved only temporary.

Katherine Clarke—the wife of Samuel Clarke—makes it clear that a similar personal experience further inclined her towards religion and towards a total submission to the will of God:

> It pleased God [she wrote] upon the death of my youngest child that it lay very heavy upon my spirit, insomuch I was brought upon my knees to beg support from God and to crave his grace and assistance that I might not break out to speak or act anything whereby God's name might be dishonoured or the gospel discredited and that he would be pleased to make up this outward loss with some durable and spiritual comforts. And I found a seasonable, gracious and speedy answer to these my requests. For though I lay long under the burden of that loss, yet in this time did the Lord sweetly manifest his special love to my soul, assuring me that he was my gracious and reconciled Father in Christ, whereby my love to him was much increased, even inflamed.[158]

It seems fairly clear, then, in these cases at least, that the experience of childbirth could 'convert' women, or at least strengthen them in their faith. Even Bishop Bridgeman's wife seems in some respects to have inclined towards puritanism, a fact which may have been associated with the anxieties of child-bearing. Eight of her children had died at birth or in infancy, and the birth of her fourteenth child roughly coincided with the arrival of the puritan minister, John Angier, at Ringley chapel.[159] Oliver Heywood in his biography of Angier tells how:

> God ordered it so by his providence that the Bishop's wife, being a gracious woman, was at that time much afflicted in conscience, and Mr Angier, by God's blessing, was an instrument of much good to her by his counsels and prayers, which became a furtherance of his liberty, for the Bishop would usually say, 'Mr Angier, you must see my wife before you go', and she interceded for him.[160]

Given the great element of risk in child-bearing, it is not surprising that when women survived the experience they should have had strong views about the manner in which they and their new-born offspring were to be treated by the Church. As we have seen already, women figured prominently in cases involving opposition to the use of the sign of the cross in baptism. But even more relevant in this connection was the opposition sometimes shown by women to the

158 Clarke, *Lives of Sundry Eminent Persons*, ii, 159.
159 The Bishop and his wife were at this time living at Great Lever, only two miles away from Ringley.
160 Heywood, *Life of John Angier*, 57.

churching ceremony—a ceremony whose implied purpose was one of penance rather than thanksgiving.[161]

In 1614, for example, one Anne Marlow from Warrington was charged 'for baptising her child in another parish and she herself not churched'.[162] In 1622 the wife of John Davison of Tatton, Cheshire, was charged at Rostherne 'for bearing a child half a year ago and not churched',[163] while at Chipping in Lancashire in 1633 Elizabeth Beasley was presented 'for not coming to church to give thanks to God after her deliverance of child'.[164]

But cases of this kind are both ambiguous and uncommon, and no justification of this particular expression of dissent appears in the sermon literature. We must therefore conclude either that opposition of this type was not common amongst puritans of this area or that the silence of the records indicates only that the authorities were not pressing the point. On this as on other aspects of puritanism, the limitations of available evidence confront the historian. Puritanism in the diocese of Chester was never systematically attacked before the 1630's and consequently the documentation relating to some aspects of its development—its social appeal, for instance—is not so explicit as the social historian would like.[165]

161 The point receives some attention in P. Higgins, 'Women in the English Civil War', M.A. thesis, University of Manchester, 1965, 59–60.
162 Chester. 1614 vis. EDV 1/19, f. 161.
163 Chester. 1622 vis. EDV 1/24, f. 42v.
164 York. 1633 vis. RVIA 23, f. 198v.
165 C. P. Clasen was able to study the social basis of Anabaptism in Germany only because the records of the relentless persecution of the movement were so detailed and abundant. ('The sociology of Swabian Anabaptism', *Church History*, 32, 1963.) Similarly, the copious records kept by the Quakers before and after the Act of Toleration have permitted work to be carried out on the social composition of the Friends. (A. Cole, 'The social origins of the early Friends', *Journal of the Friends' Historical Society*, 48, 1957, and R. T. Vann, 'Quakerism and the social structure in the interregnum', *Past and Present*, 43, 1969.)

Chapter four

The role of patrons

The countenance . . . which a man of great estate and power does
give to a minister is of great import and influence unto his ministry.

Samuel Clarke, *Lives of Sundry Eminent Persons*, I, 169

1 *Aristocracy*

The growth and organisation of puritanism usually involved contributions from three main groups. Two of these—the clergy and
the godly laity—have been discussed in preceding chapters. So, to
gain an overall picture of puritanism and of the forces at work
within it, the third element must now be considered: the role of lay
patrons.

Effective patronage of puritanism presupposed social influence
as well as the willingness to dispose of wealth and property. Not
unnaturally, then, since the opportunities available to them were
often greatest, members of the aristocracy could become conspicuous
as supporters of puritan ministers. The strong aristocratic pressures
which were brought to bear, for example, in the Elizabethan Privy
Council undoubtedly made it easier for puritanism to develop.
Through their influence preachers were sometimes sheltered from
official censure. John Field, for instance, was protected by the Earls
of Leicester and Warwick:

> When the Earl of Leicester lived [wrote Thomas Digges] it went for
> current that all the Papists were traitors in action and affection. He was
> no sooner dead but . . . puritans were traduced as troublers of the State.[1]

Of more immediate relevance to the present study, however, is
the career of Henry, Earl of Huntingdon. The Earl's activity on
behalf of the puritans was summed up by his brother, Sir Francis
Hastings:

> He never set a straying foot in any place [he wrote] where he did
> not labour at the least to settle the preaching of the Word to the
> people. And in many places, I know, he brought it to pass to the com-
> fort of many consciences and the knitting of their hearts in all loyalty

1 Quoted in Stone, *Crisis of the Aristocracy*, 737.

and obedience to their Sovereign and Queen; and in whomsoever he found either backwardness or blind ignorance, he would seek lovingly to have them instructed or else by just severity to correct and reform them.[2]

To begin with, Huntingdon had exploited his position as the leading figure in Leicestershire society to full advantage. In Leicester itself he had re-founded the grammar school on puritan lines and had promoted the extension of preaching in the town. But in 1572 Huntingdon became Lord President of the Council in the North and was thus given greater scope to exert his influence on behalf of puritanism. He led the campaign against recusants in the North and was instrumental in founding lectureships in York and Doncaster:

> I do all I can to get good preachers planted in the market towns of this country [he wrote to the Bishop of Chester in 1584], in which somewhat is already done but much remains to be done . . .[3]

The difficulty was that— apart from his own private chaplains— Huntingdon was in direct control of no ecclesiastical appointments in the North. However, at least in Yorkshire, there are signs that Huntingdon was winning over members of the gentry to support puritan ministers.[4] Some indication of the Earl's contribution to the religious development of the North is given in Christopher Fetherstone's dedication of a translation of his to Huntingdon. There he praised the Earl's:

> singular zeal, your unfeined faith, your sincere profession, your especial care to advance God's glory and to root out Papistry, [for which] this realm generally but my countrymen in the north parts— my native soil—especially have and shall have great cause to praise God for you in the day of their visitation.[5]

The Earl was praised, too, by Bishop Chaderton of Chester as 'a rare man of this age'. 'Truly,' the Bishop went on, 'his Lordship

---

2 Quoted in C. Cross, 'Noble patronage in the Elizabethan Church', *Cambridge Historical Journal*, III, 1960, 9. The local aspects of the Earl's career are discussed in the same author's 'The Earl of Huntingdon and Elizabethan Leicestershire' *Trans. Leics. Arch. Soc.*, 36, 1960, and all aspects are dealt with in her book *The Puritan Earl*, 1966.

3 Peck, *Desiderata Curiosa*, 151.

4 The nonconformist Robert Moore, for example, was indirectly indebted to Huntingdon for his living of Guisley, Yorkshire. (Cross, *The Puritan Earl*, 264.)

5 Quoted in Cross, 'Noble patronage', 14.

is more zealously affected and takes more pains in this action of reformation than any two bishops of this land.'[6]

Huntingdon's presidency of the Council in the North, however, gave him little direct authority in the diocese of Chester, since the two palatine counties of Lancashire and Cheshire lay outside his jurisdiction. But he was also a leading member of the northern High Commission, which had powers over the whole northern province, including the diocese of Chester.[7] In this capacity, he had joined with Archbishop Grindal as early as 1575 in an attack on the performance of the traditional mystery plays in Chester.[8]

Lancashire especially was a county which Huntingdon could not reasonably afford to ignore.

> It will be very hard [so it was noted in 1591] for the Lord President of the north parts to keep in order the counties of York and other counties adjoining upon Lancashire within that commission so long as Lancashire shall remain unreformed.[9]

Realising this, Huntingdon had written to the Bishop of Chester in 1582 recommending the establishment of lecturers and stressing the profit to be gained from 'an hour spent every morning from six to seven or from seven to eight in prayer and a lecture'.[10] But in the development of puritanism in the diocese of Chester the role of the Lord President was in the main limited to the giving of advice. Aristocratic patronage—such as there was—came rather from the Earls of Derby.

The fourth Earl of Derby (d. 1592), though not a puritan himself, was certainly anti-Catholic, and his activities against the Lancashire recusants were praised on more than one occasion. For example, he was informed in 1589 that it was the Queen's view that 'next unto God's goodness, she thinks your Lordship to have been the principal cause of the staying of the country from falling to Popery'.[11] Again, in the following year the Privy Council wrote to the Earl, praising:

> the accustomed great care your Lordship does use in those things that concern the public service and amongst the rest we cannot but greatly

---

6 P.R.O. State Papers Domestic. SP 15/27/28. Chaderton to the Earl of Leicester, 1580.

7 Cross, *The Puritan Earl*, 233.

8 G. Ormerod, *History of the County Palatine of Chester*, Helsby edition, 1882, I, 236. See Cross, *op cit.*, 247–8, for details of the close co-operation which existed between Huntingdon and Grindal.

9 P.R.O. State Papers Domestic. SP 12/240/138.   10 Peck, *op. cit.*, 110.

11 Peck, *op. cit.*, 140.

commend the good order your Lordship has lately begun to take amongst your own servants, tenants and retainers to bring them to conformity . . .[12]

This same Earl invited the leading puritan divines of the diocese to preach before him at Lathom and Knowsley. William Leigh, rector of Standish, would appear to have been most popular with the Earl, for he is known to have preached before him on no fewer than eleven occasions between 1587 and 1590. John Caldwell, rector of Winwick, preached at Lathom or Knowsley nine times in the same period. Richard Midgley, vicar of Rochdale, gave seven sermons before him in these years, as did Robert Eaton, vicar of Leigh. Oliver Carter of Manchester preached three times at the Earl's request, while Peter Shaw of Bury preached twice. Thomas Hunt, puritan curate of Oldham chapel, on the other hand, preached only once at Lathom, as—rather surprisingly—did Edward Fleetwood, the leading Lancashire divine of his day.[13]

Those ministers from this group who published, acknowledged the Earl of Derby as their patron. It was, for example, at the Earl's instigation that a sermon preached before him by John Caldwell in 1578 came to be printed. So Caldwell, in the dedication to this work, declared that:

I am thereby emboldened to crave patronage of you now it is printed and further published abroad, especially because it now has more need thereof, most humbly desiring your honour to take it in good part now as you did then and to continue your good will to the faithful ministers and preachers of the Word and to seek ever more and more to promote the honour and glory of our good, utter hatred and detestation of the lying, false doctrine of Antichrist, as well as it is known to me

---

12 *Acts of the Privy Council*, 25 July 1590. The Council wrote again on this subject on 25 March 1592.

13 Fleetwood—as we shall see (pp. 172–3)—had taken great pains to expose the corrupt state of the civil administration in Lancashire—a fact which is not likely to have endeared him to Derby, the Lord Lieutenant.

  Robert Nicholls of Wrenbury, Cheshire, probably preached one sermon before the Earl.

  These details of the preaching at Lathom have been obtained from F. R. Raines (ed.), *Derby Household Books*, Chet. Soc., old series, 31, Manchester, 1853. Some of these very entries, however, indicate the limitations of the Earl's puritan sympathies. Such for example, is one under 11 January 1589 which states that 'Sunday Mr Caldwell preached and that night the players played'.

and others that daily have experience of your honourable disposition herein . . .[14]

Oliver Carter, preacher at the Manchester Collegiate Church, dedicated his *Answere . . . unto certaine Popish Questions* to the Earl of Derby in 1579.[15]

James Stanley, Lord Strange (1607–51), later seventh Earl of Derby, was also to some extent a patron of the puritan divines in the diocese of Chester.[16] Charles Herle, for example, was tutor or chaplain to his lordship in the 1620's, and it was to the Stanleys that Herle—like Caldwell before him—owed his advancement to the wealthy rectory of Winwick. It was to Lord Strange, therefore, that Herle dedicated his book of *Contemplations and Devotions on the several passages of our blessed Saviour's Death and Passion* in 1631, the year of its publication.

> If I dare print a book [wrote Herle] no question I dare not think of any other patron than your Lordship, to whom by all the engagements of preferment, favour, gratitude, duty and domestic service I stand so strictly obliged. To whom should the book belong but to him to whom the author [belongs]?

Though he later became a leading Presbyterian, Herle was a moderate in politics and never completely severed his connection with the Earl his patron. Strongly disapproving of the execution of Charles I, Herle returned from London to Lancashire and probably associated himself with the troops raised by the Earl of Derby in 1650. He is even said to have sheltered the Earl after the latter's defeat at Wigan.[17]

Other puritan divines of the diocese of Chester, however, were indebted to Lord Strange for their advancement. One of these was John Broxopp, whom Strange had presented to the vicarage of

14 Caldwell, *A Sermon preached before the right honorable Earle of Darbie . . .*, 1577.
15 A commendatory Letter to the Reader was supplied by the Leicestershire divine Anthony Gilby.
16 In this connection the influence of the Earl's wife, Charlotte de la Tremouille, should not be overlooked.
17 The Commonwealth Church Surveyors of 1650 classed Herle as 'an orthodox godly divine' but added that he had not prayed for the success of the Commonwealth on 13 June of that year as was required of ministers. (H. Fishwick (ed.), *Commonwealth Church Survey*, Rec. Soc. Lancs. and Ches., 1, 1879, 47.) The action did not go unnoticed and Herle was for a time kept under restraint.

Ormskirk in 1628.[18] Another who enjoyed the patronage of Lord Strange was Christopher Hudson, lecturer at Preston in the 1630's. One of the sermons in the surviving volume of Hudson's manuscripts is described as having been 'preached at Lathom in the monthly course of my attendance there, 6 November 1636, before my Lord Strange, and afterwards presented unto him upon his own entreaty by me'.[19] Hudson, it is stated in the same volume, was chaplain to Lord Strange, and it was to his patron that he dedicated this sermon on 'The Triumph of Gods Grace over Mans Sinne'.

> This small treatise [Hudson wrote] I make bold upon your command to present unto your Lordship as a poor testimonial of my thankful heart for your undeserved favour constantly exhibited to me, beseeching you to entertain it as attentively in the reading as you did attentively in the hearing, and to receive it with as willing a hand as I tender it with a loyal heart and a mind most conscious to myself of many infirmities which would have discouraged me from this dedication if my soul had not been possessed with a full persuasion that your accustomed goodness and love will cover the multitude of my imperfections.[20]

But apart from the support they gave to individual ministers such as Herle and Hudson, there is no evidence to suggest that the Stanleys were intimately involved in the puritanism of the diocese. This impression of a limited social role being played by the aristocracy in Lancashire is borne out by Professor Jordan's work on regional philanthropy. For, speaking of the part played by the Lancashire nobility in framing the social institutions of the area, Jordan observes that after the Reformation there can be seen 'an almost complete abnegation of social responsibility on the part of a class which after 1530 may be regarded as without great cultural significance in the county'.[21]

18 Broxopp was also made Archdeacon of Man. All ecclesiastical patronage in the Isle of Man, it should be noted, was in the hands of the Earl of Derby.
19 Preston. Hudson's MSS sermons. DP 353, f. 62v. It would seem likely that Hudson intended his collection of sermons to be published.
20 *Ibid.*, f. 62. Hudson spoke of Lord Strange's having 'a love to worship and such a melting heart at the hearing of the Word'. Samuel Hinde—the son of the Bunbury minister William Hinde—was also for a time chaplain to Lord Strange in the 1630's.
21 W. K. Jordan, *The Social Institutions of Lancashire 1480–1660*, Chet. Soc., third series, 11, Manchester, 1962, 107.

2 Gentry

Gentry patronage of puritanism in the diocese of Chester was much more important.[22] Jordan found that, in the period he reviewed, the Lancashire gentry gave over a fifth of the county's charitable funds, and that of the gifts of the lesser gentry about a tenth was donated by puritan gentlemen for religious uses.[23] Richard Blackburn, for example, a puritan landowner of Newton-le-Willows, left £400 in 1615 to support 'a learned man to preach and teach the word of God at Newton'.[24] The position of Denton chapel was made more secure in 1618 when Richard Holland endowed it with £100 to be used to provide a regular stipend for 'a godly minister to preach the word of God and read divine service'.[25] Nor was this the end of the interest the Hollands showed in the chapel. The family, in fact, continued to take an active part in the affairs of the chapelry, and maintained a close control over the appointed ministers.[26]

Another illustration of the importance of gentry patronage is provided by the case of Salford chapel. The lead in its foundation in 1634 had been taken by Humphrey Booth, a local gentleman-clothier, who spent nearly £500 on the enterprise.[27] Booth—who had been presented in the 1633 visitation for failing to kneel at the receiving of the communion—made further provision for the chapel in the following year. The endowments so far made had been only for the chapel building itself. Arrangements were therefore made for the support of 'a godly, learned, able, fit, zealous and faithful man for a preaching minister', whose appointment was to be in the hands of the chapel trustees and their descendants. At Bradshaw the puritan family of that name rebuilt the chapel there in 1640.[28]

Numerous other, though less substantial, gifts were made by members of the gentry to further the puritan cause. An increase in

22 For comparative purposes J. T. Cliffe, *The Yorkshire Gentry, from the Reformation to the Civil War*, 1969, ch. 12, 'The growth of puritanism', 256–81, is extremely valuable.
23 Jordan, *op. cit.*, 106, 110.
24 *Ibid.*, 80–81.
25 *Ibid.*, 81.
26 John Angier came to be appointed to Denton because he was acceptable to the Hollands. A rival candidate—Henry Hoot—had been disapproved of by the patron. (Heywood, *Life of John Angier*, 59.)
27 Jordan, *op. cit.*, 18. Lesser amounts, ranging from £5 to £20, had been contributed by others, including Sir Alexander Radcliffe of Ordsall. (Hollingworth, *Mancuniensis*, 117.)
28 *V.C.H. Lancs.*, v, 272.

the endowment of the Bolton lectureship, for example, was given in the will of Robert Lever of Darcy Lever, gent., proved in 1621. Lever set aside the sum of £20 which was 'to be paid yearly by 20s a year towards Mr Gosnell his wages, and if God call him away, then to what preacher shall be placed in his place so long and until twenty pounds shall be paid'. Lever's benefaction, however, went further than this:

> Whereas I did promise to give a hundred marks [he went on] towards the buying of a stipend for the continuance of wages to a preacher at Bolton if there be a stipend bought within four years after my departure, then I do give towards the purchase thereof an hundred marks and then the payment of the reversion of the said twenty pounds to cease, provided that the stipend be thirty pounds by year at least . . .[29]

But the contribution of the gentry to the development of puritanism in the diocese of Chester was not only of a financial nature; the support which they gave was more varied than Jordan's statistical study suggests. This is clearly illustrated, for example, by the career of John Bruen, of Stapleford, Cheshire.

Sabbath Clark, later minister at Bruen's parish church of Tarvin, summed up his patron's contribution to the local development of puritanism as follows:

> He was the chief instrument [wrote Clark] to plant and establish the preaching of the Gospel in this congregation, first by providing divers of God's ministers to preach here oftentimes when the incumbent was grown old and decrepit [and] afterwards by maintaining a preacher at his own proper cost and charges, and lastly by being a means to obtain the place for me in reversion and allowing me the greatest part for my maintenance, so that this parish has cause for ever to acknowledge him a nursing father of religion amongst them.[30]

These claims were not exaggerated. Bruen had made determined efforts to deal with problems of Popery and profaneness which faced him at Tarvin. For example, William Hinde tells how Bruen over-hauled the parish church, bringing it belatedly in line with Eliza-bethan requirements. 'He presently took order to pull down all these painted puppets and Popish idols in a warrantable and peaceable manner, and of his own cost and charge repaired the breaches and beautified the windows with white and bright glass again'.[31]

---

29 Lever also gave £4 to James Gosnell 'to buy him a cloak' and left 40s a year towards the maintenance of a preacher at Rivington.

30 Quoted in Hinde, *Life of John Bruen*, 88.   31 Hinde, *op. cit.*, 79.

Further information of this kind is found in the records of a case heard by the Bishop of Chester in 1603.[32] The charges were directed not against Bruen personally but against some of his servants— William Lowe, Richard Jackson, John Platt, Robert Lloyd, Ralph Darington, James Harte and John Bones. The accused men confessed that on one particular Sunday:

> they did with their staves throw down a stone cross standing in the churchyard of Warton and in the very same night the said William Lowe and Robert Lloyd, the others not being in their company, did break down about three or four foot of glass of the great window in the chancel of the parish church of Tarvin, wherein was the image of St Andrew and Lazarus.

The men denied that they had been urged on to these actions either by a minister or by their master and claimed that in fact the latter had been offended by their rashness. But even if this last statement is taken at face value—and one wonders whether it ought to be—indirect responsibility for the outbursts of iconoclasm still rests with Bruen. For, aiming at the conversion of the parish, he had first of all erected the godly discipline within his own household, allowing only the godly to have a place within it. The Bruen household went to church as a body, in procession, singing psalms as they went, 'leaving neither cook nor butler behind him nor any of his servants but two or three to make the doors and tend the house until their return'.[33] Bruen, in short, set up a miniature religious community and created the atmosphere which it breathed. Iconoclasm was no more than a natural result of this situation.

The Bruen household became, in fact, a puritan seminary, the influence of which extended far beyond its immediate neighbourhood:

> Many passengers from London to Ireland and from Ireland into England [declared Hinde], many travellers, horsemen and others out of Lancashire and the farthest parts of Cheshire, who would as they had occasion to come to the courts or fairs of Chester take up his house for their lodging place, not so much, I conceive, for the ease and refreshing of their bodies as for the comfort and rejoicing of their hearts in seeing his face, in hearing his voice, in conferring and advising with him, in having a portion in his prayers and a part in his praises unto God with him.[34]

---

32 Chester. Quarter sessions records. QSF 1/80. 1603.
33 Hinde, *op. cit.*, 210.   34 *Ibid.*, 186.

Towards the end of his life—he died in 1625—John Bruen assessed the religious changes which had come about in his time. 'Now the borders of the Church are much enlarged,' he wrote, 'the number of believers wonderfully increased, and blessed be God, every quarter and corner of the country is now filled with the sweet savour of the Gospel.' Conversely, he recalled 'when first I began to profess religion there was almost none in the whole shire that were acquainted with the power and practice of it'.[35] In Tarvin the religious transformation was mainly Bruen's work. Patronage, when so determined, could carry all before it.

Other members of the gentry, of course, besides Bruen helped to steer the puritan clergy of the diocese through difficult times. Edmund Hopwood, Esq., of Hopwood, in the parish of Middleton, for example, came to the defence of the Lancashire preachers at the time of Archbishop Piers' metropolitan visitation of the diocese in 1590. In his correspondence with the Archbishop Hopwood conceded that the ministers in question displayed irregularities, such as the failure to wear the surplice. He pointed out, however, that:

> some of them have been planters or founders of religion in these parts, continual well users of their liberty so many years enjoyed, and therefore it behoves me to use all good means I may that this corner of my country might still enjoy them.

Hopwood later made a special plea for Richard Midgley, vicar of Rochdale, whom he described as:

> a country scholar, yet discreet, sober and very peaceable, the only first planter of sound religion in this corner of our country in Her Majesty's time, and since his first entrance has not used the surplice in his church, yet has used his ministry very peaceably and had at his monthly communions above eight hundred communicants that zealously cried 'Thy kingdom come'.[36]

In 1604 a more general petition on behalf of the Lancashire preachers was sent to the King by their local supporters amongst the gentry about the time of the Hampton Court conference. Chief among the petitioners was Sir Richard Assheton of Middleton (d. 1617), head of a noted Puritan family and twice Sheriff of Lancashire.[37] Assheton's son-in-law, John Holt of Stubley, also signed the petition, as did James Assheton, Esq., of Chadderton.

35 Hinde, *op. cit.*, 216.
36 *Kenyon Mss.*, H.M.C. 598–9, 602.
37 In 1598 and 1607.

The remaining signatories were Randle Barton of Smithills, Alexander Rigby, John Wrightington, Richard Fleetwood, Nicholas Banister, John Bradshaw of Bradshaw, Richard Holland, Sir Edmund Trafford and Nicholas Mosley.

The petitioners gave a spirited defence of the nonconformist preachers, declaring that:

> We have known them . . . for all the time of their continuance amongst us to be men worthy to be respected as the ministers of Christ. Some of them [they went on] have continued amongst us well near forty years and the most of them above twenty, diligent and painful preachers, and that with such fruit and blessing upon their labours that whereas in the beginning of her late Majesty's reign . . . this county was generally overgrown with Popery and profaneness, it is now—and especially in the places in which these men have continued—so reformed that they are become unfeigned professors of the Gospel, and many recusants are yearly conformed. Divers of the said preachers [the petitioners continued] were men of great years, some gentlemen by birth, and according to their ability great housekeepers, some of good reputation for learning and all of them of honest conversation and peaceable among their neighbours.

The petitioners stressed that if the Lancashire preachers were deprived for their admitted nonconformity, the county as a whole would lose by the action. Such an attack upon them, the petitioners argued, would 'bring exceeding much grief to all the godly, too great rejoicing to the common adversaries and further endanger the progress of religion in these parts'.[38]

The ministers' patrons again came to their defence at a later date when Bishop Morton of Chester was trying to bring them to conformity. The precise date of the petition is not known but it must be within the period 1616–19, the years of Morton's episcopate. The actual signatories to the petition, unfortunately, are not known, but in the preface to his brother's *Defence of Church Government*[39] Thomas Paget explained that when the position of the puritan divines of the diocese was threatened, 'it pleased God to stir up some of the eminent and well affected knights and esquires inhabiting in that diocese to consult and agree together to write a letter to the Bishop.'

Individual case histories of puritan divines clearly illustrate the support which was often forthcoming from the gentry. Richard

38 P.R.O. State Papers Domestic. SP 14/10/62.
39 John Paget's work was published in London in 1641.

Mather of Toxteth, for example, undoubtedly benefited from his contacts with the gentry.[40] Mather was silenced for his nonconformity by the metropolitan visitors of Archbishop Neile in 1633. 'But then,' wrote his biographer, 'by means of the intercession of some gentlemen in Lancashire and by the influence of Simon Byby, a near alliance of the Bishop's, he was restored again to his public ministry.'[41]

John Angier, too, owed much to the support he received from members of the gentry. During his stay at Denton he had the Holland family as patrons. Much later—after the Five Mile Act of 1665—a vagrant Angier was welcomed as a guest into the homes of Cheshire gentry families such as the Crewes of Utkinton.[42]

The young Henry Newcome enjoyed the patronage of his wife's kinsman, Henry Mainwaring, who nominated him to the chapelry of Goostrey in Cheshire and even provided accommodation for his relative.[43] It was to the same gentleman that Newcome owed his remove to Gawsworth. Of this event he wrote:

> My cousin Mainwaring bestirred himself and made use of his interest with the gentlemen and it was effected. Also he employed his solicitor, Mr Thornicroft, to transact the business above, and he was forced to give pretty largely to some.[44]

As Newcome''s case reminds us, the most direct way in which the gentry could materially influence the growth of puritanism was by their control of advowsons. Patronage of this kind was sometimes of the utmost importance. In Caroline Yorkshire, for example, no fewer than eighty benefices were controlled by puritan lords and gentry.[45] Again, in Lincolnshire puritan gentry such as Sir William Wray, Sir George St Paul, Sir William Armyne and Sir Thomas Grantham used their control of advowsons to great advantage. Between them they presented to twenty-seven livings and they saw to it that only puritan divines were admitted.[46] In Suffolk much the same process was taking place. The puritan Sir Robert Jermyn, for

40 Mather's links with the gentry were strengthened still further by his marriage to Katherine, the daughter of Edmund Holt, Esq., of Bury. (Mather, *Life of Richard Mather*, 8.)
41 Mather, *op. cit.*, 10. Their intervention in 1634, however, could not save him from suspension.
42 Heywood, *Life of John Angier*, 92.
43 Newcome, *Autobiography*, I, 11.   44 *Ibid.*, 17.
45 Cliffe, *The Yorkshire Gentry*, 268.
46 F. Hill, *Tudor and Stuart Lincoln*, Cambridge, 1956, 116.

example, controlled eleven advowsons and promoted only clergymen who shared his views.[47] In Caroline Essex the patronage of the Earl of Warwick was even more extensive. He was without question the county's most important single patron. In the Rochford hundred alone he presented to ten livings. The Earl also controlled Felsted school, to which he appointed the puritan clergyman John Preston in 1627.[48] In the Midlands the Earl of Huntingdon held seven advowsons, and by this means puritan divines such as Arthur Hildersham and Anthony Gilby were advanced.[49]

It would appear, however, that in the diocese of Chester the use of advowsons played a less prominent part in the development of puritanism than it did elsewhere in the country. No single member of either the aristocracy or the gentry held a large number of livings. Even the Stanleys had very few within their gift. They presented to Winwick and Ormskirk, and also to Bury in 1623 and 1633, but to no others in Lancashire.[50]

Good use, however, could be made by puritan patrons of the limited opportunities available to them in this field. As an example, one can point to the fact that the Assheton family, of Middleton, held the wealthy rectory there and that although the living was invariably given to a member of the family they proved that nepotism and puritanism could go together.[51] The Chadderton branch of the Assheton family presented to Prestwich, with similar results, the living being occupied from 1569 to 1632 by William and John Langley, both of whom were staunch puritans.

It was to the Hoghton family, on the other hand, that the puritan divine Isaac Ambrose owed his appointment to the vicarage of Preston. Ambrose's indebtedness to his patrons was acknowledged in his dedication of a part of his theological work *Three Great*

47 Collinson, 'Puritan classical movement', 870–71.
48 W. Addison, *Essex Heyday: a study in seventeenth-century social life*, 1949, 226.
49 Cross, 'The Earl of Huntingdon and Elizabethan Leicestershire', 10.
50 In Lancashire the patronage of the Crown included the Wardenship of Manchester and the livings of Wigan, Eccles and Deane. Within the gift of the Archbishop of Canterbury were the Lancashire livings of Rochdale, Blackburn and Whalley, while the Bishop of Chester presented to Bolton, Childwall, Chipping and Bolton-le-Sands (after 1587). King's College, Cambridge, had the advowson of Prescot and Christ Church, Oxford, those of Kirkham and Great Budworth in Cheshire.
51 This and other information about presentations has been obtained from the parish clergy lists in the *V.C.H. Lancs*.

Ordinances of Jesus Christ to Sir Richard Hoghton and his wife in 1662.

Turning from Lancashire to Cheshire, it can be seen that the patronage of the puritan Sir William Brereton, though its scope was limited, was used to some effect. In 1616 Brereton had presented Robert Halliley to the living of Middlewich. Halliley was a thoroughgoing puritan, being charged at various times with failing to wear the surplice, to use the sign of the cross and for administering the communion to non-kneelers. Later, in 1632, Brereton presented the puritan Ralph Stirrop to the rectory of Ashton on Mersey.[52] Lastly we may note that it was through the patronage of Sir William Brereton that the Yorkshire divine John Shaw was in 1643 presented to Lymm in Cheshire.[53]

3 Merchants and tradesmen

In the case of the Cheshire parish of Bunbury, unlike those instances cited above, the advowson was held not by a member of the gentry but by a company of merchants. In 1594 Thomas Aldersey, a Cheshire-born merchant who had prospered in London, purchased the tithes of Bunbury and used them to endow a preachership and curacy there.[54] To administer the benefaction Aldersey appointed the London Company of Haberdashers as his trustees.[55]

Aldersey—who stipulated that all the clergy chosen to fill the Bunbury preachership and curacy were to be university men with at least an M.A.—made the first appointments himself. Christopher Harvey M.A. was chosen as the preacher[56] and in his will in 1596 Aldersey offered to forgive him an outstanding debt on condition that he would remain in his place seven years longer, 'God sparing him life further to plant the true knowledge of God there which is

52 Ormerod, *op. cit.,* 1, 561.
53 *Life of Master John Shaw,* 137.
54 Thomas Aldersey (1522–96), a merchant tailor, was the son of John Aldersey, gent., of Aldersey and Spurstow. He was City Auditor for London in 1572 and was four times an M.P. for the city.
55 Bunbury was the first living of which the Haberdashers gained control. Through later bequests the Company's patronage came to include lectureships at Newland, Monmouth and St Bartholomew's, London. (D. Williams Whitney, 'London puritanism: the Haberdashers' Company', *Church History,* 32, 1963.)
56 Harvey was charged in 1601 with not wearing the surplice. (Chester. 1601 vis. EDV 1/12a, f. 64v.)

so graciously begun by his ministry . . .' Harvey, however, died in 1601, but in accordance with Aldersey's own preferences and wishes a puritan succession at Bunbury was maintained by the Haberdashers.

The preachership left vacant by Harvey's death was filled first by the more famous William Hinde, the biographer of John Bruen, who remained at Bunbury until his death in 1628. Hinde was then succeeded by Samuel Torshell. The curacy was filled successively by the puritans Richard Rowe, Richard Oseley and John Swan.[57]

Puritanism, then, was expressed by virtually all the clergy appointed to this parish, but to the authorities they constituted a particularly serious problem in virtue of the fact that their position gave them virtual immunity. Archbishop Neile summed up the situation in his report on the visitation of 1633:

> The haberdashers of London [he wrote] pretend to have power to place and displace [the clergy they support] at their pleasure without any respect of episcopal jurisdiction. And their grants to the preacher and the curate run 'To have and to hold *quam diu se bene gesserint*'. The place is said to be a good nursery of Novelists, and the curate and lecturer there [the Archbishop continued] were found altogether unconformable, presuming that the Bishop of Chester had no power over them, which I wonder that the Bishop of Chester endured.[58]

Ministers of Bunbury paid tribute to the patronage of the London Haberdashers' Company in their published writings. William Hinde, for example, dedicated his treatise *A Path to Pietie*[59] to Sir Thomas Lowe, Master of the Company, and the four Wardens. Hinde declared:

> It were my part . . . and my people's, too, were it in our power, to raise a monument of eternal memory both for the author and instrument of so rich mercies as we of this place do enjoy both for soul and body. For whereas the author and giver of every good gift . . . [Hinde went on] was pleased to cast his eye of pity and compassion upon this parish, living yet in darkness while the light shone round about them . . . to raise . . . a place for his true worship, houses and maintenance for learning and religion, with annual and ample allowance for the poor, and all by the hand and travail, care and cost of our famous and worthy founder Thomas Aldersey . . .

---

57 Ormerod, *op. cit.*, II, 260.
58 P.R.O. State Papers Domestic. SP 16/259/78. Neile to the King, January 1634.
59 The book was published at Oxford in 1613.

Again, in 1623, when Hinde published a work entitled *The Office and Moral Law of God*, he addressed his dedication in part to:

> my worthy patrons, the right worshipful Nicholas Ranton, Master of the Worshipful Company of the Haberdashers in the City of London, [and to] the worshipful . . . Wardens of the same Company.

Samuel Torshell—who in 1629 succeeded Hinde as preacher at Bunbury—followed the precedent by dedicating his *Three Questions of Free Justification, Christian Liberty, the Use of the Law* (1632) to the Master and Wardens of the Haberdashers' Company. Similarly, when in the following year Torshell published his treatise on *The Saints Humiliation* he again addressed himself to the ruling body of the Company. 'Excellent,' he wrote, 'is the wise and faithful use of entrusted power in placing of able men in ministry . . .'

But it is clear that it was not only at Bunbury that the development of puritanism in the diocese of Chester was influenced by the intervention of London merchants. John Shaw tells us that by 1633 there had grown up:

> a custom for the merchants and other tradesmen that lived in London, so many of them as were born in the same county, to meet at a solemn feast, upon their own charges, together in London and there to consult what good they might do their native county by settling some ministers—
> —or some other good work—in that county.[60]

County loyalty was a powerful force in seventeenth-century England. Jordan found that the Londoners who gave over £29,000 to Lancashire charities (about 28 per cent of the total) were predominantly local men.[61] In 1629, for example, Thomas Stones, a Lancashire-born London haberdasher, gave about £1,200 for the building and endowment of a church at Much Hoole, near Preston.[62]

It was primarily to the Lancashire-born members of the London mercantile community that around 1641 George Walker—himself a

60 *Life of Master John Shaw*, 126. It was in this way that Devonshire-born merchants came to invite Shaw to settle at Chelmsleigh as their stipendiary preacher.

61 Forty-four of the fifty-five Londoners who gave donations were born in Lancashire. (Jordan, *op. cit.*, 98–9.) For general comments on the strength of county loyalties in the seventeenth century see A. M. Everitt, *The Local Community and the Great Rebellion*, Historical Association pamphlet, 1969, and in the same author's *Change in the Provinces: the Seventeenth Century*, mentioned earlier. For a case study of this subject Professor Everitt's *Community of Kent and the Great Rebellion*, Leicester, 1966, is valuable.

62 Jordan, *op. cit.*, 81, 60.

native of the county—addressed his *Exhortation for contributions to
maintain preachers in Lancashire.*[63] The clergyman's pamphlet is
worthy of close investigation, for, as Fuller pointed out, Walker's
'example and persuasion advanced about a thousand pounds towards
the maintenance of preaching ministers in his native county'.[64]

Walker reminded his readers—and potential patrons—of the
deplorable state of religion in the county, and argued that this situation would continue unless the number of preaching ministers there
was increased. He urged his readers to assume responsibility for this
important work. 'We ought to honour God with our wealth,' he
wrote, 'by spending a great part thereof in works of piety and
charity upon the poor members of Christ.'

Remembering the type of audience he was addressing, Walker
spent much time underlining the results to be expected from his
scheme:

> This work [he wrote] is not one of those alms deeds and works of
> charity which are done in secret which few see but God; this is a public
> work like a candle upon a candlestick which gives light to many.

The scheme, he went on, should be viewed as a profitable invest-
ment; no element of risk was involved:

> Here is no great sum to be adventured or put forth upon uncertainties
> [he wrote] but a small yearly benevolence to be paid quarterly and
> continued so long as it shall manifestly appear to be well employed to
> good purpose and for present profit.

The profits of the enterprise, in fact, would be such as any businessman could feel pleased with:

> Whosoever has a desire to put forth his talent of worldly wealth, what-
> soever it is [Walker declared] more or less, to the best advantage and
> so employ it that it may bring in double or treble gain, surely he cannot
> find a better way than this pious work which is here commended unto
> you.

Walker drew attention to the benefits which accrued from the
reformed religion. Since the Reformation, he argued 'this land and

63 Walker's *Exhortation* is printed in C. W. Sutton (ed.), *Miscellany, vol. 1,*
Chet. Soc., new series, 47, Manchester, 1902. George Walker M.A. (1581–
1651) was born at Hawkshead and educated at the grammar school there.
He later entered St John's College, Cambridge, where he graduated B.A.
in 1608 and M.A. in 1611.
64 Fuller, *History of the Worthies of England*, 118.

Church has prospered in all worldly peace, plenty and prosperity, excelled all other nations and Churches of the world'. His merchant hearers would be wise, therefore, to bring the Reformation to those parts of Lancashire which it had so far failed to reach:

> If you heartily and unfeignedly desire to see your native county and kindred flourish in all worldly wealth and prosperity [wrote Walker] you cannot for the obtaining of your desire in all the world find a more ready way than this work of piety, which I here commend unto you, which, as it tends first to plant the Gospel and true religion, so it will draw on all other blessings by means of them.[65]

It was this desire to help his native county which in 1625 had prompted Nathan Walworth to endow Ringley chapel in Prestwich parish. Walworth (1572–1640) was a native of the parish and had prospered in the service of the Earls of Pembroke and through his mercantile connections in London.[66] In the first instance about £250 was given for the building of the chapel but further benefactions followed towards the minister's stipend.

The contribution made by merchants to the development of puritanism in the diocese of Chester, then, was of considerable importance. Jordan, in his analysis of the social origins of charitable giving in Lancashire, found that merchants and tradesmen between them gave as much as 27 per cent of the county total.[67] But this financial assistance, of course, came from the local trading and merchant classes as well as from the London mercantile community.

Thomas Benson, for example, the Chester brewer whose proselytising activities have already been described in the previous chapter, made bequests to ministers in his will in 1614. First, the sum of 10s was given to his minister to preach his funeral sermon. But, more revealingly, Benson bequeathed 20s to the puritan divine Nicholas Byfield 'as a token of my love, and on him and his God show mercy both now and ever, for by the blessing of God in his ministry my soul many times has received comfort'. Around 1616 the much more substantial sum of £20 a year was given to the Lan-

---

65 Walker, *op. cit.*, 4, 5, 6, 10, 11. Walker himself made provision in his will for £20 a year to be paid to the preacher at his native Hawkshead. (Jordan, *op. cit.*, 82.)

66 The early history of Ringley chapel is well documented in J. S. Fletcher (ed.), *The Correspondence of Nathan Walworth and Peter Seddon*, Chet. Soc., old series, 109, Manchester, 1880.

67 Jordan, *op. cit.*, 106. Merchants alone gave about 21 per cent.

cashire chapel of Didsbury by the Manchester clothier Rowland Mosley.[68]

In the following year Thomas Breres of Bolton, chapman, made known in his will:

> that if the inhabitants of the town of Rivington or thereabouts do hire a preacher to preach at Rivington church that they have forty shillings every year so long as they shall so hire a preacher towards the better maintenance and finding of such a preacher as shall be by them so hired as aforesaid and my will and mind is that the said forty shillings shall be yearly paid as aforesaid and shall issue out of my said lands in Rivington.

John Ratcliffe, brewer and alderman of Chester, by his will in 1633 contributed towards the maintenance of a lecturer in the city. He gave:

> to my loving friend Mr Ley,[69] preacher of God's Word and now lecturer in the said city of Chester, the sum of forty shillings yearly during so many years as he shall live and continue lecturer in the said city or else in lieu of the said yearly payment of forty shillings my will and mind is he shall have one piece of plate of the value of five pounds at his election . . .

Four years later, when the Manchester haberdasher George Clarke died, he made bequests to the puritan Warden and Fellows of the Collegiate Church.[70] In 1638 the Bolton mercer John Marsh left sums of 10s each to the ministers Robert Parke, Timothy Aspinwall, William Gregg, Alexander Horrocks and Mr Johnson. He requested that one of them should preach at his funeral, and even supplied the text for the occasion![71] Finally, it may be noted that Henry Kelly of Manchester, chapman, in his will in 1640 bequeathed £10 to William Bourne, the Fellow of the Collegiate Church whose nonconformity has been repeatedly mentioned elsewhere in the present study.[72]

68 Jordan, *op. cit.*, 80.
69 Incumbent of Great Budworth, Cheshire.
70 Clarke had been presented in the 1633 visitation for failing to kneel at the required times in the service. (York. 1633 vis. RVIA 23, f. 612.)
71 Marsh had also been charged in the 1633 visitation for not kneeling at the receipt of the communion (f. 561).
72 Kelly had been churchwarden in 1622, and along with the two others who held this office had been presented for refusing to disclose the names of those who were nonconformists at the communion. (Chester. 1622 vis. EDV 1/24, f. 129v.)

4 Women

Elsewhere in this book attention has been drawn to the important role of women in the expression and organisation of puritanism, especially at the domestic level. But it is of particular relevance to the subject now under discussion to observe that women often distinguished themselves not only as participants in, but also as patrons of, puritanism.

Some indication of the importance of women as patrons can be gleaned from sermon dedications. John Ley, for example, the leading puritan divine in Cheshire in the generation before the Civil War, addressed the 'Epistle dedicatory' of his description of *A Patterne of Pietie*, published in 1640, to Lady Brilliana Harley and Lady Alice Lucy.[73] And his dedication was no mere formality. He pointed out that 'Your respects both to preachers and people have been uniformly carried with religious favour without any compliment to irregular faction.'

The pattern of piety described in this work was that which had been exemplified in the life of Mistress Jane Ratcliffe of Chester. She was the niece of Edward Brerewood, the puritan professor at Gresham College in London, and the wife of John Ratcliffe, brewer and alderman of Chester and himself an ardent puritan. It was to Jane Ratcliffe that Byfield had dedicated his treatise on *The Signes*.[74] There he had acknowledged:

> your singular love and liking of my ministry, together with your reverent and willing entertainment of faithful ministers . . .
> I have had occasion to know [Byfield went on] your order and manner of life, your desires, purposes, tears and uprightness, your faith, your love, your obedience . . . And I am well assured that his treatise will find good access unto the hands and hearts of divers in these parts, even for the love they bear to you, and for the good they now hear you have by experience reaped from these [writings].

Mistress Ratcliffe became a widow in 1633, and it was in these circumstances that John Ley acquired the position of her spiritual

73 The puritanism of Lady Brilliana Harley comes out unmistakably in her *Letters*, ed. T. T. Lewis, Camden Soc., 58, 1854. It was through the sponsorship of her husband, Sir Robert Harley, that John Ley came to preach a fast sermon before the House of Commons in 1643. Clarke's *Lives of Sundry Eminent Persons* includes a brief biography of Lady Alice Lucy.
74 Byfield, *The Signes, or an essay concerning Gods Love and Mans Salvation . . .*, 1637, newly corrected and amended.

adviser.[75] Ley paid tribute to the generosity of his patron in *A Patterne of Pietie*:

> When she heard of the irreligious parsimony of some towards the public ministration in this city [of Chester] [wrote Ley] she professed—and that without both ostentation and hypocrisy . . .—that she had rather be at all the charge of the common contributions herself, if her estate would bear it, than that God should be grumbled at or his service poorly prized, or the wages of his work unwillingly paid.[76]

While still on the subject of sermon dedications it should be noted that Samuel Torshell, the Bunbury preacher, dedicated one of his works to a godly gentlewoman of Cheshire, Mrs Jane Done of Utkinton. Two reasons were given for the dedication. First, it was particularly appropriate:

> because you are and have been long an eminent example of that which the treatise commends. I know you will neither be afraid nor ashamed to own that course of religion and society now which you were not afraid to practise nor ashamed to countenance heretofore when the times were suspicious of all the meetings of godly professors and threatened and raged against them . . . It is your praise [Torshell concluded] that you have learned what I am teaching unto others.

Second, Torshell wished to leave on record 'a testimony of the sincere and great respect I bear and have ever borne to you since I had the happiness to have acquaintance with your gifts and graces'.[77]

It is as a patron of puritan ministers that Mrs Heywood—the wife of a Bolton merchant and mother of Oliver Heywood, the preacher —is most appropriately discussed. As a boy, Oliver Heywood had been taken by his mother to hear all the locally well known preachers of the day. But Mrs Heywood was not merely content to hear sermons where they happened to be preached; she herself actively furthered the propagation of the gospel by inviting preachers to give sermons where there was greatest need.

> She had a friendly correspondence with the best ministers in the country, who were ordinarily willing to condescend to her request for preaching [wrote Oliver Heywood], which good exercises she was very forward to promote. She had [for example], [he went on] prevailed with my

---

75 Ley, however, had been associated with the Ratcliffe household in her husband's day.   76 Ley, *op. cit.*, 83.
77 Torshell, *A Helpe to Christian Fellowship . . .*, 1644.

K

father Angier and Mr Gee for their pains at Bolton or Cockey . . .
[Such was her reputation] for her love to, care of and prevalency
[*sic*] with ministers, a reverend divine used to call her 'the mother
of the clergy'.

Heywood elaborated these points elsewhere. 'When the chapels in
the neighbourhood were vacant,' he wrote, 'she used every means
in her power to procure the settlement of pious ministers in them.'[78]
Almost the last action of her life was to work for the settlement
of a minister at Ainsworth chapel.

An indication of the financial support given by women to puritan
ministers is also provided by probate records, although it must
always be borne in mind that because of the laws of property far
fewer wills were made by women than by men. Jordan, in his
work on English philanthropy, found that half the women donors
were widows, but since such women enjoyed a considerable degree
of economic liberty this is not altogether surprising. But significantly
Jordan found that a quarter of the women donors were married.
Clearly, then, 'women possessed far more of disposable wealth and
certainly far greater independence of judgement than has commonly
been supposed'.[79]

Moreover, when Jordan came to analyse the direction of their
gifts he found that women donors as a group were apparently far
more secular-minded than men. On average, throughout the country,
women directed only about 18 per cent of their gifts to religious uses.
But, as Jordan himself points out, there were significant regional
variations. In Lancashire, over a third of women's gifts were for
religion.[80] The outlook here was different. The strengthening of
religion was a pressing need in Lancashire, and the total sum
bequeathed by women in the county for this purpose was only
slightly less in value than that expended on their top priority, which
was education.[81]

78 Heywood, *Autobiography, diaries, etc*, I, 47: Hunter, *Life of Oliver Heywood*, 26.
79 W. K. Jordan, *Philanthropy in England, 1480–1660*, 1959, 354.
80 This high proportion—34.37 per cent—given by the women of Lancashire for religious uses was, in Jordan's sample, second only to that of Somerset's 34.84 per cent.
81 Jordan, *op cit.*, 382–3. In Lancashire 34.66 per cent of women's donations were for education, 34.37 per cent for religion. The women of the county, then, put religion higher in their priorities than did men. Of the total charitable gifts of Lancashire, 41.79 per cent went towards education, 31.94 per cent to religious uses.

For example, Judith Foxe, widow, of Manchester, made bequests to five puritan ministers in her will, which was proved in 1624.[82] To William Hinde, her brother-in-law, and to Thomas Paget of Blackley 20s each was given. To Mr Gee of Newton £5 was allowed. Mr Norman, preacher at Gorton chapel, and Mr Root were each given 10s. Mrs Foxe also bequeathed 'unto some others five pounds six shillings and eightpence as shall be thought fit to have legacies at the discretion and disposing of my kind friends Mr Bourne, John Gilliam and Ralph Kenyon'.[83]

But these bequests—although they provide a further indication of her puritanism—hardly emphasise sufficiently the closeness of Judith Fox's relationship with the preachers. She was, as has been pointed out earlier, related by marriage to the puritan divine William Hinde and it was to him that she entrusted the wardship of her daughter Sarah. Mr Gee of Newton was made guardian of her son John. Finally, she made her 'dear friend and pastor' William Bourne supervisor of her last will and testament.

Other women made bequests to preachers in their wills. For example, Anne Baguley, of Newton, Manchester, who had been presented for her failure to kneel in the 1619 visitation, left the sum of 22s to the local minister, Mr Gee. The puritan divines Paget and Root were each given 10s. Martha Bate, the widow of a Chester physician, left the sum of 40s to Nathaniel Lancaster, later minister at Tarporley, when she died in 1628 and specifically requested him to preach her funeral sermon.[84] In 1647, when Mary Reynolds, widow, of Chester died, she bequeathed 20s each to the puritan divines John Glendole, Nathaniel Lancaster, Thomas Langley and Samuel Eaton. Glendole, minister at St Oswald's, Chester, was given a further £1 for his pains in preaching her funeral sermon. But Mrs Reynolds also left the very substantial sum of £100 to be:

given and distributed to certain godly persons who have been spoiled in their estates, at the discretion of my executors with the assistance of

82 Judith Fox had been twice charged with refusing to kneel at the communion in 1608 and in 1623.
83 William Bourne's puritanism has been noted elsewhere. The other two executors were also puritans. Gilliam, a tailor, was presented for non-kneeling in 1617, as was Kenyon in 1619 and 1633.
84 Her will provides a further indication of the solidarity of the puritan group in Chester. One of Mrs Bates' executors was Calvin Bruen, the son of John Bruen of Stapleford. Among the witnesses were William Trafford and Richard Golborne—both of whom, like Calvin Bruen, were later involved in the reception given to William Prynne in Chester in 1637.

Mr Lancaster, Mr Glendole, Mr Boat[85] and who else they shall consider meet to assist therein.

To conclude this examination of the financial support given by women to puritan ministers, the efforts of two more women patrons can be noted. First, in 1638 Dame Dorothy Leigh of Worsley gave the very substantial sum of £400, which was partly to be used to maintain a minister at Ellenbrook chapel. Her aim was to make the chapel independent of outside controls, for, as she herself declared, she was determined 'that the Bishop should have no hand in the putting in, placing or displacing of the minister there . . .'[86]

Second, one can note the importance of the contribution made by Lady Bowes of Coventry, later Lady Darcy, a sister of Sir William Wray, who was one of the key figures in the puritan organisation in Lincolnshire.[87] Lady Bowes invited the fiery Lancashire-born preacher Richard Rothwell to minister in the Barnard Castle area, where she had estates, and maintained him with a liberal stipend of £40 a year. But this was not the only example of her generosity. According to Rothwell's biographer, she 'gave about one hundred pounds per annum to maintain preachers where there were none nor any means for them, and all her preachers', he went on, 'were men silenced by reason of nonconformity'.[88]

5 Municipalities

So far in this chapter attention has been focused on individual lay patrons. But municipal patronage could be of equal or, in some circumstances, of more importance. In Congleton, Nantwich and Liverpool, for example, the town corporations were financially responsible for the maintenance of their curates and were therefore in a position to secure the type of puritan preaching they preferred.

In Congleton, first of all, the town account books record payments

85 This minister has not been identified.
86 E. Axon, 'Ellenbrook chapel and its seventeenth-century ministers', *Trans. Lancs. and Ches. Antiq. Soc.*, 38, 1920, 1.
87 Hill, *Tudor and Stuart Lincoln*, 116.
88 S. Gower, *Life of Richard Rothwell*, Bolton, 1787, 172–3. Rothwell (*c*. 1563–1627) later moved to Nottinghamshire and was popularly known as 'the rough hewer'. An eighteenth-century descendant of his, a Bolton wig-maker, is said to have boasted 'I'm a real Rothwell . . . a descendant of him that beat the devil'. (J. Clegg, *Annals of Bolton*, Bolton, 1888, 49.)

being made to preachers from as early as 1584.[89] And, very revealingly, in 1637 the corporation:

> ordered by common consent that Mr Redman, the minister of this town, shall have his former wages allowed him by the town well and duly paid him, he contenting himself therewith . . . and in default thereof a new minister to be chosen and provided by the mayor with the consent and privity of the aldermen and council of the town.[90]

Moreover—as has been shown—it was the corporation which financed the preaching Exercises which were held in the town from the 1630's.

Gentry-dominated Nantwich, too, was financially responsible for its curate, the latter being allowed—in the seventeenth century—£10 a year. Since the town was the paymaster, it would tolerate no interference in its choice of clergymen. As Thomas Mainwaring, Esq., put it in 1629:

> I do remember and will testify that these ministers which have been of the Nantwich church have been placed and displaced by the gentlemen and others of the town without the consent or approbation either of the Lord Bishop or any other person whatsoever.[91]

Similarly, in Liverpool it was an officially sponsored puritanism which developed in the town, a fact witnessed by the strict regulation of the Sabbath and by the corporation's control of its chosen clergy.[92] One seventeenth-century curate—Liverpool, like Congleton and Nantwich, had no rector or vicar, being only a chapelry—was even instructed in 1612 'to cut his hair of a comely and seemly length as best beseems a man in his place'.[93]

These cases suggest that the growth of puritanism in urban areas was not unrelated to a growing insistence on corporate independence. Congleton, Nantwich and Liverpool, or at least the influential citizens controlling them, were determined to maintain their autonomous position in religious affairs. Puritanism could easily enter into and colour these struggles. Urban puritanism and

89 R. Head, *Congleton Past and Present*, Congleton, 1887, 176–8.

90 *Ibid.*, 81. See also Stephens (ed.), *History of Congleton*, 209.

91 Quoted in J. Hall, *History of Nantwich*, Nantwich, 1883, 291.

92 The town's determination to be master of its own affairs is also seen in the control it exercised over its M.P.'s and in its preference for local men in this office. (W. D. Pink and A. B. Beavan, *The Parliamentary Representation of Lancashire*, 1889, 177–88.)

93 G. Chandler and E. Saxton, *Liverpool under James I*, Liverpool, 1960, 166.

municipal patronage of it, however, can be further illustrated by an examination of the available evidence concerning lectureships.

Lecturers should be viewed as public servants rather than as independent agents. Whether they were maintained by municipal salary, by public subscription or by private benefaction, they were in each case ultimately dependent upon lay support. The Laudian Peter Heylyn, in fact, denounced lecturers as mere puppets in the hands of their patrons. Lecturers, he wrote, were not:

> raised so much out of care and conscience for training up people in the ways of faith and piety as to advance a faction and to alienate the people's minds from the government and forms of worship here by law established. For these lecturers, having no dependence upon the bishops, nor taking the oath of canonical obedience to them, nor subscribing to the doctrine and established ceremonies, made it their work to please those patrons on whose arbitrary maintenance they were planted, and consequently to carry on the puritan interest which their patron drove at. A generation of men [he went on] neither lay nor clergy, having no place at all in the prayers of the Church, where we find mention only of bishops, pastors and curates, nor being taken notice of in the terms of law as being neither parsons nor vicars, or, to speak of them in the vulgar proverb, neither flesh nor fish nor good red herring.[94]

Despite exaggeration and bias, Heylyn made a valid point. An examination of lectureships tells us as much about patronage as about the preachers themselves.

Liverpool, for example, had its lectureship by the early 1590's. Discussion is known to have taken place in the town assembly in 1591 about:

> Master Carter, the preacher, concerning what allowance the inhabitants of this town will, of their own voluntary and free wills, yield and give towards his better maintenance, in consideration of his great good zeal and pains in bestowing the good talent to him given by God by his often and diligent preaching of God's Word amongst us . . .[95]

This was in June. By October of the same year the decision had been made for the corporation to augment his salary by £4.[96]

The responsibility for paying the lecturer, however, seems to have alternated for a time between the town and the people themselves. In 1593, for example, the lecturer was being maintained by volun-

94 Heylyn, *Cyprianus Anglicus*, 1671, 9.
95 J. A. Twemlow (ed.), *Liverpool Town Books*, Liverpool, 1935, II, 596–7. 21 June 1591.
96 *Ibid.*, 608.

tary contributions only.[97] By the 1620's, however, the Liverpool lectureship was recognised as a munical appointment with a salary of £25 a year.[98]

Liverpool—as we have seen—already had a preaching curate, similarly appointed by the corporation, but his services, combined with those of the regular lecturer, were still apparently insufficient to satisfy the town's demand for sermons. Additional preaching, therefore, in the form of another weekday lecture, was requested in 1629 in a council petition to the Bishop of Chester. 'They humbly entreat your Lordship,' so the councillors wrote, 'to grant them so much favour as to afford them once a month two sermons upon some weekday which they shall think most fit and convenient.'[99] The request was granted, but with the proviso that a watch was to be kept to prevent the lectureship from becoming a puritan base. Be this as it may, however, the surveillance cannot have been very rigid, for the weekday lecturers appointed included Richard Mather of Toxteth and Mr Kay of Walton, a later Presbyterian.[100]

Although far less is known of its origin and development, at Chester also it would appear that, by the 1580's at least, there was a municipal lecturer established in the city. The weekly lecture was held on Fridays at St Peter's, and in the corporation orders for 1583 it was laid down:

for the better furniture of the auditory at lecture time . . . [that] all the citizenry of this city, being not justly accustomed to the contrary, [were] to make their repair to every such lecture and there during the same in decent order to remain.[101]

In the 1630's John Ley, minister of Great Budworth, is known to have been giving the weekly lecture, and it was in respect of these visits that he was rewarded in the will of John Ratcliffe, the puritan brewer and alderman of Chester, in 1633.

97 Twemlow, *op. cit.*, 656.
98 Chandler and Saxton, *op. cit.*, 93–4. J. Touzeau, *The Rise and Progress of Liverpool*, 1912, I, 158–9.
99 Touzeau, *op. cit.*, 171.
100 Davies, *Toxteth Chapel*, 13; *V.C.H. Lancs*, VIII, 20. Richard Mather also preached a lecture in the nearby parish of Prescot. According to his biographer, this was held 'once a fortnight on the third day of the week'. (*Life of Richard Mather*, 8.) In 1633, however, a charge against Mather includes the information that he 'read *weekly* lecture at the parish church of Prescot'. (York. 1633 vis. RVIA 23, f. 345v.)
101 Cambridge. Gonville and Caius MSS, 197, f. 56. 'Orders set down by Mr Robert Brerewood, mayor of Chester. 25 October 1583.'

At Bolton—as befitted this 'Geneva of Lancashire'—there was also a lectureship in existence by the middle years of Elizabeth's reign. The most prominent, but probably not the first, of the Bolton lecturers was James Gosnell. Gosnell, originally from Leicestershire, settled in the town early in the 1580's and remained there until his death in 1622. Little is known, unfortunately, about the maintenance of the lectureship, but from the available evidence it would seem that Gosnell depended upon the voluntary gifts of his hearers rather than upon a fixed stipend from the town government. Be this as it may, Gosnell's income was clearly more than adequate and he became a prosperous man. To the Palatinate loan raised in the diocese in 1620 he contributed £2, while the vicar of Bolton paid only 6s 8d. In 1622, when further contributions for the same cause were demanded, Gosnell gave £5 and the vicar 13s 4d.[102] A further indication of Gosnell's prosperity is provided by the fact that he himself placed the Bolton lectureship on an even firmer footing by a bequest made in his will in 1622. He left lands yielding an annual income of £30, which was to be given to 'a preacher, as distinct from the vicar of Bolton, to preach in the parish church upon every Lord's day and Monday'.[103]

Gosnell's will reminds us that in Bolton, as in Liverpool, the lectureship was designed to supplement the efforts of the incumbent. Gosnell himself had fulfilled this role, since Ellis Sanderson, vicar from 1598, was also a puritan and was presented in 1605 for his failure to wear the surplice.[104] Seventeenth-century vicars of Bolton, as well as the lecturers, were consistently puritan in temper, but one preaching minister in the town was clearly not enough to satisfy the demand for sermons.

The documentation relating to the lectureship at Preston is similarly inadequate. It would seem likely, however, that the lectureship grew out of the stipendiary curacy which the corporation had maintained in the town since at least the early sixteenth century. At what date the transition occurred it is impossible to say, but that it was after 1590 is certain, since in that year the Lancashire J.P. Edmund Hopwood had told the Archbishop of York that there was no place which would be more suitable for a weekly lecture than Preston.[105]

102 Scholes, *History of Bolton*, 255.
103 F. R. Raines (ed.), *Notitia Cestriensis*, Chet. Soc., old series, 8, 19, 21, 22, Manchester, 1845–50, II, Pt. I, 9–10.
104 Chester. 1605 vis. EDV 1/14, f. 94v.
105 *Kenyon Mss.*, H.M.C., 601. 23 February 1591.

The town is known to have moved towards puritanism in the early seventeenth century, and in the 1630's Christopher Hudson M.A.—whose sermons have been quoted elsewhere in this book—is known to have been lecturer there and still held the post in 1642 when the Protestation returns were made.[106] Although his office was a municipal appointment, Hudson was at the same time also indebted to individual patrons.[107]

That puritanism in Preston gained strength from the patronage of an influential group is made clear in the letters of James Martin, the vicar who was ejected from his living in the 1620's. For Martin claimed that he had been opposed in Preston by 'the principal puritans, my adversaries the richest men of the town', and in a letter to Secretary Windebank proceeded to describe them.[108]

First in rank was Sir Gilbert Hoghton, who according to Martin had maliciously insinuated to the King that he had acquired his living by simony. But Sir Gilbert, Martin wrote, took more immediate measures to remove the unwanted incumbent. He took advantage of an unpaid debt owed to him by Martin and had the latter imprisoned in Lancaster gaol, and with the vicar thus safely out of the way Sir Gilbert, we are informed, took further steps to sequester him of his living.

The chief of Martin's local opponents in Preston, however, was William Lemon, 'a burgomaster of Preston and ringleader of my adversaries, the chief fomenter of Inskip[109] with money and a great supporter of schismatics in that county'. Martin's opponents also included Adam Mort, 'another rich burgomaster there of the same tribe who contributed largely in the suit against me by Inskip'.[110] Then there was Edmund Werden, 'a rich shopkeeper, a conventicler, a malapt censurer of my sermons'. Also listed in this same dramatis personae of the plot against Martin was Roger Langton, who, although not a puritan himself, 'yet at their instance when he was mayor entered the church while I read divine service and inhibited me . . .' The others listed were John Singleton, Seth Bushell, William Haydock, Henry Breres and John Jameson—all

106 H. Fishwick, *History of Preston*, Rochdale, 1900, 425.
107 To William Haydock, for example, to whose son Hudson was godfather.
108 P.R.O. State Papers Domestic. SP 16/236/42. 11 April 1633.
109 Inskip, it will be remembered, was the puritans' rival clergyman to Martin.
110 Some account of Adam Mort is given in E. Axon, 'The Mort family in connexion with Lancashire nonconformity', *Trans. Unitarian Hist. Soc.*, 3, 1925, 135–47. Adam Mort, gent., in his will of 1630 made a substantial bequest towards the maintenance of a preacher at Astley chapel.

of them wealthy citizens of Preston.[111] 'They are twelve in all,' the embittered Martin concluded, 'whereof Lemon, Mort and Bushell may well spare a thousand pounds apiece [i.e. in fines], Sir Gilbert and Packer[112] £1,500 apiece and the other six among them £3,000.'

6 *The godly discipline: the alliance between patrons and preachers*

A study of patronage reminds us that puritanism and its attendant godly discipline took firmest root not when they were in opposition to influential laymen but when they had their support. Adam Martindale at one time almost made up his mind to minister in Yorkshire, since 'the noble spirit of the gentry and others in those parts was very attractive.'[113] And such success as the puritan divine John Murcot achieved in the Cheshire parish of West Kirby owed much, as we have seen in an earlier chapter, to the co-operation of the local magistrate.

Richard Eaton, minister at Great Budworth, took occasion in a funeral sermon preached in 1614 to exhort the civil authorities to impose the godly discipline.

> You that are rulers in this our Israel [he declared], execution of justice upon riotous and inordinate livers is for the present a sweet-smelling sacrifice unto God . . . It will procure you even in this life many sweet blessings from above. And thereafter it shall be a crown upon your heads.[114]

With a similar end in view, Gilbert Nelson, rector of Tatham, in Lancashire, reminded the J.P.'s in 1634 of the co-operation which ought to exist between ministers and magistrates.

> You are the hand of the commonweal [he wrote], whereinto God has put his sword of justice. Ministers [he continued] are the mouth of the Church: where we see abuses in either we may only reprove and complain. You have power to correct.

---

111 When the minister, John Inskip—then of Garstang—died in 1631, he nominated as the executors of his will William Werden, draper, and William Haydock, salter, of Preston. (T. C. Smith, *Records of the Parish Church of Preston*, Preston, 1892, 51.)

112 John Packer's opposition to Martin had been shown at Ormskirk, where the latter had been Queen's Preacher.

113 *Life of Adam Martindale*, 76.

114 Eaton, *A Sermon preached at the funeralls of . . . Thomas Dutton*, 1616, 21.

The conclusion, therefore, was obvious. 'A mutual help may work a better reformation.'[115]

Christopher Hudson, lecturer at Preston, was even more explicit on this question in a sermon he preached before the Lancashire assizes in 1632. Hudson's argument was that without a godly magistrate:

the kingdom of darkness is exalted in the kingdom of light . . . the magistracy and ministry as the elm and the vine, the garden and the bees, flourish pleasantly together, or else decay and wither together.

Lest any of the judges and assembled company had still not taken the point, Hudson repeated his central message in even more explicit terms:

Excommunication [he confessed] is but . . . a hurtless thunderbolt; we are forced for help to have recourse to your secular arm, the sword of Gideon . . .

It is religion only [he went on] which knits together the heterogenean parts of any kingdom . . . Oh remember, therefore, I beseech you, that you owe your lives, your gowns and all that you have to the Gospel, and if our ministry should not keep the consciences of men in awe, neither you nor the world should endure one year longer, and if you assist not religion you should cut off your left hand with your right.[116]

What Hudson and other preachers were doing, then, was to remind those in authority of the social benefits of puritanism. John White, for example, at one time vicar of the Lancashire parish of Eccles, spoke of that 'general barbarousness [which] did abound in the people until it pleased God by the ministry of his Gospel to convert them'. He contrasted the situation which prevailed in parishes unserved by a puritan minister with that to be found in:

other parishes where the gospel has been taught being reduced to civility.

There is but one way to prevent the danger that may be feared from this generation and their practices [he went on], and that is that sin be severely punished and a preaching ministry settled, as much as is possible, in all places of the land, and painful preaching effectually maintained against the manifold discouragements of this iron age,

---

115 Preston. Quarter sessions. QSB 1/136/27, 1634. Professor Walzer contends that 'by the 1640's the minister had become the adviser and exhorter of the gentleman in office, training him in the style and method of conscientious activity'. (*Revolution of the Saints*, 233.)
116 Preston. DP 353. Hudson's MSS sermons, ff. 47v and 54.

whereby the subject may be taught obedience, and ignorance and superstition—the root of disloyalty—may be expelled.[117]

There is no doubt that arguments of this kind found acceptance
in those circles the preachers were trying to convince. Members of
the Elizabethan Privy Council, for example, encouraged the planting
of puritan preachers in Lancashire, since they knew that the latter
would 'instruct the people the better to know their duty towards God
and Her Majesty's laws and to reduce them to such conformity as
we desire'.[118] Again, those members of the Lancashire gentry who
petitioned on behalf of the county's puritan preachers in 1604 emphasised that 'by means of their good doctrine and example we have
found it more easy to contain the common people in the duties of
their subjection and loyalty to the supreme power'.[119] Fear and dis-
trust of the common people—the 'many-headed monster'— haunted
politicians and administrators, as it did preachers, and it was this
meeting point which often helped to make possible an alliance
between them.[120] Even if magistrates themselves did not actively
espouse puritanism, then at least they could recognise the advantages
of its imposition on society.[121]

Puritanism, they saw, stood for order, and the godly discipline
was a means of achieving that end:

Of all commonwealths [wrote Christoper Hudson, to confirm this im-
pression], that is most miserable where wickedness is committed without
punishment in great and small.
    It is a miserable thing [he went on] to live under tyranny, where
nothing is lawful, but far more miserable to live under anarchy, where

117 White, *A Defence of the Way to the True Church*, 51; *The Way to the True
    Church*, 111, and epistle dedicatory—both in White's collected *Works*,
    1624.
118 Peck, *Desiderata Curiosa*, 113.
119 P.R.O. State Papers Domestic. SP 14/10/62.
120 The subject is discussed in C. Hill, 'The many-headed monster in late Tudor
    and early Stuart political thinking', in C. H. Carter (ed.), *From Renaissance
    to Counter Reformation: Essays presented to Garrett Mattingly*, 1966.
121 'The very existence and spread of Puritanism in the years before the
    Revolution,' declares Walzer, 'surely suggest the presence in English society
    of an acute fear of disorder and "wickedness"—a fear . . . attendant upon
    the transformation of the old political and social order.' (Walzer, *op. cit.*,
    302.)
        Few members of the gentry were presented as puritans in the visitations.
    But there is no means of knowing—and this would be more meaningful
    —how many of them set up puritan devotions in their own households.

nothing is unlawful, for then the commonwealth falls down as a house without foundation.

It was absolutely necessary, then, that restraints should be placed upon the people. 'Happy is that commonwealth,' wrote Hudson, in contrast to the picture already presented, 'where the bridle of government is put upon the people, which otherwise is as a beast with many heads.'[122] The view of the Cheshire gentleman John Bruen was remarkably similar. He wrote in his commonplace book that 'it is a miserable thing when governors humour the people in their sins. Sin will take heart by the approbation of the meanest looker-on, but if authority once second it it grows impudent.'[123]

Bruen's own views on puritanism and the godly discipline, like those of the preachers, were based on conviction. But although identity on this point was desirable, it was not essential. To a considerable extent, magistrates and ministers faced common problems and had common objectives, and in the pursuit of the latter expediency and sincerity could quite easily merge.

The issue which brought the civil authorities and the preachers closest together was that of Sunday observance, for there was considerable agreement amongst them that the profaning of the Sabbath threatened the well-being of society besides that of religion. The views of the preachers on this point were repeatedly expressed, but what must be noted here is that their forthright opposition to Sabbath-breaking often corresponded closely with the line taken on this question by municipal authorities and by the J.P.'s.

Official concern for religion was shown, for example, at Chester in the corporation's orders for 1583. Significantly, the list began with regulations concerning attendance at church. It was ordered:

first that every citizen, their wives, journeymen and apprentices, except as by sickness or other lawful cause can excuse them, upon every Sunday and holy day repair to every their parish churches both at morning and evening prayer and to such time and church where by tolling of the bells they shall perceive any sermon to be preached. And there quietly and orderly to attend during the time of the sermon . . . upon pain of such

---

122 Hudson, 'The happines of governement', ff. 48, 49, 48v. Cf. Nicholas Bownde in *The True Doctrine of the Sabbath*, 1595: 'the chiefest end of all government [is] that . . . the parts of God's true worship might be set up everywhere and all men compelled to stoop unto it and make profession of it at leastwise in the outward discipline of the Church . . .' (Quoted in R. Cox, *The Literature of the Sabbath Question*, I, 150.)

123 British Museum. Harleian MSS 6607, f. 92.

fine, penalty and imprisonment as by the statutes, ordinances and injunctions thereof is in the case made and provided.[124]

Shopkeepers were banned from trading on the Sabbath.

Similar regulations were made in Liverpool and Manchester. In Liverpool a fine of 1s was imposed on those who indulged in work or recreation on Sundays.[125] In Manchester in 1611 fruit dealers, pedlars and street traders were forbidden to sell their wares on the Sabbath.[126] The authorities at Warrington in 1617 placed a ban on Sunday amusements and recreations.[127]

Attempts to keep order on Sundays were also made by the J.P.'s, though since the Commission of the Peace—especially in Elizabethan Lancashire—invariably and unavoidably included many with pronounced Roman Catholic sympathies, a united front on this question was not possible. But be this as it may, the records of the quarter sessions show that some effort was being made to deal with the problems posed by Sunday amusements and trading.

At Preston, for example, in 1590, the J.P.'s took action against one Christopher Poulton of Merscough, alehouse keeper, for holding a bear-baiting. At the quarter sessions at Wigan in 1592 the assembled J.P.'s dealt with 'Richard and William Buckley, of Charnock Richard, labourers, and Richard Sharrock, of Heath Charnock, butcher, [who] on the day called Relic Sunday[128] 1592 in time of divine service at Chorley played at bowls'.[129]

But even more explicit than these cases were the regulations concerning Sunday observance made by the J.P.'s at Manchester in 1616. It was ordered on this occasion that:

> there be no wares or victuals sold or showed upon any Sunday, necessary victuals only excepted, and that no butcher sell any flesh upon any Sunday after the second peal ended to morning prayer nor yet at any time in the afternoon upon the Sabbath day.

Second, the J.P.'s laid down that:

> no householder after the beginning of the last peal to morning prayer suffer any person, not being of the household, to eat, drink or remain

---

124 Cambridge. Gonville and Caius MSS 197, f. 55.
125 Chandler and Saxton, *op. cit.*, 94.
126 *V.C.H. Lancs.*, IV, 199.
127 R. S. France (ed.), *The Statutes and Ordinances of Warrington, 1617*, in *A Lancashire Miscellany*, Rec. Soc. Lancs. and Ches., 109, 1965, 29.
128 The third Sunday after midsummer day.
129 J. Tait (ed.), *Lancashire Quarter Sessions*, Chet. Soc., new series, 77, Manchester, 1917, 11, 64.

in their house in time of divine service, but shall shut their doors up, to the end that all persons within the said house may go to the church.

Ample provision was made for the enforcement of these regulations. Offenders against the first order were to be bound over to appear at the next assizes. In connection with the second regulation, any alehouse which remained open and entertained guests during service time was to be closed down and never re-licensed. It was also ordered that anyone found wandering abroad during time of service was to be fined twelve pence for the offence and be required to appear at the next assizes.

The J.P.'s at Manchester on this occasion also made determined efforts to come to grips with the problem of Sunday recreations. It was expressly stated in the orders that there was to be 'no piping, dancing, bowling, bear- or bull-baiting or any other profanation upon any Sabbath day in any part of the day or upon any festival day in time of divine service'.[130] It was these regulations, forbidding amusements at any time on the Sabbath—not only during service time—which prompted James I's Declaration of Sports for Lancashire in 1617.

7 The scope and results of patronage

An attempt has been made in this chapter to describe the origins of the various forms of patronage which puritan ministers enjoyed in the diocese of Chester. In this context the respective contributions of the aristocracy, gentry, merchants and tradesmen, women, and collective bodies such as merchants' companies and town corporations have been discussed. The forms which this patronage took—bequests, maintenance of chaplains and lecturers, the use of advowsons, and (less tangibly) the defence of preachers in difficult times—have been considered, and also, so far as it is known, the motivation.

Enough has been said to indicate the importance of patronage in the development of puritanism in the diocese. It is equally clear, however, that this patronage was mainly local in range and character. There was, as we have seen, no concentration of ecclesiastical livings in the hands of a single patron of any class. Huntingdon controlled no Northern advowsons. The Earls of Derby had few at their

130 E. Axon (ed.), *Manchester Quarter Sessions, 1616–23*, Rec. Soc. Lancs. and Ches., 42, 1901, 15–17.

command, and this was true of the gentry. In consequence, the
scope of patronage was more limited than was often the case elsewhere in the country.[131]

Since this was so, the results of patronage were also limited. The
patrons whose activities have been discussed in this chapter had
little influence outside the diocese and were thus unable to promote
ministers to positions of national importance. This was true even of
the Earls of Derby, who were county aristocracy, lacking and—at
least in the case of the seventh Earl—not wanting influence at court.
John Broxopp and Christopher Hudson, both of whom enjoyed
Lord Strange's patronage, remained purely local figures. Only Charles
Herle, presented by the Stanleys to the rectory of Winwick, rose
to take his place amongst the leading puritan divines of the 1640's,
and this advancement was in no way the result of his patron's
efforts.

Most of the puritan ministers of the diocese of Chester, then,
remained only locally significant, like their patrons. Of the 160 divines
in the diocese during this period, only twenty-four got into print.
And of these, at least eight made their mark outside the diocese. Such
was the case with Nicholas Byfield, Samuel Clarke, Christopher
Goodman, Thomas Case, Richard Mather, John and Thomas Paget
and John White. A further indication both of the inability of the
puritan divines of the diocese to attract national notice and become
leading spokesmen of English puritanism and also of the limited
influence of their patrons is provided by the list of those who preached
before the Long Parliament.

Only four of the puritan clergy of the diocese of Chester preached
before the House of Commons in the 1640's.[132] The first to do so was

131 The character of Catholicism in Lancashire was similar. According to
   W. R. Trimble, 'Lancashire had few Catholics of any wealth and none of
   national standing. Its strong Catholicism was a very localized matter'
   (Trimble, *The Catholic Laity in Elizabethan England*, Cambridge, Mass.,
   1964, 206–7.) Cf. J. B. Watson, 'The Lancashire gentry and public service,
   1529–58', *Trans. Lancs. and Ches. Antiq. Soc.*, 73–4, 1966, for a further
   indication of the essentially local influence and interests of the gentry.
132 Much useful background material on this subject is provided by H. R.
   Trevor-Roper, 'The fast sermons of the Long Parliament', in *Essays in
   British History*, ed. Trevor-Roper, 1964, although the author is primarily
   interested in showing that the fast sermons were instruments of policy. It
   is the details of sponsorship given in the Commons' journals with which
   we are concerned here.
   On aspects of the fast sermons, see also E. W. Kirby, 'Sermons before the

Thomas Case, whose provocative sermons preached in Manchester in the late 1630's have been commented upon elsewhere. It was upon 26 October 1642 that Case preached before the House on *Gods Rising, His Enemies Scattering,* thanks largely, it would appear, to Sir William Brereton (1604–61), the Parliamentary general and county member for Cheshire.[133] It was usually the preacher's original sponsor who was later instructed by the House to convey its thanks to the minister for his services. In this instance it was Brereton whom the House requested to thank Thomas Case. Case again preached before the House of Commons on 9 April 1644, a fast sermon entitled *The Root of Apostacy and Fountain of True Fortitude.* Again it was Brereton who conveyed to the preacher the thanks of the House. In view of this link between sponsor and preacher, it was particularly appropriate that Case should have been chosen to preach on the day of thanksgiving (19 February 1646) for Brereton's taking of Chester.[134]

Charles Herle, rector of Winwick, preached a fast sermon before the House of Commons on 30 November 1642, a sermon which was afterwards printed as *A Payre of Compasses for Church and State.*[135] Herle's sponsor was John Moore (*c.* 1599–1650) of Bank Hall, the member for Liverpool and one of a family which was intimately involved in the growing puritanism of that town. It was Moore who later had a share in introducing Richard Heyricke as a preacher before Parliament. But this was not until 27 May 1646, when Heyricke preached a sermon subsequently published as *Queen Esthers Resolves.* As in Herle's case, Moore was again requested to thank the preacher on behalf of the House.[136]

Like Case, Herle and Heyricke, John Ley of Great Budworth was a member of the Assembly of Divines, and he too preached before the House of Commons. His sermon—on *The Fury of Warre and Folly of Sinne*—was given on 26 April 1643. Unlike the three others, it was to a non-local patron that Ley was indebted for his appearance before the House. It was, in fact, Sir Robert Harley (1579–1656), the county

Commons, 1640–42', *American Hist. R.,* xliv, 1938–9, and J. C. Spalding, 'Sermons before Parliament, 1640–49, as a public puritan diary', *Church History,* 36, 1967.

133 Brereton's patronage of ministers in the diocese has already been noted.

134 In the absence of Brereton, the vote of thanks was on this occasion made by Francis Rous, the member for Truro.

135 In June of the following year Herle preached before the House of Lords a sermon later printed as *Davids Song in Three Parts.*

136 It was Mr Ashurst—Governor of Liverpool from 1645—whom the House had asked to invite Heyricke to preach before them.

L

member for Herefordshire and an active puritan, who originally sponsored him and later conveyed to him the thanks of the Commons for his preaching.[137]

But the experience of these four ministers—members of the Westminster Assembly and preachers of fast sermons before the House of Commons—was the exception, not the rule. At local level, preachers in the diocese of Chester could become well known, and patronage— that exercised by John Bruen, for example—might be able to triumph. Outside the diocese this was rarely the case, and most of these preachers and their patrons lived and died in provincial obscurity.

137 Ley's dedication of his book *A Patterne of Pietie*, 1640, to Lady Brilliana Harley, Sir Robert's wife, has been noted earlier in the present chapter.

Chapter Five

Catholic and puritan

I was but lately removed into these parts, and one of special note fore-warned me I should be crucified as Christ was between two thieves: the Papist [and] the Puritan . . .

Richard Heyricke, *Three Sermons preached at the Collegiate Church in Manchester . . .*, 1641, epistle dedicatory

1 *Puritan versus Catholic*

Although in this study attention has been focused on puritanism, it should never be forgotten that the opposite religious extreme still remained widely acceptable in the diocese of Chester throughout the whole period which has been reviewed. But Catholicism provided more than a mere background. In the first place, there is no doubt that the presence and challenge of the old religion acted as a constant stimulus to the rise and consolidation of puritanism. Second, it is equally clear that the Catholic problem directly influenced the attitude of the authorities towards puritanism. Faced with the disturbing threat of Catholicism, Church and government needed an alliance with the puritan preachers. So there came to exist, at least throughout Elizabeth's reign, a working co-operation between the authorities and the puritan clergy.

The peculiarities of the situation in the diocese of Chester, then, must be borne in mind when exploring the relations between puritans and Roman Catholics. Generally speaking, the puritan onslaught on Catholicism was a part of the wider, official campaign to extirpate the old religion. Sixteenth- and seventeenth-century puritan divines in the diocese, therefore, could rightly claim to be the champions of the reformed order. It was only when the attitude of the authorities to both puritanism and Cathlocism began to change as the seventeenth century progressed that such ministers were left more or less out on a limb.[1]

---

1 In a sermon preached in 1637 Richard Heyricke took occasion to deplore the change in official attitude towards puritans. 'When drunkenness and blasphemy dare outface the pulpit,' he lamented, 'refusing puritans are put down, when recusant Papists are set in places of honour.' (Manchester Central Library. Worsley MSS, M 35/5/3/7.)

Puritan divines always provided the most determined opposition to Catholicism.

> The quarrel betwixt Rome and us [declared Richard Heyricke in 1639] is not like Caesar and Pompey, which should be chief, but like that betwixt Rome and Carthage, which should not be. If Rome prevail [he went on] we shall not stand; and if we prevail they should not stay long.[2]

Not surprisingly, it was the puritan clergy of Lancashire, where Catholicism was strongest and most extensive, who were the most conspicuous in the attack on the old religion and its adherents.

As far as the printed works of Lancashire divines are concerned, the earliest onslaughts on the Catholic position was made by Oliver Carter, Fellow of the Manchester College, in his *Answere . . . unto Certaine Popish Questions and Demaundes*. Published in 1579, the book attempted to expose the errors of Popery—an urgent task—'for partly by these Popish whisperers [i.e. the priests], and partly for lack of true and faithful teachers, shipwreck is made of the Gospel of Christ'.

It was in fact the Catholic priests—his professional opponents, as it were—whom Carter most bitterly opposed. He denounced them for leading laymen astray, and dwelt particularly on their failure to make the scriptures available for general reading 'lest the misty clouds of your superstitious devices would vanish away if the bright beams of Christ his Gospel might shine in simple men's minds'.[3] And, like any Protestant, Carter attacked Catholic belief in the mass and poured scorn on the trappings of the old religion. 'For all such kind of trumpery,' he concluded of the Roman Catholic Church, 'be her very marks. As there was none of these toys in the primitive Church, neither in any true reformed Church since that time.'[4] But although Carter's criticism was general, his purpose was local and immediate. He wrote 'for the comfort of my poor neighbours, whom I perceive to be over much seduced—the more it is to be lamented—by these and such like popish devices'.[5]

John White, vicar first of Leyland and then of Eccles, continued this attack on Catholicism; his treatise outlining *The Way to the True Church*, first published in 1608, was explicitly directed 'to the

2 Heyricke, *Three Sermons* . . ., 164
3 Carter, *op. cit.*, 8.
4 Carter, *op. cit.*, 34
5 *Ibid.*, epistle dedicatory.

glory of God and confusion of Papistry'. But like Carter, White had local conditions in mind as he wrote:

> They that live in these parts among people popishly addicted [he declared] live in the midst of Sodom. And let it be observed if all disorder be not most in those parts among us where the people are most Pope-holy—other parishes where the Gospel has been taught being reduced to civility and the rest that swarm with priests and recusants remaining savage and barbarous . . .[6]

He continued the same theme in his later *Defence of the Way to the True Church*:

> The condition of the place where sometimes I lived [he wrote] [was] transported with much superstition and importuned with Romish priests and their books, and sometimes their libels [were] set upon our church doors.[7]

Again, as in Carter's case, it was not so much the local recusants themselves but their priests whom White most bitterly opposed:

> I speak not of simple recusants [he wrote] but of fugitive Jesuits and seminarists that have renounced their allegiance to their natural sovereign and made themselves the Pope's creatures and vowed him blind obedience in all that he shall command them. For many Papists [White was convinced] when their seducers are removed shall come home to obedience, and repenting them of their idolatry and superstition embrace . . . the religion established.[8]

To say the least, the opportunity for discrediting Catholicism afforded by the Gunpowder Plot was not missed by the puritan divines. William Leigh, vicar of Standish, was the first of the Lancashire preachers to use this event as a weapon against the Papists, his sermon on *Great Britaines Great Deliverance from the great Danger of Popish Powder* being published in 1606.

The history of post-Reformation Catholicism in England, Leigh contended, was the record of a continuous conspiracy. But even against this long record of Popish treachery the Gunpowder Plot, Leigh argued, stood out as the most infamous action of all:

> We should have seen these miscreants [he declared] never sated with the blood of the saints till they had changed our religion for

6 White, *Works*, 1624, III.
7 *Ibid.*, epistle dedicatory.
8 White, *Defence*, epistle dedicatory.

superstition, our knowledge for ignorance, our preaching for massing, our subjects for rebels, our councellors for conspirators . . .[9]

Much later in the century—on 5 November 1638—Richard Heyricke, Warden of Manchester, preached on this subject in the Collegiate Church. 'Believe me,' he declared, 'I cannot think on the horror of the treason but my spirit is moved within me, my indignation is stirred as often as the very mention of the name Papist is made.'[10] He continued the same theme in a sermon preached on 5 November the following year:

> To speak of the murders, massacres, treacheries, cruelties of the Papists [Heyricke declared], it is so large a field that entering into it I know not where to begin nor where to end. I could, my brethren [he went on], show you a sea of blood flowing from the sea of Rome.[11]

Later still, on 5 November 1644, Charles Herle, rector of Winwick, preached before the House of Commons the sermon later printed in the following year as *Davids Reserve and Rescue*. The defeat of the conspiracy in 1605, Herle emphasised, had not removed the Popish threat. The danger still remained:

> The same brood of enemies [he declared], that then dared venture but on an undermining, dare now attempt an open battery. Nor are they without their pioneers too still at work and now busier than ever in digging vaults such as may reach from Oxford, Rome, Hell to Westminster, and there to blow up if possible the better foundations of your Houses—their liberties and privileges.[12]

The battle between puritanism and Catholicism, however, in Lancashire was not fought over purely religious issues. As some of the extracts quoted above suggest, the religious struggle tended to merge with the simultaneous puritan assault on ignorance, superstition and pagan survivals. 'This county,' wrote Thomas Fuller of seventeenth-century Lancashire, 'may be called the cock-pit of conscience, wherein constant combats between religion and superstition' took place.[13] Lancashire, for example, provides some of the clearest supporting evidence for Professor Trevor-Roper's point that the persecution of witches was particularly intensive in areas where puritanism and Catholicism were in collision.[14]

9 Leigh, *op. cit.*, epistle dedicatory.
10 Heyricke, *Three Sermons . . .*, 55.   11 *Ibid.*, 140.
12 Herle, *op. cit.*, epistle dedicatory.
13 Fuller, *History of the Worthies of England*, 124.
14 H. R. Trevor-Roper, 'The European witch craze in the sixteenth and seventeenth centuries' in *Religion, the Reformation and Social Change*, 1967. But

Although Catholics and puritans were poles apart in religion, what helped to intensify the desperate rivalry between them was the issue of the godly discipline:

> For my own part [wrote the puritan divine John White], having spent much of my time among them, this I have found, that in all excess of sin, Papists have been the ringleaders, in riotous companies, in drunken meetings, in seditious assemblies and practices, and in profaning the Sabbath, in quarrels and brawls in stage plays, greens, ales, and all heathenish customs. The common people of that sort [are] generally buried in sin, swearing more than can be expressed, uncleanness, drunkenness, perfidiousness, vile and odious, their families untaught and dissolute, their behaviour fierce and full of contumely injury [and] inhumanity...[15]

Of all the 'heathenish customs' encouraged or condoned by Catholics, that which the puritan divines most opposed was Sabbath-breaking. The inevitable result of this common practice, so the puritan ministers of Lancashire argued in 1590, was that:

> the youth will not by any means be brought to attend the exercise of catechising in the afternoon, neither the people to be present at the evening service, so that it were hard for the preacher to find a competent congregation in any church to preach unto.[16]

Puritan divines firmly believed that this result had come about through deliberate policy on the part of the papists. Not surprisingly, they viewed James I's Declaration of Sports for Lancashire as being an edict of toleration for Papists and a deliberate attempt to undermine the authority of the preachers. 'Who are greater maintainers of this impiety [Sunday pastimes] than our recusants?' wrote William Harrison, for example, in *The Difference of Hearers*. 'By these means they keep the people from the Church and so continue them in their Popery and ignorance.'[17] Attendance at church could be increased only by removing the distractions which kept people away.

---

see A. Macfarlane, *Witchcraft in Tudor and Stuart England*, 1970, 186–91, who argues against a direct correlation between witchcraft persecution and religious tension.

15 White, *The Way to the True Church*, in his *Works*, 1624, 111–12. Precisely the same argument was used by William Harrison in his work *The Difference of Hearers* . . ., 1614, 400.

16 F. R. Raines (ed.), *Miscellany*, vol. V, Chet. Soc., 2.

17 Harrison, *op. cit.*, epistle dedicatory.

By opposing sports and pastimes, then, puritans hit at Catholicism. The use of this policy can be well illustrated by the case
of John Bruen of Stapleford, Cheshire, for although puritan opposition to Papists came mainly from Lancashire—where the problem
was greatest—it was not restricted to that county. Like the Lancashire preachers of 1590, Bruen found that in his own parish of
Tarvin he was faced with the dual threat of Popery and profaneness.
So, in order to obstruct celebrations around St Andrew's day, for
example, Bruen:

> observed many years together to invite two or three of the best affected
> preachers in the diocese that spent most of three days in preaching and
> praying in the church so as the pipers and fiddlers and bearwards and
> players and gamesters had no time left them for their vanities, but went
> away with great fretting, and yet multitudes of well-affected people filled
> the town and the church and that with much rejoicing . . .[18]

And in 1603 Bruen's servants were charged with throwing down
maypoles and crosses 'because they saw much abuse of those things
by many of the people'.[19]

At a rather later date Adam Martindale led a no less determined
attack on maypoles and their supporters. Preaching a sermon on the
text 'How long, ye simple ones, will you love simplicity?' (Proverbs,
1, 22), Martindale:

> calmly reproved their folly in erecting a maypole in that way they had
> done, told them many learned men were of opinion that a maypole was
> a relic of the shameful worship of the strumpet Flora in Rome, but
> however that was, it was a thing that never did, nor could do good,
> [and] had occasioned and might occasion much harm to people's
> souls.

Martindale's wife, however, took more practical action. 'Not long
after,' Martindale tells us, 'my wife, assisted with three young
women, whipped it down in the night with a framing saw, cutting
it breast high so as the bottom would serve well for a dial post.'[20]

Puritan divines were adamant that with the Catholics there could

---

18 Hinde, *Life of John Bruen*, 90. This description of Bruen's activities was
approvingly quoted as late as 1845 by the Rev. Alfred Hewlett of Astley,
Cheshire, to support his own efforts to prevent the annual Wakes holiday
from being wholly wasted 'in riotous mirth'. (Hewlett, *Christian Cottager's
Magazine*, I, 1845, 241–3.)
19 Chester. Quarter sessions records. QSF 1/80, 1603.
20 *Life of Adam Martindale*, 157.

be no accommodation; the gulf separating them from the true Church was too great to be bridged.

> As the difference is real and of long continuance [wrote John White], so is there no hope to reconcile it. The Papacy that stands in opposition against us was brought in by Satan at the first and is still continued only to seduce the world. And what fellowship [he asked] has righteousness with unrighteousness? What communion has light with darkness? Or what concord has Christ with Belial? Or the temple of God with idols?[21]

But White, like other puritan divines, had great faith in the efficacy of preaching, and believed that by this means some at least of the Catholic laity could be won over to the reformed religion.

> The Protestant ministry has not been fruitless among the people [he declared]. . . . Many people have joyfully received the truth and acknowledged the errors wherein the guile of seminarists has held them and many that appeared to be sound Catholices have done this.
>   Popish superstition [White concluded] would soon be rooted out there and those locusts soon blown away if the word were effectually preached among them.[22]

But the puritan argument in favour of preaching as an antidote to Catholic superstition was nowhere more explicitly and eloquently stated than by George Walker. Like John White, Walker, in his *Exhortation for contributions to maintain preachers in Lancashire,* showed that he was convinced that the ignorance of the people and the lack of preaching were closely connected. Walker was himself a native of Lancashire and, recalling his own experience of the county, declared that:

> I myself do know and can name, for instance, if need require, divers parishes which within my memory were so deeply plunged in super-stition, and even drowned in ignorance, that the name of a preacher was as much scorned of many as the name of a babbler and of some as much hated as the name of a heretic. But now of late years [Walker wrote] I have seen with my eyes such a wonderful alteration wrought by God's grace and blessing accompanying the labours of some holy and godly preachers sent among them . . .[23]

Puritan criticism of Catholicism, then, was not purely negative and vindictive in purpose. 'I do not wish their punishment,' wrote

21 Heyricke, *Three Sermons* . . ., 104–5.
22 White, *Defence*, 51.
23 Walker, *Exhortation*, 18.

Oliver Carter, for example, 'but desire their reformation.'[24] More informal methods, however, than public preaching were used by puritan ministers to win over members of the Catholic laity. For instance, in Elizabeth's reign use was made of private conferences. Some Cheshire recusants, for example, were ordered to confer with the puritan divine Christopher Goodman 'for their better resolution in matters of religion wherewith they are entangled'.[25] Edward Fleetwood of Wigan, too, used this method, and John White advocated its extension.[26]

But there is no evidence to show that this method—like the sermons preached by puritan divines to their literally captive audience of imprisoned recusants—was attended with any success, and the ministers themselves soon tired of it.[27] Some of the puritan divines, therefore—especially in the seventeenth century, by which time they had had a long experience of failure—despairing of ever winning over the Catholics to their side, abandoned the attempt altogether. Instead of trying to advance their cause they adopted a defensive policy, aiming only to preserve the identity of the godly element in their charge and thus in practice to segregate the Catholics.

Richard Heyricke—who in his day was undoubtedly the leading spokesman of puritanism in Lancashire—was one who advised the godly puritans to ostracise all Catholics.

> Have no converse [he declared], no acquaintance, no familiarity, no friendship, have nothing to do with Papists. Depart from them that you be not partakers in their sins. They are of an infectious nature [he went on] and a man cannot touch pitch and not be defiled by it.
>
> I pity those that have Papists lying in their bosoms [he continued], those children that have Popish parents, those servants that have Popish masters, those tenants that have Popish landlords, those poor neighbours that have great Popish friends.[28]

---

24 Carter, *Answere . . . unto Certaine Popish Questions and Demaundes*, epistle dedicatory.

25 York. 1578 vis. RVIA 8, ff. 10–10v, 16v, 36.

26 Letter from Fleetwood to the Lord Treasurer, 12 October 1590. B.M. Add. MSS 48064, ff. 68–9.

27 White, *Way to the True Church*, epistle dedicatory. Edward Fleetwood found recusants 'contemptuous of the due order of conference'.

Private conferences of this kind were similarly unsuccessful in the West Riding of Yorkshire—an area whose religious development was not unlike Lancashire's. (H. Aveling, 'The Catholic recusants of the West Riding of Yorkshire, 1558–1790', *Proceedings of the Leeds Phil. and Lit. Soc.*, x, 1963, 256.)   28 Heyricke, *Three Sermons . . .*, 98–9.

This was in 1638. In the previous year John Broxopp, vicar of Orms-kirk, was said to have preached a similar sermon in which he laid down that 'a Protestant that married with a Papist was damned, or to that effect'.[29]

2 *Parochial studies of the conflict*

The struggle between puritans and Catholics can be illustrated best, perhaps, by examining in detail the situation in individual parishes. For this purpose, as far as Lancashire is concerned, the predomi-nantly Catholic Fylde provides the most interesting examples.

Looking at Garstang first of all, we find that this was a recusant stronghold throughout the period under review, large numbers of Catholics being presented in almost every visitation. In 1605, for example, 190 recusants in the parish were named.[30] Catholicism here, organised on a household basis, survived all attempts to overthrow it, a fact which is made clear in a presentment in the 1619 visitation. In that year Anna, wife of John Butler of Kirkland in Garstang parish, was charged 'for being of bold, insolent and offensive behaviour in maintaining of Popish superstitions and making choice of Popish recusants to be her servants'.[31] Moreover, the Catholicism of the parish—as the same visitation records show —was reinforced by the ministrations of seminary priests. William Walmsley and Henry Butler, gent., were presented for 'christen-ing their children privately and, as is thought, by Jesuits and seminarists'.[32]

Given this situation, it is not surprising that when in 1599 the four Queen's Preachers for Lancashire were appointed, one of them —William Forster D.D.—should have been settled at Garstang. Nor is it surprising that Forster's preaching and attempts to impose orthodoxy—with a puritan bias!—prompted extreme reaction amongst the Garstang Catholics.

On one memorable occasion, while Forster and the pursuivant of the Ecclesiastical Commission were in Garstang opening proceed-ings against the recusants of the district, an organised assault was made upon them.[33] Bishop Vaughan of Chester was quick to inform

29 Chester. Consistory Court papers. EDC 5, 1637. Deposition of Peter Cropper.
30 Chester. 1605 vis. EDV 1/14, ff. 176–8.
31 Chester. 1619 vis. EDV 1/22, f. 144.
32 *Ibid.*, f. 145v.
33 P.R.O. State Papers Domestic. SP 12/275/64, 1.

Cecil of the outrage. He wrote to him on 16 September 1600 and described how:

> about twenty persons, all in armour with muskets and other weapons, marched through the town to the vicar's house, where they purposed to have massacred Her Majesty's preacher, the vicar and one of the messengers attending on the Ecclesiastical Commission here for some service that he had done in that part of the country.[34]

Despite the efforts of the Queen's Preacher and of successive vicars, the Garstang area remained relatively unaffected by the Reformation even in the second half of the seventeenth century. Isaac Ambrose, appointed vicar in 1654, reflected thus upon the hopelessness of the task before him:

> In so great a parish [he wrote], consisting of fourteen or fifteen hamlets, and containing many thousands of people in it, I shall willingly undertake to do what I can but not to do all that a pastor ordinarily ought to do, for it is beyond me. If the adverse party—for there are multitudes of Papists with us—think there is work enough for four or five priests who have their constant residence in that parish, what work may you imagine for one Gospel minister, especially having no assistant at all, nor knowing for the present, notwithstanding his desires and endeavours that way, how he shall be able to procure one.[35]

Poulton-le-Fylde, like Garstang, was a parish which was dominated by the old religion. Large numbers of recusants were regularly presented at the visitations, and the Catholic rites and ceremonies were still clandestinely performed. In 1619, for example, a group of six Papists were charged that they 'have their children baptised by unlawful ministers', while in the same year Alice, wife of John Davie of Carleton, was presented 'for pulling down the corpse of Richard Silcock, deceased, as they were going with the dead corpse to the church to have them kneel at a cross'.[36] In 1633 William Cotton, 'being a layman, [was presented] for making graves in the night for recusants and burying them'.[37] Six recusants had been previously presented—in 1623—on the charge that they 'deprave publicly the religion now established and openly maintain Popery, wearing crosses in their hat as badges thereof'.[38]

34 *Salisbury Mss,* H.M.C., x, 315.
35 Ambrose, *Three Great Ordinances of Jesus Christ,* 1011–12.
36 Chester. 1619 vis. EDV 1/22, f. 150v.
37 York. 1633 vis. RVIA 23, f. 225.
38 Chester. 1623 vis. EDV 1/25, f. 29.

As at Garstang, seminary priests were present in this parish. In 1604, for example, John Whiteside, John Kisbrowe, Edmund Russell and Mistress Collas of Marton were 'suspected to relieve seminary priests and Jesuits'. Mistress Singleton, Janet Kirkham, widow, and Ellen Richards, widow, were similarly charged, and William Russell of Marton 'had a priest taken in his house'.[39]

Vicar of Poulton from 1582 was Peter White, a nonconformist presented in several visitations.[40] His refusal to use the sign of the cross in baptism—as we have seen—caused many of his parishioners to have their children baptised outside the parish. But their resistance to their puritan vicar was shown in other ways as well. For example, Catholic women were apparently refusing to be churched by him. In 1623 it was said of Isabella, wife of Richard Silcock, that she was 'now relapsed and become a great recusant, [and that she] refused to be churched [and], as is thought, was churched by a priest'.[41] She was by no means alone, however, in taking this stand. Ten others, in fact, were similarly charged in the same visitation.

Resistance was also expressed in the parish's refusal to accept responsibility for providing the sacramental bread and wine, for in 1623 the wardens were presented on the charge that they 'do not provide bread and wine at the parish charge at Easter according to the Book of Common Prayer and canons'.[42]

Presentments for Sabbath-breaking at Poulton seem to have occurred fairly regularly in the visitations—in 1608, 1611, 1614, 1619 and 1623—which may represent an aspect of an attempt by White alone, or along with sympathetic churchwardens, to impose the godly discipline. The tone of at least some of these presentments does suggest a puritan inspiration. In 1611, for example, two men were charged 'for keeping pipers . . . on the Sabbath day and drawing the people from the church'.[43] While in 1619, a group of five were presented as 'tablers, carders, players at shuffleboard, and bowlers upon the Sabbath day in the afternoon'.[44] But in the

39 Chester. 1604 vis. EDV 1/13, ff. 198v–199.
40 White was still vicar in 1650, in which year the Commonwealth Church surveyors noted that 'the present incumbent and minister there is Mr Peter White, formerly an able and painful minister, but now very aged and infirm'. (*Commonwealth Church Survey*, 151.)
41 Chester. 1623 vis. EDV 1/25, f. 28v.
42 *Ibid.*, f. 28.
43 Chester. 1611 vis. EDV 1/17, f. 134.
44 Chester. 1619 vis. EDV 1/21, f. 25v.

absence of further background information it would be unwise, perhaps, to press the point too far.

Certainly, however, recusancy was not the only problem facing the puritan incumbent of the parish. In remote rural areas such as this, folk-lore and superstitions were so deeply ingrained that their overthrow was almost impossible; witchcraft was a feature of every-day life. In Poulton in 1611, for instance, one Robert Hey was presented 'for witchcraft, sorcery and telling fortunes, being called the Wiseman of the Fylde'.[45] Clearly, in situations such as this, superstition rivalled religion, and there was a real danger that figures like Hey would become leaders of opposition. And so, as we have seen, the puritan effort to overcome ignorance and super-stition often, and easily, merged with the assault on Catholicism. Significantly, Edward Fleetwood, vicar of Kirkham, wrote of Lancashire that 'no parts in England has had so many witches, none [is] fuller of Papists'.[46]

The situation at Kirkham—the adjacent parish—was, in fact, similar to that prevailing at Poulton. This parish, too, was over-whelmingly Catholic in inclination, a fact indicated, for example, by the presentment of some 160 recusants in the 1619 visitation.[47] Kirkham was in the gift of Christ Church, Oxford, and the conflict between the successive puritan incumbents it appointed and their stub-bornly conservative parishioners is repeatedly expressed in the records.

James Smith—one of the authors of the 1590 description of the religious state of Lancashire—was vicar from 1585 to 1591, and his relations with the parish were far from cordial. The churchwardens —favourers of Catholicism themselves—were clearly doing all they could to obstruct the vicar's attempts to establish the reformed religion. In 1590 they were presented for failing to list the recusants of the parish and for neglecting to collect from them the weekly fines for their absence from church. Smith, on the other hand, was himself presented on account of the fact that 'divers have died whom he has not buried, being required'.[48]

The vigorous attempt to introduce the reformed religion to the parish is known to have continued during the years 1594–98, when Nicholas Helme was vicar. In 1598 Helme was presented for failing

45 Chester. 1611 vis. EDV 1/17, f. 134.
46 Fleetwood, *A Declaration of a strange and wonderfull Monster born in Kirkham parish in Lancashire . . .*, 1645, 4.
47 Chester. 1619 vis. EDV 1/21, ff. 29–32.
48 York. 1590 vis. RVIA 11, f. 71v.

to wear the surplice, for omitting to use the sign of the cross in baptism and for withholding the communion from notorious offenders.[49] But Arthur Greenacre, who succeeded Helme as vicar, can hardly have been any more acceptable to the parish. There seems, in fact, to have been almost a mass boycott of the parish church and vicar in operation at this time, for in 1605 no fewer than sixty-one people were presented 'for not christening their children at their parish church'.[50]

In Kirkham, then, what was clearly taking place was a struggle for control of parochial affairs, a struggle which was constantly embittered by religious differences. The records of a case heard by the Consistory Court in 1638–39 provide the clearest indication of the situation in the parish.

On the one side, the case involved the vicar, Edward Fleetwood, a determined and uncompromising nonconformist who offended the parish by such actions as his refusal to wear the surplice and by his abbreviation of the Prayer Book services. On the other side, it involved the select vestry of the 'Thirty Men' of the parish[51] and the churchwardens they appointed.

Each aspect of Fleetwood's nonconformity was listed in the articles against him. One of the charges, however, declared that he had:

> several times locked yourself within the church and put your key into the church door on the inside to keep out the aforesaid churchwardens and such workmen as they desired to employ about the church's repair . . . [and that he] abused them and called them factious and turbulent fellows, thieves and robbers, and threatened to keep them out with a cudgel, and gave them much scandalous and opprobrious language and told them they should not proceed in any business there without your consent.[52]

---

49 Chester. 1598 vis. EDV 1/12, ff. 116–17.
50 Chester. 1605 vis. EDV 1/14, ff. 186–7.
51 The 'Thirty Men' 'formed a standing council representing the fifteen townships of Kirkham parish . . . The oath which they took was administered by the civil and not the ecclesiastical authority, and once elected, they held office for life or until they desired to resign. On a vacancy occurring in their number, the remainder selected the new member; they were above the churchwardens, whom they appointed, and acted as guardians of the parish property . . .' (R. Cunliffe Shaw, *History of Kirkham in Amounderness*, Preston, 1949, 138.)

Their activities are documented in R. Cunliffe Shaw (ed.), *Records of the Thirty Men of the Parish of Kirkham*, Kendal, 1930. Select vestries also existed at Garstang, Preston, Lancaster and Goosnargh.
52 Chester. Consistory Court papers. EDC 5, 1638–39. Article 12.

The explanation of the friction became clearer as the case progressed. To the 'Thirty Men' Fleetwood was a troublesome innovator who was exceeding his powers. To the vicar, on the other hand, the select vestry, by their persistent independence and by leading the resistance against him, had arrogated a position to which they were not entitled. He therefore opposed them and resisted such schemes of theirs as repairing the church, 'holding their pretended office or government to be unlawful', and because he was convinced that they were slandering him to the Bishop of Chester.[53]

To achieve any success in Kirkham, Fleetwood had seen that he had first to challenge and undermine the powers of the select vestry. The judgement in the case, however, went against him and he was ordered to pay his opponents' costs[54]—a result indicative of the changed official attitude to puritanism in the diocese. By this time, clearly, the ecclesiastical authorities considered aggressive puritan clergymen like Fleetwood to be a greater nuisance than their Papist parishioners.

But although in this instance he was defeated, Fleetwood did not cease to work against the Catholics. No opportunity was lost for discrediting the old religion and its adherents, a fact which can be illustrated by a fascinating anti-Popery tract which Fleetwood wrote in the mid-1640's.

This tract was entitled *A Declaration of a strange and wonderful Monster* and was published in 1646.[55] Its subject was the malformed child—'the face of it upon the breast and without a head'—born to Mistress Hoghton, a Catholic gentlewoman of Kirkham parish. According to Fleetwood the birth was undoubtedly a divine judgement against Catholicism, and it was the puritan's duty to publish it abroad 'that so all the kingdom might see the hand of God herein, to the comfort of his people and the terror of the wicked that deride and scorn them'.[56]

This task Fleetwood took up with his usual determination and enthusiasm. Dealing first in his pamphlet with the background to the event, Fleetwood described his parish as one which 'God has blessed with good ministers and some godly people—though but few—in it, who by the malice of wicked and profane wretches have

---

53 Responses 10 and 19.   54 *Records of the Thirty Men*, 29–32.
55 The tract–of which there is a copy in the British Museum (E.325(20))—
    consists of five pages of text and carries on its title page a crudely drawn
    picture of the main events in the story.
56 Fleetwood, *op. cit.*, 7.

been much abused heretofore'. Mistress Hoghton belonged to this
latter category. Her parents were both Papists[57] and she herself
married a Catholic and in her household defended the old religion
at all times.

> She has often been heard to curse against Mr Prynne, Mr Burton and
> Dr Bastwick and the Roundheads [wrote Fleetwood]. Also to revile the
> Parliament and say that she thought that the King and the bishops were
> the righter part of us . . . and that the puritans and Independents deserve
> all to be hanged . . .[58]

But of all these expressions, so hateful to the puritan Fleetwood,
one in particular stood out. Mistress Hoghton emphatically declared
that 'I pray God that rather than I shall be a Roundhead or bear
a Roundhead, I may bring forth a child without a head'.[59] In fact,
as we have seen, this is what was alleged to have happened.

It was the midwife—herself the widow of a previous vicar of
Kirkham[60]—who first informed Fleetwood of the monster's birth,
'declaring her opinion that she verily believed that it was the hand
of God upon her for those imprecations she wished upon herself'.
News of the event quickly travelled far and wide and came at
length:

> to the ears of some of the Committee. And for the further satisfaction
> of the truth thereof, Colonel Moore, an honest, godly gentleman and one
> of the committee, being there, it was desired he should send a letter to
> Mr Fleetwood, the minister of the parish, to know the certainty of it
> whether it was true or not . . .

The midwife confirmed her former testimony:

> yet, for better satisfaction, Mr Fleetwood caused the grave to be opened
> and the child to be taken up and laid to view and found there a body
> without a head as the midwife had said, only the child had a face upon
> the breast of it . . .[61]

Moving now from Amounderness to Warrington deanery, we
find indications of the collision between Catholicism and the
reformed religion at Prescot. This parish was similar to Kirkham
in more than one respect. Firstly, like Kirkham, its advowson was

---

57 Her mother cut off the ears of her pet cat and christened it Prynne.
58 Fleetwood, *op. cit.*, 6.   59 *Ibid.*, 6.
60 According to the tract, she was the widow of 'Mr Gattaker', but this is
   presumably a mistaken rendering of Arthur Greenacre M.A., Vicar from
   1598 to 1627.   61 Fleetwood, *op. cit.*, 7.

M

held by a university college—in this case King's College, Cambridge. And like Kirkham, Prescot was a stronghold of Catholic recusancy. But in Prescot the main arena for the contest between Papist and puritan was not the church itself but the town grammar school.[62]

The grammar school at Prescot was situated immediately next to the parish church—a position which enabled the puritan vicar Thomas Meade to intervene in, and indeed control, its affairs.[63]

> Our forefathers [declared Meade in 1592] from all ages until this time in all places have founded schools by churches, that the schoolmaster and scholars at all times when it should seem to the minister expedient should be, as it were, at his elbow. And as the duty of catechising [the vicar went on], both by God's law and man's law, of necessity is laid upon the minister, so it is necessary and expedient that he should have them near him whom he should instruct in the principles of Christian religion.[64]

Catechising, the puritan vicar was convinced, was of the greatest importance.

> The only reformation that we can hope for in this corrupt country [he declared on another occasion] is that children be truly and diligently catechised, for I think that superstition is so grounded in the aged that without the rare mercy of God death must part.[65]

Not surprisingly, then, under the influence of the puritan vicar Prescot Grammar School became in that parish 'a great furtherance for religion'.

But this situation was strongly deplored by the leading recusant gentry of the area, who, to thwart Meade's intentions, proposed to gain control of the endowments and then remove the school to Eccleston, where it would be out of the vicar's reach.[66] Meade, however, had powerful allies—King's College and the Earl of Derby

62　There is an interesting discussion of this subject in F. A. Bailey, 'Prescot Grammar School in Elizabethan times: a sidelight on the Reformation in Lancashire', *Trans. Hist. Soc. Lancs. and Ches.*, 86, 1935.

63　Meade was vicar of Prescot from 1583 to 1616 and was a graduate of King's, Fellow from 1573 and Vice-Provost of that college for two years from 1582.

64　Bailey, article *cit.*, 10.

65　*Ibid.*, 3. Christopher Hudson, lecturer at Preston, declared in a sermon in 1633 that 'learning is the eye of pure religion, the bulwark of the gospel and the ruin of the Papacy . . .'. (Preston, DP 353, Hudson's MSS sermons, f. 26.)

66　Bailey, article *cit.*, 3.

—and the opposition failed to achieve its object. The grammar school remained under the vicar's control.

Virtually all the illustrations so far given of the confrontation of the two religious extremes have been drawn from Lancashire. It was there that Catholicism was strongest and most deeply entrenched; of all the diocese, it was Lancashire which always caused most anxiety to the government. Recusancy in Cheshire, on the other hand, was much less extensive. In 1575 Bishop Downham could name seventy-three notorious recusants in Lancashire but only eight in the neighbouring county. Similarly, in 1582, whereas as many as 428 recusants in Lancashire were presented, only forty-one were named in Cheshire.[67] The 'manifold enormities' of which the preachers complained in the description of 1590 were to be found in 'the most parts of Lancashire' but only in 'some parts' of Cheshire. But although it was less extensive, recusancy in Cheshire still constituted a problem which was by no means of negligible importance. As has been indicated in an earlier chapter, the distribution of recusancy in Cheshire closely resembled the pattern in Lancashire. It was in the predominantly arable western half of the county—especially the south-west—that recusancy was strongest. Not surprisingly, therefore, it is in this area that the clearest indications are given of the local conflict between puritan and Papist.

One such example—that of John Bruen and his determined efforts against Catholicism at Tarvin—has already been mentioned at an earlier stage in the present chapter. What Bruen was doing, as we have seen, was to impose his puritan beliefs upon a predominantly Catholic parish. A similar process was taking place at nearby Bunbury.

The puritan influence at Bunbury, as has already been suggested, was supplied by the succession of nonconformist divines appointed to the living by the London Haberdashers' Company. It was a difficult task which faced these ministers, for the parish was a stronghold of Catholicism.

Mr Wark has found that out of a total of 302 known recusants in Elizabethan Cheshire no fewer than seventy-five came from Bunbury.[68] And this state of affairs continued in the first half of the seventeenth century. 'You of this parish,' wrote Samuel Torshell, the Bunbury preacher in 1633, 'live mixed with so many Papists

67 The 1575 and 1582 figures are mentioned in K. R. Wark, *Elizabethan Recusancy in Cheshire*, Chet. Soc., third series, 19, 1971, 13, 45.
68 *Ibid.*, 132

as nowhere more in the whole county.'[69] His contention is illustrated by the fact that at the quarter sessions of 1638 a local ale seller, Richard Brock, and his wife were presented for keeping:

> in their alehouse, which is not fully five roods distant from the chancel door of the parish church, divers pictures and other Popish relics, and namely one great crucifix of brass or copper fairly gilded, which Brock audaciously and in contempt of the statute sometimes brings forth and openly sets before such as come to drink at his house, and sometimes saying these or words to the like effect, 'Now God be thanked, all things begin to come well on, and in time, no doubt will come to good end.'[70]

According to a census of 1640, the parish contained no fewer than 112 recusants.[71]

What impact the puritan ministers made upon this stubbornly conservative parish it is difficult to judge, for they constantly came up against a front of Catholic resistance. In 1590, for example, one Thomas Huckley was presented on the charge that 'he rails against the preacher',[72] while early in the seventeenth century John Walker was charged for 'usually going forth of the church when Mr Hinde preaches'.[73] In 1604, the inhabitants were collectively charged with being 'very negligent in sending their children and servants to be catechised'.[74] And in 1614 Thomas Palin and Humphrey Peacock were presented 'for speaking against religion and the ministers'.[75]

Resistance such as this constantly hampered the work of the puritan divines in Bunbury. The situation there was accurately summed up early in the seventeenth century by the pro-puritan William Webb in his *Itinerary* of Cheshire.

> If any do complain of the small crop of that great harvest [he wrote] and indefatigable pains there taken [i.e. by the preachers] let them impute it to the barrenness of the soil and want of due care and attention in the hearers and not to the labours of the workmen, whose comforts, I know, lie stored up in the conscionable discharge of the duties enjoined them.[76]

Puritanism here, then, remained primarily clerical.

69 Torshell, *The Saints Humiliation*, 14.
70 J. H. Bennett and J. C. Dewhurst (eds.), *Cheshire Quarter Sessions*, Rec. Soc. Lancs. and Ches., 94, 1940, 94.
71 Chester. Quarter sessions. QSF 4/44, 1640.
72 York. 1590 vis. RVIA 11, f. 141v.
73 Chester. Citation book. EDV 1/11, f. 38. Cases. 7 February 1614.
74 Chester. 1604 vis. EDV 1/13, f. 41.
75 Chester. 1614 vis. EDV 1/19, ff. 40v–41.
76 Daniel King (ed.), *Vale Royall of England*, 1656, ii, 105.

3 *Exhorting the magistrate*

Of the extent of recusancy in Lancashire and of the prevalence of Popish practices the puritan divines were in no doubt, and they took pains to bring to the notice of those in authority the deplorable condition of the county. A comprehensive report on the subject was drawn up by the Lancashire preachers in 1590. The document has been previously quoted in this study, but its importance is such that it requires a fuller and more detailed discussion at this point.[77]

The authors of this fascinating account of 'the manifold enormities of the ecclesiastical state' executed their self imposed task with remarkable thoroughness, giving full information, for example, about Popish fasts and festivals. A long account was also given of the Popish practices which frequently took place at funerals:

> Some use the Popish rites of burial towards the dead corpse at home [the preachers declared], as it were, burying it before it comes to the church.
> [Some] carry the corpse towards the church . . . [and] with haste prevent the minister and bury the corpse themselves because they will not be partakers of the service said at the burial . . .[78]

Even if the minister was allowed to conduct the service, it was often the case that many of the accompanying mourners would abruptly leave.[79]

Marriage ceremonies, too, provided similar opportunities for the intrusion of Popish practices. Nor was the baptismal ceremony allowed to remain free from Popish rites. Catholic parents, the preachers found, often left the church with their child while the christening was in progress, and whenever possible they registered their preference for the old forms.[80]

But the preachers gave detailed information not only about recusants but also about church Papists.

> Those that seem to be reformed from their former state of recusancy now come so seldom to the church [they declared], and they behave

---

77 The document is printed in its entirety in F. R. Raines (ed.), *Miscellany, vol. V*, Chet. Soc., old series, 96, Manchester, 1875. The description had, in fact, seventeen authors, who have already been listed in chapter two. One of them was a Cheshire divine—Henry Sumner of Disley.

78 In 1619 at Preston Thomas Johnson was presented on the charge that he had 'buried a child of his . . . and did refuse the minister and would not suffer him to come near the corpse to take the cross towel nor suffer him to say service, but pulled his gown in pieces'. (Chester. 1619 vis. EDV 1/22, f. 137v.)

79 Raines, *op. cit.*, 6.   80 *Ibid.*, 7.

themselves so unconformably, some with withdrawing them to the
farthest parts of the church from the Word, some bestowing themselves
in their own private prayers,[81] some talking or otherwise misspending
the time, some scorning of the public action of the ministry that their
presence does more hurt than their absence did.[82]

Since the receiving of the communion at Easter was one of the
tests of conformity used by the authorities, it followed that, to
avoid the penalties attached to recusancy, many would attend church
at that time who did not normally do so. Accordingly, the preachers
found that at the Easter communion they were more than usually
troubled by Popish disorders. 'Many intrude themselves to receive
the sacrament who before have not been present at divine service,'
they declared in their report, 'nor at any part of the prayers before
the communion.' They deplored the way in which the Papists
commonly behaved at the actual administration of the sacrament;
to them, the preachers declared, the ceremony was merely a dis-
tasteful necessity to be concluded as quickly as possible.[83]

One of the authors of this description of Lancashire was Edward
Fleetwood, rector of Wigan, and of all the puritan divines in the
county at this time none tried more determinedly to come to grips
with Catholicism. However, Fleetwood recognised that, to undermine the old religion, the active co-operation of the civil authorities
was essential. But since the Lancashire J.P.'s included many who
were of pronounced Roman Catholic sympathies, the Commission
of the Peace itself had first to be overhauled.[84]

Fleetwood was himself a J.P., and it was to a considerable extent
due to his efforts that the Lancashire Commission was indeed
reformed in 1587. The puritan rector wrote to the Lord Treasurer
in the autumn of that year describing the new situation:

First, for the whole body of the Commissioners [he wrote], they are so
proportionately allotted to the shire, as our store of sound men would

---

81 Puritans consistently opposed the practice of private prayer during Church services; every aspect of worship, they argued, was a congregational experience.
'This private praying,' wrote John Angier of Denton, 'is a sin, for it is a despis-
ing of the worship of God in hand.' (Angier, *Helpe to Better Hearts*, 75.)
82 Raines, *op. cit.*, 3.   83 *Ibid.*, 8.
84 In 1564 it was estimated that six of the Lancashire J.P.'s were favourable to
the reformed religion, while eighteen were definitely unfavourable. For
Cheshire eleven were said to be favourable and nine unfavourable. (M.
Bateson (ed.), 'Collection of original letters from the bishops to the Privy
Council, 1564', *Miscellany, vol. IX*, Camden Soc., 1893.)

any way afford. Five or four or three Justices at the least unto every hundred. By means whereof every hundred has its sufficient magistracy within itself, and every quarter sessions, entertaining the most of them two hundreds, a competent number of Justices and the general assizes a full furnished bench of worshipful gentlemen to countenance and attend that great and honourable service . . . where they employed themselves so thoroughly in the cause of religion [he went on] that there ensued a most plentiful detection of six hundred recusants by oath presented, as also the indictment of eighty-seven of them, as many as for the time could be preferred to the jury. And further a notification by oath of twenty-one vagrant priests usually received in Lancashire, and twenty-five notorious houses of receipt for them. Such are the manifold commodities which we feel already by Your Honour's most sound direction.[85]

Since there were not enough sound men to go round, arrangements had been made for the J.P.'s of Salford hundred—the most puritan area—to attend, and influence, quarter sessions elswhere in the county. In this way, as in others, Manchester was to lead the way in religion.

But to order reforms was one thing; to have them carried out was another—a fact which Fleetwood made clear in another report sent to the Lord Treasurer in 1590.[86] Less than half the recusants discovered by the bishop had been indicted by the J.P.'s, and earlier presentments were neglected through the failings of the Attorney, of the Clerk of the Crown and of Mr Walmsley, a Justice of Assize, whose own wife, according to Fleetwood, was a recusant.

But according to Fleetwood, Justice Walmsley not only favoured the Papists in this way but helped them still further by actively opposing the preachers.

He not only enforced in his public charge [we are told] the matters of nonconformity in a cross or a surplice against the preachers as high points of Martinism, meet to be equally weighed in the balance with Popish recusancy, as he affirmed, but indeed with a more unequal balance than he used to the recusants, he gave out special articles extracted out of the statute . . .

for proceedings to be opened against Fleetwood and others.

The need to spur on the civil authorities to take action against recusants in Lancashire was still felt by the puritan divines of the

85 The letter is dated 7 September 1587 and is printed in full in J. Strype, *Annals of the Reformation*, Oxford, 1824, Pt. 3, vol. 11, 488–94.
86 12 October 1590. B. M. Yelverton mss. Add. mss 48064, ff. 68–9. I am indebted to Professor Collinson for drawing my attention to this document.

county in the following century. For example, in 1641 Gilbert Nelson, rector of Tatham, urged forward the campaign against the Catholics:

> not as a busy informer, but in discharge of my conscience, having *cure animarum* within the parish, and out of an unfeigned desire of suppression of Popery—that great grievance of this kingdom which by conniving in this kind were likely to grow . . . [from strength to strength].[87]

Similarly, in a sermon preached in 1638 Richard Heyricke, Warden of Manchester, took occasion to exhort all those:

> armed with authority [to] go to the utmost of your authority; you that have power to punish [he went on], punish; to indict, indict; to present, present. Let not Papists rest in peace [Heyricke declared], in safety, in security by you . . .
>
>   You that keep back the sword from doing justice when God calls for it, you may yourselves die by the sword of God, and the blood of all that perish through your neglect shall lie upon your heads.[88]

4 The nature of the conflict

Two main points emerge from the detailed discussion given in this chapter. The first is that most of the evidence concerning the confrontation of the two religious extremes in the diocese had its provenance in Lancashire, where Catholicism was most deeply embedded. Where Catholicism was strongest there was most puritan opposition.[89] In Cheshire, on the other hand, where Catholicism was weaker and recusancy less extensive, puritan attacks on the old religion were neither so numerous nor so heated. Admittedly, criticism similar to that of the Lancashire divines was occasionally made by Cheshire ministers. William Hinde, for example, who approvingly described John Bruen's efforts to deal with the local Catholic problem at Tarvin, declared in more general terms that there was 'no religion so agreeable to carnal reason and fleshly wisdom, nor

87 Preston. Quarter sessions records. QSB 1/252/17. 1641.
88 Heyricke, *Three Sermons* . . ., 104–5.
89 This contention is not undermined by the fact that the most vocal criticism of the old religion came from the predominantly puritan Manchester area. For the divines of this region were concerned not only with their own immediate problems but with the fortunes of puritanism in the county as a whole. So, in leading the anti-Catholic campaign, the puritan divines of the Manchester area were only stressing yet again their leadership.

so pleasing and plausible to natural affection, as pharisaical devotion and hypocrisy and Popish superstition and idolatry'.[90] But such attacks were uncommon, and never occupied a central position in the published work of the Cheshire divines.

The second and more general point is that nearly all the evidence of rivalry between puritans and Catholics used in the present chapter is provided directly or indirectly by the clergy. As we have seen, puritan divines such as Oliver Carter, John White, William Leigh, Charles Herle and Richard Heyricke vigorously assailed the Catholic position in their published work. And in practice as well as in print it is the clergy's lead against local recusancy which has been observed in the Lancashire parishes of Garstang, Poulton, Kirkham and Prescot, and similarly in the Cheshire parish of Bunbury.

Virtually all we know about the struggle between puritanism and Catholicism, then, comes from accounts written by or about the clergy. Now it has already been suggested earlier in the present study that allowance must be made for the fact that the historian's knowledge of puritanism is inevitably to some extent distorted by the character of his sources. These, as we have seen, mainly concern the clergy, whose nonconformity was generally most conspicuous, considered most serious by the authorities and was most written about by themselves, their defenders and detractors.

So the question arises: was fierce opposition to Catholicism a constant feature of puritanism as a whole or only of clerical puritanism? Did Catholic observance actually increase in the seventeenth century, as writers such as Richard Heyricke would have us believe?[91] Certainly the puritan ministers' assault on Catholicism intensified as the seventeenth century progressed, and their attitude noticeably hardened. But was this because Catholics were more numerous? Or was it that the puritan divines from the 1630's, faced with 'Laudian' innovations, felt a more than usually imperative need to abuse and undermine Catholicism? At a time when the official attitude in the diocese to both puritanism and Catholicism was changing, were the puritan divines more than ever anxious to stress —and so, perhaps, magnify—the Catholic threat in order to avoid persecution themselves? Was the bogey of Catholicism as useful to

90 Hinde, *Life of John Bruen*, 16.
91 Heyricke claimed in 1641 that 'Popery has multiplied abundantly'. (*Three Sermons . . .*, epistle dedicatory.) But this statement was made, after all, on the very eve of the Civil War, which should at least make us pause before immediately accepting its truth.

puritan divines in the years before the Civil War as it was to
Parliamentarians during the event?

How did Catholic and puritan laymen treat each other? Did they
always remain socially separate? Did puritan laymen always 'marry
in the Lord' as the preachers advised, and similarly, did Catholics
like Mistress Hoghton of Kirkham invariably take a co-religionist as
a marriage partner?[92] Or did lay Catholics and puritans—especially
the conformists amongst them—in a way that was impossible for
their priests and pastors—often manage to achieve a peaceful
co-existence? Could the ties which united families and neighbours
sometimes pull more strongly than those of religion? How typical,
for instance, was Adam Mort of Preston, who, though a member of
a noted puritan family, at the time of the Civil War was held to be
a Papist?[93] And how common was it to find men like Roger Kirby,
Esq., one of the county members for Lancashire in the Long Parliament and a puritan, mixing with men like 'one Chorley of Chorley,
a seducing Papist', and to find, moreover, that the two were 'very
familiar together'?[94]

In view of the almost total lack of evidence relating to lay attitudes
on the subject, these questions must unfortunately remain wholly
or partly unanswered. But the very fact that such questions have
been posed is in itself important. They should at least remind us that
the evidence of strife between Catholic and puritan comes primarily
from the clergy, and that this may be only one part of the whole
picture.

92 Mistress Hoghton had been obliged to marry a Catholic, 'for none else were
admitted to come suitors to her'. (Fleetwood, *op. cit.*, 5.) At the opposite
extreme, John Broxopp of Ormskirk preached that 'a Protestant that married
with a Papist was damned'. But the sternness of his warning may in fact mean
that however much he disapproved of them such marriages were taking place.
      Intermarriage amongst puritans and Catholics was not unknown—see the
Life of Adam Martindale, 21–2—and Dr MacFarlane has even found
instances of Quakers marrying Papists in seventeenth-century Westmorland.

93 E. Axon, 'The Mort family in connection with Lancashire nonconformity',
Trans. Unitarian Hist. Soc., 3, 1925, 139.

94 This was in July 1642. The point is mentioned by K. J. Lindley in 'The part
played by Catholics in the Civil War in Lancashire and Monmouthshire',
M.A. thesis, Manchester University, 1965, 131.
      What Dr Lindley does—and this has a particular relevance to the sugges-
tions made above—is to disprove the puritan generalisation that all Catholics
were Royalists in the Civil War. He shows that, in fact, many Catholics
remained neutral and that this was the course taken by the majority of men
lower down the Catholic social scale.

Chapter Six

Conclusion

Using a wide range of manuscript and published sources, an attempt has been made in this book to explore and analyse the various aspects of the development, distribution, organisation and structure of puritanism in the diocese of Chester. Stage by stage, the conclusions suggested by these investigations can now be summarised.

To begin with, it was found that puritanism was far stronger in the archdeaconry of Chester than in that of Richmond; most of the illustrations used in the course of the book, then, were drawn from Lancashire south of the Ribble and from Cheshire. But the real stronghold of puritanism in the archdeaconry of Chester was in the east—a pastoral area with growing trade and industry. The local evidence suggested a distinct similarity between the distribution of puritanism and that of market towns—a finding which lends weight to the frequently made generalisation that puritanism took firmest root in the most thriving and economically developed parts of the country.

Within this eastern region of the diocese of Chester, Manchester in particular stood out for its size, prosperity and puritanism. Of all towns in this part of the North, Manchester had the closest and most regular ties with London, and like the capital in many ways took a lead in religious affairs, though on a local scale. For example, when preaching Exercises were set up in the 1580's, first in Lancashire and then in the whole diocese, it was mainly from the preachers of the deanery of Manchester that the initiative came. Similarly, it is possible up to a point to view the highly organised Presbyterian experiment in Lancashire in the late 1640's as an attempt to impose the religious sympathies of the Manchester area upon the whole county.

The eastern half of the archdeaconry of Chester was also an area of expanding population, a fact which is indicated, for example, by the large number of newly founded chapels situated there. So even before the much greater population expansion of the eighteenth and nineteenth centuries, ecclesiastical provision for the area had become strained and insufficient. Even in the seventeenth century the parish as such was incapable of containing all the developments which were taking place within it. And so for the historian of puritanism it is often the smaller units of chapelry and household which occupy the centre of interest.

Of course, the role of the clergy in the development of puritanism was very significant. Although it was not invariably the case, nonetheless clerical puritanism usually preceded lay puritanism. Above all, the puritan clergy were preachers and retailers of ideas; it was they who provided a reasoned justification of religious dissent. But despite the influence and importance of the puritan clergy, puritanism as a whole should not be mistaken for what, by the seventeenth century at least, was only one of its various forms. Ministerial self-esteem needs to be scrutinised and not uncritically accepted at face value. For allowances must surely be made for the fact that a disproportionate amount of our knowledge of puritanism is derived from accounts by or about the clergy, who, writing always from their particular standpoint, naturally tended to exaggerate their own contribution. In this respect, then, the sources produce distortions in the overall image of puritanism—distortions which older historians of the subject such as R. G. Usher did nothing to correct.

It would seem to be generally true that the clergy in the diocese of Chester, as elsewhere, exercised most influence in the earliest phases of the development of puritanism, for it was at this point that the challenge facing them was greatest, and then that there would be least independence amongst puritan laymen. But the role of the clergy tended to decline as puritanism consolidated itself. Lay intervention and participation were necessary to the success of puritanism —a fact which the clergy recognised and tried to bring about. The irony was that, by doing so, the puritan clergy weakened their own position. By the eve of the Civil War it was only in predominantly Catholic areas of the diocese of Chester that the puritan clergy were continuing to play their original and central role; elsewhere they had begun to share it with the laity.

This regional study has demonstrated that puritanism did indeed possess an 'inner momentum' of the kind described by Professor Collinson. Puritan members of congregations could be quite as capable as their pastors of exerting themselves and expressing their independence. Certainly the clergy in the puritan areas of the diocese of Chester did not have a captive audience. On the contrary, puritan laymen—often themselves educated and well steeped in the scriptures—were highly critical of unsatisfactory preachers. If their enthusiasm for sermons could not be quenched locally by their own minister, then they did not hesitate to look outside their own parish and follow other preachers.

Admittedly, complete and deliberate separatism was rare amongst the early puritans of the diocese of Chester, but at the same time it is clear that godly laymen were competent to organise their own devotional life. Conventicles, for example—a natural extension of the puritan emphasis on family-based religion and one of the surest signs of the vitality of lay puritanism—were regularly being held by godly laymen in the diocese, at least in the early seventeenth century.

Puritan laymen in the diocese, trained in household devotions and in conventicles, could easily take on a role similar to that officially given to the clergyman. Time and time again, laymen were presented in the Church courts not simply for meeting together to sing psalms, repeat sermons and the like, but for expounding doctrine. It is quite clear also that the godly layman played an important part in the movement towards Reformation and the establishment of the godly discipline. He could be a proselytiser in his own right.

It was mainly this stress on the value of household religion which gave to women a role of acknowledged importance in the development and organisation of puritanism. It was in the home that women had the greatest scope not only for participating in, but for actually shaping, the religious life of the family. This was the basis of their influence over religious affairs and it was largely unaffected by the fact that, numerically speaking, puritanism in the diocese was not dominated by women.

Seventeenth-century puritanism in the diocese of Chester, organised on a household basis, could—and often did—exist without the support of lay patrons. But clearly puritanism and its associated godly discipline were able to take firmest hold not when they were opposed by influential laymen but when they had their support. The puritan divines, therefore, were constantly reminding the civil authorities of the value—indeed, necessity—of co-operation. Puritanism, they emphasised, with its high moral tone and stress on discipline and order, conferred social benefits too great to be overlooked. Preachers and magistrates, after all, they argued, faced common problems and had common objectives.

Not the least of these shared objectives was the desire to come to grips with Catholicism—still widely acceptable in the diocese, particularly in the western half. Puritan divines—especially those in Lancashire, where the problem was greatest—always provided the most determined opposition to the old faith and its adherents and did all they could to provide information on the subject and to spur on the civil authorities to deal with the Catholic problem. The preachers' description of the religious condition of Lancashire in 1590—much quoted in this study—is the most notable sixteenth-century example of their activity in this field, but the need to exhort the magistrate to take action against Catholic recusants was still felt in the following century.

It may be, however, that the sources once again produce a distortion, by magnifying the rivalry between puritanism and Catholicism. Nearly all the evidence relating to the subject is provided directly or indirectly by the clergy, who, for 'professional' reasons, may have judged it expedient to exaggerate the Catholic threat which faced them. But in the absence of information about lay attitudes on this point, the suggestion made in chapter five that fierce opposition to Catholics may have been mainly a feature of clerical puritanism rather than of puritanism as a whole must remain a hypothesis.

The conflict between Catholicism and puritanism is one of the most fascinating aspects of the religious history of the diocese in this period. But Catholicism, it should be stressed again, did more than provide a mere background to the development of puritanism in this region. There is no doubt that the challenge of the old religion constantly promoted the rise and consolidation of the opposite religious extreme. And because of the peculiarities of the religious situation in the diocese of Chester, which removed most of the hostility that the ecclesiastical authorities might otherwise have been inclined to show, it was the puritans—in Elizabeth's reign at least —who emerged and were regarded as the champions of the reformed order. Clearly, situations such as this show the limited validity of the concept of a national and monolithic 'Puritan Movement'. The chronological and regional variations within puritanism were too significant to be ignored.

Puritanism in the diocese of Chester was not—and in the nature of things could not have been—entirely self-contained physically and intellectually. First, puritan ideas current in the diocese were not conceived in isolation nor in a vacuum but were derived largely from the ministers' university training and from the digested reading of nationally available religious literature. More than half the puritan divines of the diocese, it will be remembered, had attended either Oxford or Cambridge, and a survey of their libraries revealed that they were reasonably well read and up-to-date. From an ideological point of view at least, as Professor Collinson asserts, 'clerical puritanism as a cohesive, national movement was created in the universities'.[1]

Physically, too, the puritanism of the docese of Chester was not an entirely separate phenomenon. For one thing, the preaching resources of the diocese were strengthened by assistance from outside. The links between Lancashire and Yorkshire, for example, were strong and numerous in this respect, and instances were given earlier in the book of clergymen who divided their ministries between the two counties. But it was not only from Yorkshire that assistance of this kind came—a fact which is vividly illustrated by the activities of Thomas Case, who came to Lancashire in the 1630's from the diocese of Norwich to proselytise for the puritan cause.

The influence of London on the development of puritanism in the diocese of Chester was also considerable, and provides a further insight into the social and economic transformation which the capital was working in the country as a whole. London's impact on the nation, as Dr Hill and Professor Jordan have suggested, was scarcely less important from the religious than from the economic point of view. To begin with, London's extensive mercantile connections throughout the country offered valuable channels of communication which could be utilised for the propagation of the gospel. Merchants and tradesmen congregating in the capital were able to take full advantage of the 'puritan facilities' available there. Indeed, they could scarcely fail to be aware of them. And so we find that it was common practice for provincial traders to use their business visits to London as opportunities for sampling the rich fare of preaching and for buying the latest books and pamphlets. Then as now London was the main centre of the book trade.

London also, as the chief centre of English commercial wealth, was an important source of patronage. Occasionally, in fact, London merchant companies were in direct control of puritan preachers in the diocese of Chester, as was the case with the Haberdashers' Company and the living of Bunbury in Cheshire. But a more general indication of London's importance in this respect is provided by the fact that almost a third of Lancashire's charitable funds in the early modern period were donated by Londoners, especially by natives of the Northern county living in the capital. Here, then, is a further indication of the strong county loyalties explored by Professor Everitt.[2] George Walker, the Lancashire-born London preacher,

1 Collinson, *Puritan Movement*, 127.
2 See the titles by Professor Everitt listed in note 61 on p. 130.

knew what he was doing in the 1640's when he addressed his *Exhortation for Contributions to Maintain Preachers in Lancashire* to fellow Lancastrians amongst the metropolitan trading community.[3] At times such as these the national and regional strands in the history of puritanism begin to join together.

One particular instance which stands out in this respect occurred in 1637. In that year the puritan lawyer William Prynne, newly sentenced and mutilated in London, was taken through Chester on the way to Caernarvon, where he was to serve his term of imprisonment. The event did not pass unnoticed in Chester. Bishop Bridgeman wrote to Neile on 20 August 1637, describing how Prynne had been entertained in the city 'by four factious citizens with great solemnity'.[4]

So serious was their offence considered that they were dealt with by the High Commission. One of the offenders was Calvin Bruen, the son of John Bruen of Stapleford and lately Sheriff of Chester, and he confessed in examination before Bridgeman 'that he went out of the city and fetched Prynne in and bestowed wine upon him while he was there, and rode out with him when he went thence'.[5]

The charges against another of the offenders, Peter Ince, a stationer, are perhaps the most interesting, however, since as a distributer of books he was one of the main channels along which puritanism could spread in the Chester region. 'We have no other stationer in the city,' wrote Bridgeman, 'yet no Puritanical books [appear] but our citizens get them as soon as any, which I suppose come by his means, though he be so cunning as it will hardly be discovered.'[6] Further examination of Peter Ince revealed that he 'has been of ancient acquaintance with Prynne. For when Prynne was in the Tower of London upon his first censure for his *Histrio Mastix*, this Peter Ince visited him a prisoner there.'[7]

While Prynne was in Chester arrangements were made by his

3 See pp.131–2.
4 Document printed in *Cheshire Sheaf*, old series, III, 1882, 9. The whole episode is discussed in an article by Canon Blomfield: 'Puritanism in Chester in 1637', *Chester Archaeological Jnl.*, old series, III, 1885.
5 *Cheshire Sheaf*, old series, III, 1882, 31. These two letters of Bridgeman's, unless otherwise stated, are taken as the basis of this account.
6 Compare the charges made against Thomas Smith, the Manchester stationer, in 1638. P. 10.
7 From Ince's will, proved in 1648, we learn that his son was a preacher of God's word.

supporters to have his portrait painted by a local artist. Archbishop Neile wrote to Bridgeman on this subject in October of 1637.

> It seems that Pulford the painter [wrote Neile] is both painter and poet, and may therefore dare to say and do anything. I doubt not but there was much in it of his seeking to have Prynne's picture than he acknowledges in his examination which you sent me . . . I have sent process for the innholder where Prynne was lodged, where I find there was an assembly at prayers the morning that Prynne went from Chester.[8]

In the course of the investigations further names were added to the original list of offenders, and the Prynne affair ended with those involved being heavily fined and required to make public confession of their misdeeds. The portraits painted by Pulford the artist were ordered to be burnt.

An incident such as Prynne's reception in Chester provides an additional reminder that the puritanism of this region was not a self-contained, autonomous phenomenon. It was linked with external events and developments and at times, naturally, the regional and national aspects of puritanism tended to merge.

But for all this, the puritanism of the diocese of Chester—like its Catholicism—appears in the last analysis as primarily local in character—local in organisation, local in structure, and above all local in its impact. Most of the preachers in the diocese remained only locally significant, and for this state of affairs the character and scope of patronage were primarily responsible. Through effective and influential patronage came national notice for the puritan preacher. But most of those patrons whose activities have been described in an earlier chapter were able to exert little influence outside the diocese, since they were only minor figures themselves. The fact that only four of the puritan clergy of this region preached fast sermons before the House of Commons in the 1640's provides an eloquent comment on the limited national influence of both preachers and patrons from the diocese of Chester. Developments within the diocese did not exercise a decisive influence outside, and although about a sixth of the puritan divines of this area got into print, very few of their names occupy a central place in the national history of English puritanism.

8 Bradford MSS, Weston Park, Salop. 9/8. 14 October 1637.

N

Appendix

The university background of the preachers

1. Elizabethan Cambridge

College	1561–70	1571–80	1581–90	1591–1600
Emanuel				William Harrison, B.A. 1592, M.A. 1595. Richard Rowe, B.A. 1600, M.A. 1603.
Trinity	Peter Shaw, 1564. Giles Wigginton, B.A. 1569, M.A. 1572.		Lawrence Ambler, mat. 1588.	John Paget, B.A. 1595, M.A. 1598.
Christ's		John Jackson, B.A. 1573.	William Bourne B.A. 1589, M.A. 1592. Arthur Storer, B.A. 1590, M.A. 1593.	Robert Whittle, B.A. 1596, M.A. 1599.
Queen's	Edward Assheton, B.A. 1570, M.A. 1573.	William Lawton M.A. 1580. Richard Rothwell, B.A. 1581.		Thomas Ashall, B.A. 1594.
Magdalene			Joseph Midgley, B.A. 1585, M.A. 1588.	
St John's	Oliver Carter, M.A. 1563			
Jesus		Ralph Kirk, mat. 1576.		Thomas Dod, B.A. 1596, M.A. 1599.
Corpus Christi		James Hawkesworth, B.A. 1574, M.A. 1577.		
Pembroke			Edward Tacey, mat. 1588.	
Caius			John White, B.A. 1590, M.A. 1593.	
King's		Thomas Meade B.A. 1575, M.A. 1578.		

2 *Elizabethan Oxford*

College	*1561–70*	*1571–80*	*1581–90*	*1591–1600*
Brasenose[1]		*Anthony Calcott,* B.A. 1576, M.A. 1581. *William Leigh,* B.A. 1574, M.A. 1578. *Christopher Harvey,* B.A. 1581, M.A. 1585. *Robert Eaton,* B.A. 1577, M.A. 1587.	Nicholas Helme, B.A. 1583, M.A. 1585.	
Christ Church	*Thomas Elcock,* B.A. 1562, M.A. 1566.		*Thomas Cooper,* B.A. 1590, M.A. 1593.	
Exeter				*Nicholas Byfield,* mat. 1597.
Lincoln			*Richqrd Eaton,* B.A. 1586, M.A. 1589. *Peter Blinston,* B.A. 1586.	
New College		*Edward Hollinshead,* B.A. 1577, M.A. 1581.		
Queen's				*William Hinde,* B.A. 1591.
St Mary Hall			*Miles Aspinall,* B.A. 1581, M.A. 1584.	

1 The earliest divine known to have been educated at Brasenose is Christopher Goodman who graduated B.A. in 1541, M.A. in 1544 and B.D. in 1551.

3 *Early seventeenth-century Oxford*

College	*1601–10*	*1611–20*	*1621–30*	*1631–42*
Brasenose		Richard Mather, adm. 1618. Timothy Aspinwall, mat. 1620.	William Gregg, B.A. 1622. Isaac Ambrose, B.A. 1625. Adam Bolton, B.A. 1626. Edward Gee, B.A. 1630, M.A. 1636. Richard Holker, B.A. 1626.	James Bradshaw, B.A. 1634, M.A. 1637.
Christ Church	Richard Oseley, B.A. 1604. John Ley, B.A. 1605, M.A. 1608. Sabbath Clark, B.A. 1611.	John Glendole, B.A. 1620, M.A. 1625. Thomas Case, B.A. 1620, M.A. 1623.		
Exeter		Charles Herle, B.A. 1615, M.A. 1618. John Conney, B.A. 1616, M.A. 1620. John Gee, B.A. 1617, M.A. 1621.		
St John's		Richard Heyricke, B.A. 1619, M.A. 1622.	Robert Shaw B.A. 1626, M.A. 1629.	
All Souls			Nathaniel Lancaster, B.A. 1622.	
Balliol		Richard Wilson, B.A. 1618.		
Queen's		William Shenton, B.A. 1619, M.A. 1623.		

4 *Early seventeenth-century Cambridge*

College	*1601–10*	*1611–20*	*1621–30*	*1631–42*
Emmanuel		John Broxopp, B.A. 1616, M.A. 1620. Ralph Stirrop, B.A. 1618, M.A. 1621. Robert Parke, B.A. 1619, M.A. 1622.	John Breres, B.A. 1625, M.A. 1628. John Angier, adm. 1622.	John Harrison, B.A. 1637. Jeremiah Horrocks, mat. 1632.
Trinity	Thomas Paget, B.A. 1609, M.A. 1612. Robert Cademan, B.A. 1610, M.A. 1613.			
Christ's	Richard Redmaine, B.A. 1607, M.A. 1601, Matthew Clayton, B.A. 1611, M.A. 1614,	William Curwen, mat. 1616. Thomas Shaw, B.A. 1618, M.A. 1621.	Samuel Torshell, B.A. 1625, M.A. 1628.	
Queen's	John Davenport, B.A. 1608, M.A. 1611.		William Moston, B.A. 1624, M.A. 1627.	
Magdalene			Christopher Hudson, B.A. 1626, M.A. 1629. Richard Hollingworth, B.A. 1627, M.A. 1630. Henry Dunster B.A. 1631, M.A. 1634.	
St John's	James Langley, B.A. 1604, M.A. 1607. Andrew Wood, B.A. 1605, M.A. 1609. Hugh Burrows, B.A. 1612, M.A. 1615.	Robert Fogg, B.A. 1616, M.A. 1619. Thomas Rokeby, B.A. 1615.		
Peterhouse	James Hyet, B.A. 1611, M.A. 1614.			
Clare		William Horrocks, B.A. 1618.		
Sidney Sussex	Julines Herring, B.A. 1604.			
Trinity Hall		Samuel Dale, B.A. 1620.		

Bibliography

1 *Manuscript sources*

Chester, County and Diocesan Record Office:
   Visitation records. EDV 1/series.
   Consistory Court papers. EDC 5/series.
   Consistory Court books. EDC 1/series.
   Bishop's register. EDA 2/2.
   Bishop Bridgeman's register. EDA 3/1.
   Bridgeman's act book. EDA 3/2.
   Proceedings of the Commissioners in Ecclesiastical Sources. EDA 12/3.
   Parochial records. P series. Churchwardens' Accounts for Middlewich
      (P 13/22), Frodsham (P 8/13) and Chester St Oswald's (P 29/7).
   Probate records (for Cheshire only).
   Quarter sessions files. QSF series.

York, Borthwick Institute of Historical Research:
   Metropolitan visitations. RVIA series.
   High Commission act books. RVII HC AB series.
   Probate records—will of Joseph Midgley, formerly vicar of Rochdale,
      proved 1637.

Preston, Lancashire Record Office:
   Probate records. (For Lancashire only.)
   Quarter sessions records. Recognisances. QSB 1/series (includes
      petitions).
   Christopher Hudson's mss sermons. DP 353.

Leeds, Public Libraries, Archives Department:
   Archdeaconry of Richmond, churchwardens' presentments. RD/CB
      series.
   Cause papers. RD/AC series.
   Archdeacon's act book. RD/A6.

Manchester, Central Library, Archives Department:
   Worsley mss. Sermon notes taken by Mary Booth. M 35/5/3/7.

Manchester, Chetham's Library:
   Assheton mss.

Cambridge, Gonville and Caius College:
   ms 197. (Contains details of the system of preaching Exercises set up in
      the diocese of Chester in the 1580's and also the Chester Orders of
      1583.)

Oxford, Queen's College:
MS 280, ff. 173v–175. (Letters to Edward Fleetwood, rector of Wigan.)

Weston Park, Shropshire:
Bradford MSS. Correspondence of Bishop Bridgeman of Chester. Boxes
9/8 and 18/2.

London, Public Record Office:
State Papers Domestic.

London, British Museum, Department of Manuscripts:
Harleian MSS 165/21 and 22. (Matter relating to Calvin Bruen of Chester.)
6607. (Commonplace book of John Bruen of Stapleford.)
Additional MSS 48064, ff. 68–9. (Letter of Edward Fleetwood of Wigan.)

2 *Printed sources*

Axon, E. (ed.), *Manchester Quarter Sessions, 1616–23*, Rec. Soc. Lancs.
and Ches., 42, 1901.

Bailey, F. A. (ed.), *Prescot Records, 1477–1600*, Rec. Soc. Lancs. and
Ches., 89, 1937.

Bateson, M. (ed.), *Collection of original letters from the Bishops to the
Privy Council, 1564*, in *Miscellany, vol. IX*, Camden Soc., second series,
53, 1893.

Bennett, J. H. E., and Dewhurst, J. C. (eds.), *Cheshire Quarter Sessions,
1559–1760*, Rec. Soc. Lancs. and Ches., 94, 1940.

Brasenose College Register, 1509–1909, Oxford, 1909.

Cardwell, E. (ed.), *Synodalia: a Collection of Articles of Religion, Canons
and Proceedings of Convocations in the Province of Canterbury*, Oxford,
1842.

Cheshire Sheaf, old series, III, 1882 (contains letters of Bishop Bridgeman).

Dasent, J. R. (ed.), *Acts of the Privy Council*, 1890–1907.

Fishwick, H. (ed.), *Commonwealth Church Survey*, Rec. Soc. Lancs and
Ches., I, 1789.

France, R. S. (ed.), 'The statutes and ordinances of Warrington, 1617' in
A Lancashire Miscellany, Rec. Soc. Lancs. and Ches., 109, 1965.

Harland, J. (ed.), *Lancashire Lieutenancy*, Chet. Soc., old series, 50, Manchester, 1859.

Kenyon Mss., H.M.C., fourteenth report, app. 4, 1894

Peck, F. (ed.), *Desiderata Curiosa*, 1779.

Peel, A. (ed.), *Tracts Ascribed to Richard Bancroft*, Cambridge, 1953.

Raines, F. R. (ed), *Derby Household Books*, Chet. Soc., old series, 31,
Manchester, 1853.

— *Notitia Cestriensis* (by Bishop Gastrell), Chet. Soc., old series, 8, 19, 21,
22, Manchester, 1845–50.

— *Miscellany, vol. V*, Chet. Soc., old series, 96, Manchester, 1875 (contains *A Description of the State Civil and Ecclesiastical of the County of Lancaster about the year 1590*, and correspondence relating to the 1590 metropolitan visitation of the diocese of Chester).

Salisbury Mss., H.M.C., 1883– .

Shaw, R.C. (ed.), *Records of the Thirty Men of the Parish of Kirkham*, Kendal, 1930.

Strype, J., *Annals of the Reformation*, Pt. 3, vol. 2, Oxford, 1824.

— *Memorials of the Reformation*, Pt. 1, vol. 2, Oxford, 1882.

Tait, J. (ed.), *Lancashire Quarter Sessions, 1590–1606*, 77 Manchester, 1917.

Twemlow, J. A. (ed.), *Liverpool Town Books*, two vols., Liverpool, 1918 and 1935.

Usher, R. G. (ed.), *The Presbyterian Movement in the Reign of Elizabeth*, Camden Soc., third series, 8, 1905.

3 Printed sermons, devotional literature and biographies by or about the divines of the diocese of Chester

Unless otherwise stated, the place of publication is London

Ambrose, Isaac, *Prima, Media et Ultima*, 1650.

— *Three Great Ordinances of Jesus Christ*, 1662.
   A useful selection of Ambrose's works was published in London in 1839 by Thomas Tegg.

Angier, John, *An Helpe to Better Hearts for Better Times*, 1647.

Burghall, Edward, *Providence Improved* in *Civil War Tracts*, Rec. Soc. Lancs. and Ches., 19, 1889.

Byfield, Nicholas, *The Patterne of Wholsome Words, or a Collection of such Truths as are necessary to be believed unto Salvation, separated out of the body of all Theologie*, 1618.

— *The Rule of Faith, or an Exposition of the Apostles' Creed*, 1626.

— *Directions for the Private Reading of the Scriptures*, 1626.

— *The Marrow of the Oracles of God*, seventh edition, 1630.

— *The Signes, or an Essay concerning Gods Love and Mans Salvation, gathered out of the Holy Scriptures*, 1637.

— *A Commentary upon the Three First Chapters of the First Epistle Generall of St Peter*, 1637.

Caldwell, John, *A Sermon preached before the Right Honorable Earle of Darbie . . .*, 1577.

Carter, Oliver, *An Answere . . . unto Certaine Popish Questions and Demaundes*, 1579.

Case, Thomas, *Gods Rising, His Enemies Scattering*, 1642.

— *The Root of Apostacy and Fountain of True Fortitude*, 1644.

Clarke, Samuel, *Lives of Sundry Eminent Persons in this Later Age*, 1683. (The work is prefaced by Clarke's autobiography.)

Eaton, Richard, *A Sermon preached at the Funeralls of that worthie and worshipfull Gentleman Thomas Dutton of Dutton, Esq.*, 1616.

Fleetwood, Edward, *A Declaration of a strange and wonderful Monster born in Kirkham Parish*, 1646.

Gee, John, *The Foot out of the Snare, with a Detection of sundry late Practices and Impostures of the Priests and Jesuits in England*, 1624.

Goodman, Christopher, *How Superior Powers ought to be obeyd of their subjects, and wherein they may be lawfully by Gods worde be disobeyed*, Geneva, 1558.

Gower, Stanley, *Life of Richard Rothwell*, Bolton, 1787 (a late edition of a contemporary work).

Harrison, William, *A Brief Discourse of the Christian Life and Death of Mistris Katherin Brettergh . . .*, 1612.

— *Deaths Advantage Little Regarded*, 1612.

— *The Difference of Hearers, or an Exposition of the Parable of the Sower*, 1614.

Herle, Charles, *Contemplations and Devotions on the Several Passages of our Blessed Saviours Death and Passion*, 1631.

— *A Payre of Compasses for Church and State*, 1642.

— *Davids Song of Three Parts*, 1643.

— *The Independency on Scriptures of the Independency of Churches*, 1643.

— *Abrahams Offer, Gods offering*, 1644.

— *Davids Reserve and Rescue*, 1644.

— *Wordly Policy and Moral Prudence*, 1655.

Heyricke, Richard, *Three Sermons preached at the Collegiate Church in Manchester*, 1641.

— *Queen Esthers Resolves, or a princely pattern of Heaven-born Resolution for all lovers of God and their Country*, 1646.

— *The Harmonious Consent of the Ministers within the County Palatine of Lancaster with their Reverend Brethren the ministers of the Province of London in their Late Testimonie to the Trueth of Jesus Christ and to our Solemn League and Covenant: as also against the Errours, Heresies and Blasphemies of These Times and the Toleration of them*, 1648.

Heywood, Oliver, *Life of John Angier*, Chet. Soc., new series, 97 Manchester, 1937.

— *Rev. Oliver Heywood B.A., 1630–1702: his autobiography, diaries, anecdote and event books*, ed. J. Horsfall Turner, four vols., Brighouse, 1882–85.

— *Works*, ed. J. Slate, vol. 1, Idle, 1825.

Hinde, William, *A Path to Pietie, leading to the Way, the Truth and the Life of Christ Jesus drawn upon the Ground and according to the Rule of Faith*, Oxford, 1613.

— *The Office and Moral Law of God in the days of the Gospel justified and explained at large by Scriptures, Fathers and other Orthodox Divines*, 1623.

— *A Faithfull Remonstrance of the Holy Life and Happy Death of John Bruen of Bruen Stapleford in the County of Chester, Esquire*, 1641.

— (ed.), *The Prophecie of Obediah* by John Rainolds, Oxford, 1613.

— (ed.), *The Discovery of the Man of Sinne* . . . by John Rainolds, Oxford, 1614.

— (ed.), *Bathshebaes Instructions to her Sonne Lemuel* . . . by John Dod, 1614.

Hollingsworth, Richard, *An Examination of Sundry Scriptures alleadged by our Brethren in Defence of their Church Way*, 1644.

— *Certain Queries, modestly (though plainly) propounded to such as affect the Congregational Way* . . ., 1646.

— *The Main Points of Church Government and Discipline, plainly and modestly handled by way of question and answer*, 1649.

— *Mancuniensis*, Manchester, 1839.

Jacombe, Thomas, *Abrahams Death* . . ., 1682. (Sermon preached at the funeral of Thomas Case.)

Leigh, William, *The Christians Watch, or an Heavenly Instruction to all Christians* . . ., 1605.

— *Great Britaines Great Deliverance from the Great Danger of Popish Powder*, 1606.

— *The Dreadful Day, Dolerous to the Wicked but Glorious to all such as looke and long after Christ his Second Coming*, 1610.

— *The Soules Solace against Sorrow. A Funeral Sermon preached at Childwall Church in Lancashire at the Buriall of Mistris Katherine Brettergh*, 1612.

— *The Drumme of Devotion, striking out an Alarum to Prayer by Signes in Heaven and Prodigies on Earth*, 1613.

Ley, John, *A Patterne of Pietie, or the religious life and death of that grave and gracious matron Mrs Jane Ratcliffe, widow and citizen of Chester*, 1640.

— *Sunday a Sabbath, or a preparative discourse for discussion of Sabbatory doubts*, 1641.

— *Defensive Doubts, Hopes and Reasons for refusall of the Oath imposed by the sixth canon of the Synod*, 1641.

— *A Case of Conscience concerning the Sacrament of the Lords Supper* . . ., 1641.

— *A Letter against the erection of an Altar, written June 29 1633, to the Reverend Father John Lord Bishop of Chester*, 1641.

Ley, John, *The Fury of Warre and Folly of Sinne*, 1643.
— *Light for Smoke, or a cleare and distinct reply . . . to a darke and confused answer to a Booke made and intituled 'The Smoke in the Temple' by John Saltmarsh . . .*, 1646.
Martindale, Adam, *Life of Adam Martindale written by himself*, ed. R. Parkinson, Chet. Soc., old series, 4, Manchester, 1845.
— *Divinity Knots unloosed . . .*, 1649.
— *An Antidote against the poyson of the Times, or an Axiomatical Catechism*, 1653.
Mather, Increase, *The Life and Death of that Reverend Man in God Mr Richard Mather*, Cambridge, Mass., 1670.
Morton, Thomas, *A Defence of the Innocencie of the Three Ceremonies of the Church of England, viz the Surplice, Crosse after Baptisme and Kneeling at the receiving of the blessed Sacrament*, 1618.
Murcot, John, *Several Works of Mr John Murcot . . . together with his Life and Death*, 1657.
Newcome, Henry, *Diary*, ed. T. Heywood, Chet. Soc., old series, 18 Manchester, 1849.
— *Autobiography*, ed. R. Parkinson, Chet. Soc., 26–7, Manchester, 1852.
Nicholls, Robert, *Of Kneeling in the Act of Receiving the sacramental Bread and Wine*, in J. Cotton (ed.), *Some Treasure fetched out of Rubbish*, 1660.
Paget, John, *Defence of Church Government*, 1641.
Paget, Thomas, *A Demonstration of Family Duties*, 1643.
Shaw, John, *Life of Master John Shaw* in *Yorkshire Diaries and Autobiographies in the seventeenth and eighteenth centuries*, Surtees Soc., 65, Durham, 1875.
Torshell, Samuel, *The Three Questions of Free Justification, Christian Liberty, the Use of the Law*, 1632.
— *The Saints Humiliation, being the Substance of nine profitable sermons upon severall Texts*, 1633.
— *A Case of conscience concerning flying in times of trouble*, 1643.
— *A Helpe to Christian Fellowship or a Discourse furnished with much variety of Experimentall and Historicall observations and most seasonable for these times of happy designe for Reformation*, 1644.
— *The Womans Glorie*, 1645.
— (ed.), *Commentary on Malachi* by Richard Stock, 1641.
Walker, George, *An exhortation for contributions to maintain preachers in Lancashire*, ed. C. W. Sutton, in *Miscellany, vol. I*, Chet. Soc., new series, 47, Manchester, 1902.
White, John, *Works*, 1624. (Contains, *inter al.*, White's *Way to the True Church* and his *Defence of the Way to the True Church against his Reply*.)

4 *Other sixteenth- and seventeenth-century works*

Barwick, John, *A Summarie Account of the Holy Life and Happy Death of the right reverend father in God, Thomas late Lord Bishop of Duresme*, 1660. (Thomas Morton was previously Bishop of Chester.)
Baxter, Richard, *Autobiography*, ed. J. M. Lloyd-Thomas, Everyman's Library, 1931.
Cox, R. (ed.), *The Literature of the Sabbath Question*, two vols., Edinburgh, 1865.
Fiennes, Celia, *The Journeys of Celia Fiennes*, ed. C. Morris, 1947.
Fuller, Thomas, *History of the Worthies of England*, 1662.
Gouge, William, *Of Domesticall Duties*, 1622.
Heylyn, Peter, *Cyprianus Anglicus*, 1671.
Hooker, Richard, *Of the Laws of Ecclesiastical Polity*, in the collected *Works*, 1, 1890.
Hutchinson, Lucy, *Memoirs of the Life of Colonel Hutchinson*, ed. C. H. Firth, two vols., 1885.
Josselin, Ralph, *Diary*, ed. F. Hockliffe, Camden Soc., third series, 15, 1908.
King, Daniel (ed.), *Vale Royall of England*, 1656.
Priestley Memoirs, ed. C. Jackson, Surtees Soc., 77, Durham, 1886.
Ramus, Peter, *The Logike*, 1574.
Sibbes, Richard, *The Riches of Mercie*, 1638, in the collected *Works*, ed. A. B. Grosart, VI, Edinburgh, 1863.

5 *Theses*

Blackwood, B. G., 'Social and economic aspects of the history of Lancashire, 1635–55', University of Oxford, B.Litt. thesis, 1956.
Collinson, P., 'The puritan classical movement in the reign of Elizabeth I', University of London, Ph.D, thesis, 1957.
Cosgrove, J., 'The position of the recusant gentry in the social setting of Lancashire, 1570–1642', University of Manchester, M.A. thesis, 1965.
Higgins, P., 'Women in the English Civil War', University of Manchester, M.A. thesis, 1965.
Lambert, D., 'The lower clergy of the Anglican Church in Lancashire, 1558–1642', University of Liverpool, M.A. thesis, 1964.
Lindley, K. J., 'The part played by Catholics in the Civil War in Lancashire and Monmouthshire', University of Manchester, M.A. thesis, 1965.
Newton, J. A., 'Puritanism in the diocese of York, 1603–40', University of London, Ph.D. thesis 1956.

6 *Secondary sources*

Addison, W., *Essex Heyday: a Study in Seventeenth-century Social Life*, 1949.

Aikin, J., *A Description of the Country from Thirty to Forty Miles around Manchester*, 1795.

Anderson, O., 'Women preachers in mid-Victorian Britain. Some reflections on feminism, popular religion and social change', *Historical Jnl.*, XII, 1969.

Anstruther, G., 'Lancashire clergy in 1639', *Recusant History*, 4, 1957.

Ariès, P., *Centuries of Childhood*, 1962.

Aveling, H., 'The Catholic recusants of the West Riding of Yorkshire, 1558–1790', *Proceedings of the Leeds Philosophical and Literary Soc.*, x, 1963.

Axon, E., 'The King's Preachers in Lancashire, 1599–1845', *Trans. Lancs. and Ches. Antiq. Soc.*, 56, 1944.

— 'Ellenbrook chapel and its seventeenth-century ministers', *Trans. Lancs. and Ches. Antiq. Soc.*, 38, 1920.

— 'The Mort family in connexion with Lancashire nonconformity', *Trans. Unitarian Historical Soc.*, 3, 1925.

Axon, W. E. A., 'Early booksellers and stationers of Manchester', *Trans. Lancs. and Ches. Antiq. Soc.*, 6, 1888.

Bailey, J. E., *Life of a Lancashire Rector in the Civil War*, Manchester, 1877.

Baines, T., *History of Liverpool*, 1852.

Bennett, H. S., *English Books and Readers, 1558–1603*, Cambridge, 1965.

Blomfield, Canon, 'Puritanism in Chester in 1637', *Chester Archaeological Jnl.*, old series, 3, 1885.

Booker, J. E., *A History of the Ancient Chapel of Birch in Manchester Parish*, Chet. Soc., old series, 47, Manchester, 1859.

— *History of Blackley Chapel*, Manchester, 1854.

— *A History of the Ancient Chapels of Didsbury and Chorlton*, Chet. Soc., old series, 42, Manchester, 1856.

Bossy, J., 'The character of Elizabethan Catholicism' in T. Aston (ed.), *Crisis in Europe, 1560–1660*, 1965.

Bouch, C. M. L., *Prelates and People of the Lake Counties: a History of the Diocese of Carlisle, 1133–1933*, Kendal, 1948.

— and Jones, G. P., *A short Economic and Social History of the Lake Counties, 1500–1830*, Manchester, 1961.

Brailsford, H. N., *The Levellers*, 1961.

Bridgeman, G. V. O., *History of the Church and Manor of Wigan*, Chet. Soc., new series, 15, 16, 17, 18, Manchester, 1888.

Brook, B., *Lives of the Puritans*, three vols., 1813.

Brown, R. S., The stationers, booksellers and printers of Chester to *c.* 1800', *Trans. Hist. Soc. Lancs. and Ches.*, 83, 1931.

Cardwell, E., *A History of Conferences*, Oxford, 1840.

Chandler, G., *Liverpool under James I*, Liverpool, 1960.

— *Liverpool under Charles I*, Liverpool, 1965.

Clark, A., *The Working Life of Women in the Seventeenth Century*, 1919.
Clasen, C. P., 'The sociology of Swabian Anabaptism', *Church History*, 32, New York, 1963.
Clegg, J., *Annals of Bolton*, Bolton, 1888.
Cliffe, J. T., *The Yorkshire Gentry from the Reformation to the Civil War*, 1969.
Cole, W. A., 'The social origins of the early Friends', *Jnl. of the Friends' Historical Society*, 48, 1957.
Collinson, P., *The Elizabethan Puritan Movement*, 1967.
— 'John Field and Elizabethan puritanism' in *Elizabethan Government and Society: Essays presented to Sir John Neale*, ed. S. T. Bindoff, J. Hurstfield and C. H. Williams, 1961.
— 'The beginnings of English Sabbatarianism' in *Studies in Church History*, ed. C. W. Dugmore and C. Duggan, 1964.
— 'The role of women in the English Reformation, illustrated by the life and friendships of Anne Locke' in *Studies in Church History*, ed. C. W. Dugmore and C. Duggan, II, 1965.
— 'The godly: aspects of popular Protestantism in Elizabethan England', *Past and Present Conference Papers*, 1966.
Cross, C., *The Puritan Earl: the Life of Henry Hastings, third Earl of Huntingdon, 1536–95*, 1966.
— *The Royal Supremacy in the Elizabethan Church*, 1969.
— 'Noble patronage in the Elizabethan Church', *Cambridge Historical Jnl.*, III, 1960.
— 'The Earl of Huntingdon and Elizabethan Leicestershire', *Trans. Leicestershire Archaeological Soc.*, 36, 1960.
Curtis, M. H., *Oxford and Cambridge in Transition, 1558–1642*, Oxford, 1959.
— 'The Hampton Court conference and its aftermath', *History*, XLVI, 1961.
Davids, T. W., *Annals of Evangelical Nonconformity in Essex*, 1863.
Davies, C. S. (ed.), *A History of Macclesfield*, Manchester, 1961.
Davies, H., *The Worship of the English Puritans*, 1948.
Davies, V., *Toxteth Chapel, Liverpool*, 1884.
Dickens, A. G., *Lollards and Protestants in the Diocese of York*, 1959.
— *The English Reformation*, 1964.
Dictionary of National Biography, ed. L. Stephen and S. Lee, 1885–1900.
Everitt, A. M., *The Community of Kent and the Great Rebellion*, Leicester, 1966.
— *The Local Community and the Great Rebellion*, Historical Association pamphlet, 1969.
— *Change in the Provinces: the Seventeenth Century*, 1969. University of Leicester, Department of English Local History occasional papers, second series, I.

Everitt, A. M., 'Nonconformity in country parishes' in J. Thirsk (ed.), *Land, Church and People: Essays presented to Professor H. P. R. Finberg*, 1970.

Foster, J., *Alumni Oxonienses*, four vols. Oxford, 1891–92.

Gardiner, S. R., *History of England from the Accession of James I to the Outbreak of Civil War, 1603–1642*, ten vols. 1883–84.

Garrett, C. H., *The Marian Exiles: a Study in the Origins of Elizabethan Puritanism*, Cambridge, 1938.

Gooch, G. P., *Political Thought in England from Bacon to Halifax*, 1914.

Hall, J., *History of Nantwich*, Nantwich, 1883.

Haller, W., *The Rise of Puritanism*, New York, 1938.

— *Liberty and Reformation in the Puritan Revolution*, New York, 1955.

— and M., 'The puritan art of love', *Huntington Library Quarterly*, 5, 1941–42.

Halley, R., *Lancashire, its Puritanism and Nonconformity*, 1869; second edition, Manchester, 1872.

Hart, A. T., *The Man in the Pew*, 1966.

Head, R., *Congleton Past and Present*, Congleton, 1887.

Heginbotham, H., *Stockport Ancient and Modern*, two vols., 1882–92.

Hill, C., *Economic Problems of the Church from Archbishop Whitgift to the Long Parliament*, Oxford, 1956.

— *Puritanism and Revolution*, 1958.

— *Society and Puritanism in Pre-revolutionary England*, 1964.

— *Intellectual Origins of the English Revolution*, Oxford, 1965.

— 'Propagating the Gospel' in *Historical Essays 1600–1750 presented to David Ogg*, ed. H. E. Bell and R. L. Ollard, 1963.

— 'Puritans and the "dark corners of the land" ', *T.R.H.S.*, fifth series, 13, 1962.

— 'The many-headed monster in late Tudor and early Stuart political thinking' in *From Renaissance to Counter Reformation: Essays presented to Garrett Mattingly*, ed. C. H. Carter, 1966.

Hoskins, W. G., *Provincial England*, 1963.

Howell, R., *Newcastle-upon-Tyne and the Puritan Revolution*, Oxford, 1967.

Howell, W. S., *Logic and Rhetoric in England, 1500–1700*, Princeton, 1956.

Hunter, J., *Life of Oliver Heywood*, 1842.

Inglis, K. S., *Churches and the Working Classes in Victorian England*, 1963.

— 'Patterns of religious worship in 1851', *Jnl. of Ecclesiastical History*, 11, 1960.

Jordan, W. K., *Philanthropy in England, 1480–1660*, 1959.

— *The Social Institutions of Lancashire, 1480–1660*, Chet. Soc., third series, 11, Manchester, 1962.

Kearney, H. F., *Scholars and Gentlemen: Universities and Society in Pre-industrial Britain, 1500–1700*, 1970.

Kirby, E. W., 'Sermons before the Commons, 1640–42', *American Historical Review*, XLIV, 1938–39.

Knappen, M. M., *Tudor Puritanism*, second impression, Chicago, 1965.

Laslett, P., *The World We Have Lost*, 1965.

Leatherbarrow, J. S., *The Lancashire Elizabethan Recusants*, Chet. Soc., new series, 110, Manchester, 1947.

Macfarlane, A., *The Family Life of Ralph Josselin, a Seventeenth-century Clergyman*, Cambridge, 1970.

— *Witchcraft in Tudor and Stuart England: a regional and comparative study*, 1970.

Madan, F. (ed.), *Brasenose College Quatercentenary Monographs*, two vols., Oxford, 1909–10.

Marchant, R. A., *The Puritans and the Church Courts in the Diocese of York, 1560–1642*, 1960.

Miller, P., *The New England Mind: the Seventeenth Century*, New York, 1939.

Morgan, E. S., *The Puritan Family*, Boston, Mass., 1944.

Morris, R. H., *Chester in the Plantagenet and Tudor Reigns*, Chester, 1894.

Muir, R., *History of Municipal Government in Liverpool*, Liverpool, 1906.

— *History of Liverpool*, Liverpool, 1907.

Mullinger, J. B., *The University of Cambridge*, three vols. Cambridge, 1884.

Ormerod, G., *History of the County Palatine of Chester*, ed. Helsby, three vols., 1882.

Palatine Note Book, four vols., Manchester, 1881–85.

Paul, R. S., and Smith, W. J., *A History of Middleton Grammar School*, Middleton, 1965.

Pink, W. D., and Beavan, A. B., *The Parliamentary Representation of Lancashire*, 1889.

Raines, F. R., *The Vicars of Rochdale*, Chet. Soc., new series, 1 and 2, Manchester, 1883.

— *The Rectors of Manchester and the Wardens of the Collegiate Church*, Chet. Soc., new series, 5 and 6, Manchester, 1885.

— *Lives of the Fellows of the College of Manchester*, Chet. Soc., new series, 21 and 23, Manchester, 1891.

Robson, D., *Some Aspects of Education in Cheshire in the Eighteenth Century*, Chet. Soc., third series, 13, Manchester, 1966.

Rodgers, H. B., 'The market area of Preston in the sixteenth and seventeenth centuries', *Geographical Studies*, III, 1956.

Rylands, W. H., 'Booksellers and stationers in Warrington, 1639–57', *Trans. Hist. Soc. Lancs. and Ches.*, 37, 1885.

Scholes, J. C., *History of Bolton*, Bolton, 1892.

Schücking, L. L., *The Puritan Family: a Study from the Literary Sources*, English trans., 1969.

Shaw, R. C., *History of Kirkham in Amounderness*, Preston, 1949.

Simon, J., *Education and Society in Tudor England*, Cambridge, 1966.

Spalding, J. C., 'Sermons before Parliament, 1640–49, as a public puritan diary', *Church History*, 36, 1967.

Spufford, M., 'The schooling of the peasantry in Cambridgeshire' in J. Thirsk (ed.), *Land, Church and People: Essays presented to Professor H. P. R. Finberg*, 1970.

Stephens, W. B. (ed.), *History of Congleton*, Manchester, 1970.

Stone, L., *The Crisis of the Aristocracy, 1558–1641*, Oxford, 1965.

— 'The educational revolution in England, 1560–1640', *Past and Present*, 28, 1964.

Strype, J., *Life and Acts of Bishop Aylmer*, Oxford, 1821.

Tait, J., 'The Declaration of Sports for Lancashire', *E.H.R.*, 32, 1917.

Tawney, R. H., *Religion and the Rise of Capitalism*, Pelican Books edition, 1964.

Thirsk, J. (ed.), *The Agrarian History of England and Wales, 1500–1640*, Cambridge, 1967.

— 'The family', *Past and Present*, 27, 1964.

Thomas, K., 'Women and the Civil War sects', in T. Aston (ed.), *Crisis in Europe, 1560–1660*, 1965.

Touzeau, J., *The Rise and Progress of Liverpool*, Liverpool, 1912.

Trevor-Roper, H. R., *Religion, the Reformation and Social Change*, 1967.

— 'The fast sermons of the Long Parliament' in *Essays in British History*, ed. H. R. Trevor-Roper, 1964.

Trimble, W. R., *The Catholic Laity in Elizabethan England*, Cambridge, Mass., 1964.

Usher, R. G., *The Reconstruction of the English Church*, two vols., New York, 1910.

— 'The people and the puritan movement', *Church Quarterly Review*, LVIII, 1904.

Vann, R. T., 'Quakerism and the social structure in the interregnum', *Past and Present*, 43, 1969.

Venn, J. and J. A., *Alumni Cantabrigienses*, four vols., Cambridge, 1922–27.

Victoria County History of Lancashire, ed. W. Farrer and J. Brownbill, eight vols., 1906–14.

Wadsworth, A. P., and Mann, J. de L., *The Cotton Trade and Industrial Lancashire*, Manchester, 1931.

Walzer, M., *The Revolution of the Saints*, 1966.

Wark, K. R., *Elizabethan Recusancy in Cheshire*, Chet. Soc., third series, 19, 1971.

Watson, J. B., 'The Lancashire gentry and public service, 1529–58', *Trans. Lancs. and Ches. Antiq. Soc.*, 73–4, 1966.

Whitaker, W. B., *Sunday in Tudor and Stuart Times*, 1933.

White, H. C., *The Tudor Books of Private Devotion*, Madison, Wis., 1951.

Whitney, D. Williams, 'London puritanism: the Haberdashers' Company', *Church History*, 32, 1963.

Williams, F. B., *Index of Dedications and Commendatory Verses in English Books before 1641*, Bibliographical Soc., 1962.

Wrigley, E. A., 'A simple model of London's importance in changing English society and economy, 1650–1750', *Past and Present*, 37, 1967.

Zagorin, P., *The Court and the Country: the Beginning of the English Revolution*, 1969.

Index

Acton, puritan element in, 88
Adams, Barnard, 20n.
Advowsons, puritan use of, 126–30
Alcester, Warwickshire, 48
Alderley, puritan element in, 87, 90
Aldersey, Thomas, 128, 129
Allance, John, 80
All Souls College, Oxford, 61, 187
Ambler, Lawrence, of Colne, 185
Ambrose, Isaac, of Preston, 53, 63, 70n., 95, 105, 107, 127, 162, 187
Andrew, Mistress, 80
Angier, John, of Denton, 42, 43 (biog.), 48, 50, 61n., 64n., 70, 91, 98, 104, 113, 121n., 126, 136, 172, 188
Answere . . . unto Certaine Popish Questions and Demaundes, 154
Areholme, conventicles at, 37
Ariès, P., 93n.
Armyne, Sir William, 126
Ashall, Thomas, of Swettenham, 185
Ashurst, Mr, 151n.
Ashworth, John of Warrington, 69n.
Aspinall, Miles, of Blackburn, 64n., 69n,. 186
Aspinwall, Timothy, of Knutsford, 63, 133, 187
Assheton, family, 127
    Edward, of Middleton, 64., 66n., 69n., 185
    James, Esq., 124
    John, 44n.
    Sir Richard, 124
Astbury, puritan element in, 76
Astley, Elizabeth, 94
    Margaret, 94
    Mary, 94
    Ralph, 94
Axon, E., 20n.
Aylmer, John, Bishop of London, 17

Baguley, Anne, 137
Balliol College, Oxford, 61, 187

Bancroft, Richard, 15
Bangor, deanery of, absence of puritanism in, 7
Banister, Nicholas, 125
Baptism ceremony, Popish practices during, 171; puritan attitudes towards, 28–9; puritan opposition to use of sign of cross in, 26–7, 79–80
Barber, Robert, of Manchester, 70
Barnet, Daniel, 80
Barrow, preaching Exercise at, 68
Barton Cuthbert, irreligion in, 4
Bastwick, Dr John, 167
Bate, Martha, 137
Baxter, Richard, 26n., 35, 47n., 49n., 59
Beasley, Elizabeth, 114
Beckett, John, 87
Beedal, preaching Exercises at, 66n.
Bellot, Hugh, Bishop of Chester, 1
Bennett, H. S., 38n.
Benson, Thomas, brewer, 90, 103–4, 132
Berry, William, 89
Bible, place of, in puritan preaching, 101, 102
Blackburn, preaching Exercise at, 67
Blackburn, Richard, 121
Blackrod, preaching Exercise at, 67
Blinston, Peter, 186
Blundells of Ince and Crosby, 5
Boat, Mr, 138
Bolton, Adam, of Blackburn, 63, 187
Bolton, extent of parish of, 15; puritan element in, 77, 80, 89, 96, 98–9
Bones, John, 123
Book of Martyrs, 56
Books owned by clergy, 56–8
Booksellers, 181; at Chester, 10, 182; at Manchester, 10; at Warrington, 10
Booth, Humphrey, clothier, 83, 121
Boroughbridge, deanery of, absence of puritanism in, 7
Bossy, J., 6, 110n.

Office and Moral Law of God, The, 130
Okey, James, 96
Oldham, Edward, 87, 88, 90
Oldham, puritan element in, 16, 76, 87, 103
Ormskirk, conventicles in, 37; extent of parish of, 15; puritan element in, 100, 109–10
Osbaldeston, Robert, of Whalley, 61n., 64n., 66n., 69n.
Oseley, Richard, of Weaverham, 129, 187
Over Peover, puritan element in, 85
Oxford University, puritan clergy trained at, 61–3

Packer, John, 144
Padiham, preaching Exercises at, 66n.
Paget, Thomas, of Blackley, 67, 90, 93, 106, 125, 137, 150, 188
    John, 150, 185
Palin, Thomas, 170
Pareman, Anne, 84
Parishes, vastness of, in diocese of Chester, 15–17, 177
Parke, Robert, of Bolton, 61n., 133, 188
Parkinson, Robert, 66n.
Pasfield, Robert, servant, 102
Path to Pietie, A, 129
Patronage, of puritanism, by aristocracy, 115–20; by gentry, 121–8; by merchants and tradesmen, 128–133; by municipal corporations, 138–43; by women, 134–38; limitations of, 149–52
Patterne of Pietie, A, 105, 134, 135
Payre of Compasses for Church and State, A, 151
Peacock, Humphrey, 170
Pedlars, and distribution of tracts, 10
Pembroke College, Cambridge, 60, 185, 188
Pembroke, Earls of, 132
Pendle, hostility to religion at, 4
Pendlebury, Adam, 88, 94
    James, 88, 94
    William, 88, 94
Perkins, William, 11, 57, 60

Peterhouse College Cambridge, 60, 188
Petitions in defence of puritan clergy, 124–5
Piers, John, Archbishop of York, 1, 21, 69, 124, 142
Platt, John, 123
Porter, Henry of Lancaster, 66n.
Poulson, Bartle, 84
    George, tailor, 84, 85
Poulton, Christopher, 148
Poulton-le-Fylde, struggles between Catholics and puritans at, 162–4
Powell, Alexander, 85
Practice of Christianity, The, 57
Prayer, extemporary nature of, 46, 54; importance of, to puritans, 45, 81n.
Preaching Exercises in diocese of Chester, 18–19, 65–9
Presbyterian experiment in Lancashire, 67, 177
Prescot, grammar school, 168; preaching Exercises at, 66n.; struggles between Catholics and puritans in, 168–9
Preston, Edward, unlicensed schoolmaster, 88, 103
Preston, preaching Exercises at, 66n.; puritan element in, 100, 103
Prestwich, puritan element in, 103
Priestley, Grace, 109n.
Privy Council, 5, 6, 18, 19, 65, 100, 115, 117, 146
Prophecie of Obediah, 58
Proselytising by laymen, 78, 103–5
Prynne, William, 137n., 167, 182–3
Pulford, a painter, 183
Puritanism, distribution of, 7–17, 177; local character of, 183
'Puritan Movement', concept of, 180

Quakers, 80, 108
Queen Esthers Resolves, 151
Queens' College, Cambridge, 60, 185, 188
Queen's College, Oxford, 61, 186, 187
Queen's Preachers in Lancashire, 20, 161

Radcliffe, Sir Alexander, 121n.

Skillicorne, Thomas, 99
Smith, Ellen, 110
  James, of Kirkham, 25, 69n., 164
  Jeremy, 77
  Mary, 110
  Thomas, stationer, of Manchester,
    10
Smyth, William, Bishop of Lincoln,
    61, 62
Sports, Declaration of, 21, 149, 157
Spufford, Margaret, 101n.
Stalmine, witchcraft at, 4
Stirrup, Ralph, of Ashton-on-Mersey,
    61n., 128, 188
Stoke, puritan element in, 80
Stone, L., 102, 111–12
Stones, Thomas, 130
Storer, Arthur, 60n., 185
Stourbridge Fair, 11
Street, Thomas, 87
Suffolk, puritan patrons in, 126–7
Sumner, Henry, of Disley, 69n.
Sunday a Sabbath, 50, 70
Sutton, Sir Richard, 61
Surplice, economic factors affecting use
    of, 25, 26; failure to wear, 23–6;
    lay opposition to, 75–6
Swan, John, of Bunbury, 28, 32, 38–9,
    48, 129
Swinton, Isabella, 87
Symons, Elizabeth, 108

Tacey, Edward, of Manchester, 64,
    185
Tarporley, opposition to puritanism
    in, 27; puritan element in, 78, 99
Tarvin, destruction of church windows
    at, 122, 123; preaching Exercise at,
    68
Tawney, R. H., 74
Thirsk, Joan, 15n., 93n., 94
Thomas, K., 108n.
  Oliver, 55, 56
Thompson, James, of Moncaster, 7
  William, of Newton, 29, 31
Thomson, Elizabeth, 85
Thornton, preaching Exercise at, 68
Thornton-le-Moors, objections to
    catechism at, 39

*Three Great Ordinances of Jesus
    Christ*, 70, 178
*Three Questions of Free Justification,
    Christian Liberty, the Use of the
    Law*, 130
Tildesley, John, of Deane, 70, 76, 88
Tonge, M., 3n.
Torshell, Samuel, of Bunbury, 33
    (biog.), 42, 44–5, 60n., 105, 106,
    107, 129, 130, 135, 169, 188
Townley, John, 6n.
Toxteth, puritan element in, 16–17,
    98
Trafford, Sir Edmund, 125
  William, 137n.
Trevett, Elizabeth, 87
Trevor-Roper, H. R., 4n., 150n., 156
Trimble, W. R., 150n.
Trinity College, Cambridge, 60, 185,
    188
Trinity Hall, Cambridge, 60, 188
Tylecote, Humphrey, of Stretford,
    31

Ulverston, preaching Exercises at, 66n.
University background of puritan
    clergy, *see under* Clergy
Usher, R. G., his views on puritanism,
    72, 74, 178

Vann, R. T., 114n.
Vaughan, Richard, Bishop of Chester,
    1n., 20, 64, 123, 161
Visiting preachers in diocese of
    Chester, 53, 181

Wainwright, Ann, 110
Walker, George, 2, 15, 84, 130, 131
    (biog.), 132, 159, 181–2
  John, 170
Walmsley, Justice, 173
  William, 161
Walsh, Edward, of Blackburn, 64n.,
    66n., 69n.
Walton, Margaret, 109
Walworth, Nathan, 132
Walzer, M., 64n., 145n., 146n.
Warburton, M., 66n.
Wark, K.R., 5n., 169n.

Warrington, preaching Exercise at,
68–9; puritan element in, 77;
Sabbatarianism in, 148
Warwick, Earl of, 115, 127
Watson, J. B., 150
Watts, Robert, 86
Way to the True Church, The, 154,
155
Webb, William, 170
Wemming, Anna, 110
Werden, Edmund, 100, 143
William, 144
West, Richard, 77
Whalley, extent of parish of, 15
Whately, Thomas, of Banbury, 42n.
Whitaker, W. B., 50n.
Whitall, Ralph, 89
White, John, 145, 150, 154–5, 157, 159,
185
Peter, of Poulton-le-Fylde, 27, 64n.,
69n., 163
Whitehaven, 14
Whiteside, John, 163
Whitestones, Robert, wife of, 110
Whitgift, John, Archbishop of Canter-
bury, 18, 21
Whittle, Robert, of Tarporley, 60n.,
70n., 185
Widowson, William, 80
Wigan, puritan element in, 87
Wigginton, Giles, 185
Williamson, Thomas, of Eccles, 66n.
Wilson Richard, of Chester, 70n.,
187
Windebank, Secretary, 143

Winwick, puritan element in, 88
Wirral, economic backwardness of,
14; weakness of puritanism in, 7
Witchcraft, 3–4, 56, 164
Witter, John, 99
Witton, puritan element in, 77
Womans Glorie, The, 106, 107
Women, role of, in puritanism, 105–
114, 134–8, 179
Wood, Andrew, of Knutsford, 70n.,
188
Matthew, of Wybunbury, 66n.
Worthington, Hugh, 84
Wray, Sir William, 126, 138
Wright, James, 87
L. B., 38n.
William, of Waverton, 66n.
W. J. Payling, 111n.
Wrightington, John, 125

Yate, Ellen, 94
George, 94
John, 94
Robert, 94
William, 94
Yates, Thomas, Senior, 87, 94
York, Archbishops of, *see* Grindal,
Edmund; Harsnett, Samuel;
Hutton, Matthew; Matthew,
Tobias; Neile, Richard; Piers,
John; Sandys, Edwin
York, lectureship at, 116
Yorkshire, links with Lancashire puri-
tanism, 53–4; puritan patrons in,
126; puritanism in, 18n.